Alexander .. ᴋneyfits

Arithmetic
Through
Precalculus

A Primer and Study Guide

From Elementary Mathematics
To College Calculus

Volume 1

Create Space

NEW YORK, 2017

ISBN 13: 978-1548102548

ISBN 10: 1548102547

Email: Alexander.Kheyfits@gmail.com

Volume 1

Part I. Arithmetic

and Introductory Algebra

Part II. Minimal Plane Geometry

Contents

Introduction   7

How to Approach and Solve Typical Problems   13

Index of Important Algorithms. How To Do This: 15

I   Arithmetic and Elementary Algebra   19

0   Arithmetic of Whole Numbers   21
   0.1   Addition and Subtraction of Whole Numbers 21
      0.1.1   Digit-Addition Table 21
      0.1.2   Addition of Positive Many-Digit Numbers 26
      0.1.3   Subtraction of Whole Numbers 29
      0.1.4   Multiplication of Digits 33
      Answers 0.1 35

1   The Integers   39
   1.1   Terminology 39
   1.2   Natural Numbers 40
      Answers 1.2 41
   1.3   Inequalities 41
      Answers 1.3 45
   1.4   Decimal Place-Value System 45
      1.4.1   Place-Value Systems 45
      1.4.2   Significant and Insignificant Digits 47
      1.4.3   Rounding 47
      Answers 1.4 49
   1.5   Negative Numbers 50
      Answers 1.5 52
   1.6   Addition of Signed Numbers 52
      1.6.1   Properties of Addition 52
      Answers 1.6 53
   1.7   Inverse Operations I. Subtraction 54

1.7.1   Addition of Signed Numbers   55
1.7.2   Addition and Subtraction of Signed Numbers   60
1.7.3   Order of Operations I   64
Answers 1.7   65
1.8   Multiplication and its Properties   66
1.8.1   "If And Only If" Statement   66
1.8.2   Odd and Even Numbers   66
1.8.3   Properties of Multiplication   67
Answers 1.8   72
1.9   Powers   72
1.9.1   Basic Properties of Powers   72
1.9.2   Powers of Ten   74
Answers 1.9   75
1.10 Long Multiplication   75
1.10.1 Multiplication of a Many-Digit Number by a One-Digit
        Number   75
1.10.2 Multiplication of Many-Digit Whole Numbers   77
Answers 1.10   79
1.11 Inverse Operations II. Division of Whole Numbers   79
1.11.1 Long Division of Natural Numbers   79
1.11.2 Multiplication and Division Involving Zero   84
1.11.3 Multiplication and Division of Signed Numbers   84
1.11.4 Order of Operations II   86
Answers 1.11   87
1.12 Prime Numbers. Prime Factorization   88
Answers 1.12   90
1.13 GCF and LCM   90
Answers 1.13   93

2   Rational Numbers   95
2.1   Introduction to Rational Numbers   95
2.2   Fractions and Mixed Numbers   97
2.2.1   Meaning of Fractions   97
2.2.2   Properties of Fractions 100
2.2.3   Like and Unlike Fractions 102
2.2.4   Arithmetic Operations with Fractions 103
2.2.5   Mixed Numbers 108
2.2.6   Comparing Fractions 111
2.2.7   The Average 113
2.2.8   The Mode and the Median 115
Answers 2.2 116
2.3   Proportions 118
Answers 2.3 121
2.4   Decimals and Percents 121
2.4.1   Decimals. Basic Properties 121
2.4.2   Comparing Decimals 124

2.4.3 Arithmetic Operations with Decimals 124
2.4.4 Percents 131
Answers 2.4 134
2.5 Like Terms 135
2.5.1 Algebraic Expressions 135
2.5.2 Transposition 136
2.5.3 Combining Like Terms 138
Answers 2.5 139
2.6 Linear Equations and Inequalities 140
2.6.1 Linear Equations 140
2.6.2 Interval Notation 145
2.6.3 Linear Inequalities In One Unknown 146
2.6.4 Operations with Powers. Negative Exponents 149
2.6.5 Scientific Notation 151
Answers 2.6 152
2.7 Arithmetic Operations With Mixed Units 153

3 Radicals and Irrational Numbers   155
3.1 Square Roots and Beyond 155
3.1.1 Properties of Square Roots 158
Answers 3.1 163
3.2 Order of Operations. III 164
Answers 3.2 166
3.3 Radicals in Statistics 166
Answers 3.3 168
3.4 Real Numbers 169
Answers 3.4 171

II   Minimal Plane Geometry   173

4 Lines and Angles   175
4.1 Basic Definitions 175
4.1.1 Lines and Angles 175
4.1.2 Circles 179
Answers 4.1 181
4.2 Measuring Angles and Arcs 181
Answers 4.2 183
4.3 Two Parallel Lines and a Transversal 183
Answers 4.3 188

5 Polygons   189
5.1 Basic Definitions 189
Answers 5.1 191
5.2 Triangles 191
5.2.1 Congruent and Similar Triangles 195

      5.2.2   Right Triangles. The Pythagorean Theorem 202

      5.2.3   More Triangles 205

      Answers 5.2 207

  5.3 Parallelograms 208

      Answers 5.3 210

  5.4 Perimeter and Area 210

      5.4.1   Perimeter 210

      5.4.2   Area 212

      Answers 5.4 217

6 Disc, Circle, Circumference   219

  6.1 The Circumference of a Circle 219

      Answers 6.1 221

  6.2 The Area of a Disc 221

      Answers 6.2 222

Contents of Volume 2   223

Bibliography   225

Introduction

According to recent ACT tests[1], about three-quarters of U.S. high-school graduates are not ready for college-level mathematics courses. The situation does not seem to improve – see, for example, "8 things to know about Michigan's ACT scores" by Lori Higgins in "Detroit Free Press" of 08/16/2016, especially her Thing 4, and Katherine Mangan article in "The Chronicle of Higher Education" of 09/21/2016. According to the Mangan's paper, two-thirds of community college freshmen need remediation, and as the reader of this book will learn, 2/3 is smaller than 3/4, but the difference is not too large to stop our efforts to improve the mathematical education of our students.

That is why, *remedial mathematics* courses, that is, classes intended to remedy this unpreparedness, are so widespread nationwide: colleges and universities try to help their incoming freshmen who are not ready for college. One reason for this unpreparedness is the lack of substantive knowledge of mathematics. Another, perhaps even more important reason, is that students lack the necessary skills and habits required for successful study at college. What is more, these problems are not specific to American students [5].

There is also another big group of people, who often need the remediation, just help, in mathematics – those who after several years in workforce realized that to advance their careers, they have to return to college and get higher education. And one of the major stumbling blocks for these people as well as for high-school graduates, is mathematics.

Well, why do we need mathematics? Do we need it at all? There are different possible answers to these questions, and the author does not pretend to know all or even the best of them. Nevertheless, the fact is that from Ancient Greece up to now, the curricula of almost all majors at all colleges and universities worldwide, both in sciences and in liberal arts and humanities, contain some mathematics. Certainly, many generations of people worldwide would not waste time and money for nothing.

Of course, mathematics, or rather arithmetic, is of certain utility in housekeeping, bookkeeping, etc., – this use of mathematics is familiar to everyone. What maybe is less familiar to the majority of people, is that mathematics is indispensable in engineering and sciences, so-called STEM disciplines. A simple

---

[1] http://www.insidehighered.com/news/2013/08/21/act-scores-fall-lowest-level-five-years, accessed on Aug. 24, 2013

example, that everyone has in a purse or in a pocket, is a cell phone – it is packed with mathematics. Modern communication is impossible without some mathematics that was developed by pure mathematicians a century ago, well before physicists and engineers started thinking about digital technology.

Modern biology and life sciences cannot succeed without mathematics; this has been witnessed by a new discipline called the mathematical biology, which has emerged just recently and is now taught at top-level universities. Scientists use very sophisticated mathematical tools to model economy. Computer graphics is based on very simple mathematics, which can be taught to some extent at high school. Such examples can fill out a separate book.

Hence, if we do not want to impede the future developments in life and medical science, technology, economy, etc., we need mathematics and have to study and develop it. What is more, on top of its utility, and this was recognized millennia back, as early as in Ancient Egypt and Greece, mathematics is a subject, which trains our reasoning abilities, our mental discipline. In this regard, mathematics is of everyday and everyone use. A chemist M. Lomonosov said almost three centuries back, "Mathematics must be studied just because it puts our brains in proper order". Still earlier, a universal genius Leonardo da Vinci wrote: "Human investigation cannot be called real science, unless it can be demonstrated mathematically".

Definitely, most people do not need the advanced mathematics studied by mathematics majors at universities. Nonetheless, mathematics is very systematical subject, and its advanced chapters are based on certain simple, mostly very intuitive parts. These basic parts, called usually *elementary mathematics*, were singled out during centuries and are currently studied in high school. Of course, *elementary* does not always mean simple, however, the topics in this "Primer" for the most part are the simple and important parts of the traditional middle- and high-school mathematics.

However, there is an unfortunate terrible misconception in society, which is sometimes transferred to the students, and every mathematics teacher hears again and again: "I am bad in math!" This attitude results in a huge impediment for the students[2]. Mathematics is not easy, but it is no harder than any other subject. It is maybe even easier, since it is very logical and does not require extensive memorizing. Based on many years of experience, I claim that every pupil has enough inborn capabilities to successfully learn the high-school mathematics curriculum – if she or he is persistent, is properly taught, and does exercises systematically.

The goal of the book is to help the readers to refresh (or sometimes to learn from scratch) the most important parts of elementary (= pre-college) mathematics, to close certain gaps in their high-school mathematical education and to accelerate their transition from high-school to college by removing the

---

[2]See, e.g., the discussion of this issue in [4].

need for remediation; the author's philosophy is *You Can Do It Yourself*! The text is self-contained, so that the reader does not have to use other books to pass any remedial mathematics class. This explains the structure, the contents, and the style of the "Primer".

Every new concept, a new notion in the "Primer" is introduced by making use of several model examples. After the introduction, this notion is illustrated by more examples of gradually increased difficulty. A new type of problems is accompanied by exercises for the reader's individual work. If you feel that you have mastered this particular type of problems – move to the next type. But if you feel you need more practice, then continue reading, maybe reading backward, and exercising. Moreover, an exercise you will see again and again in the book, is "Design two more exercises similar to the previous one." And after some effort you will convince yourself that this task of designing new problems is not as impossible for a persistent student as you may think. The book contains about 500 exercises for individual work; all these exercises are provided with the answers in the end of every chapter.

There is no reason here to join discussions about conceptual (or misconceptual?!) and other kinds of understanding; see, for example, a good discussion in [8]. It is obvious, however, that to develop any kind of understanding, a student needs certain minimal factual and procedural background. That is why, to succeed in solving elementary problems, one needs to have some basic knowledge in 'eyes and fingertips', that is, to learn by heart a certain, actually very small amount of information .

If one sees a group of no more than 4 or 5 objects, say, dragons, everyone can *instantly* say how many dragons are there, but with 7 or more objects in view we must count them one by one[3]. This observation is consistent with the current research in psychology and cognitive science (see [1] and the references therein), that bring more and more evidence that certain arithmetic and geometric abilities are hardwired in our brain by nature.

Hence, an important task in teaching arithmetic is to preserve and develop these existing associations within the neural structures of the brain. In turn, this implies that premature introduction of calculators leaves these associations unemployed, whence, they eventually deteriorate and disappear. Therefore, the first part of this "*Primer*" is devoted to thorough development of arithmetic without any use of calculators. This approach is based on the many-year observations of the straggling calculus students, who fail not because of any difficulty they encounter in calculus, but because they lack any simple but indispensable arithmetic background, any arithmetic facilities, necessary not only in elementary algebra, but in higher mathematics as well. For instance, to combine like terms we actually must only add/subtract their numerical coefficients. And if the student cannot do it fast enough, she or he is lost – the student is still inside this small auxiliary problem, while the class is discussing another, maybe more

---

[3]Maybe that is why, since ancient times 7 is considered a magic number, since it is not immediately comprehensible.

advance issue.

Due to the same reason, the "Primer" opens with Chapter 0, devoted to certain introductory arithmetic problems at the level of elementary school. Unfortunately, some (and many more than a few) students in every class in remedial mathematics must review this material. If the reader is fluent in arithmetic, she or he can skip Chapter 0, or otherwise use it for review, as needed.

The students often ask, why then were they taught to use calculators? And my answer is always the same – that was not necessary, that was ahead of time, and this is one of the reasons why now you are not in a college-level, but rather in this remedial class and have to study this elementary stuff again. The experience shows that without the firm arithmetic skills "in fingertips" no real success in learning mathematics is possible.

The "Primer" starts with arithmetic and proceeds on through high-school mathematics. There are many properties that cannot be rigorously proven at the level of this book. If appropriate, I follow H. Wu [9, p. 376] and *explicitly* or *implicitly* employ the

Fundamental Assumption of School Mathematics:

Any formula or weak inequality that is valid for all rational numbers, is also valid for all real numbers.

However, the "Primer" is not a regular textbook, its readers do not have 10 or 12 years for the systematical study of the high-school curriculum. All the students and all the teachers/ know firsthand that our time is always limited. The potential reader of this book had studied this material before, but due to various reasons, has to review it. Keeping this in mind, we have sometimes deviated from a standard order of topics and put them in a more straightforward order, which is appropriate for the intended, more mature readers. We have constantly used the "no-frills" approach and included only concepts and problems, which are absolutely necessary not only to successfully pass remedial mathematics classes, but also to succeed in calculus at a college or university. A couple of exclusions, like the short chapters on the determinants and the vectors in Vol. 2, can be safely omitted by the reader.

A good human tutor can answer a student's questions in any order and pick up from any point. This "Primer" also was designed with many entry and exit points. The student, who knows addition, can skip the corresponding sections and proceed to subtraction; the same can be said regarding any other section in the book. If the reader needs some preliminary definitions or notions, she or he should use the detailed Index in the back of the book.

The "Primer" also contains another index, "How To" of algorithms and procedures on p.p. 15-17, which contains references to basic procedures considered in the text. For instance, to quickly refresh in memory how to convert decimals to fractions, you should go to "How To" and look for "Convert decimals to fractions". The entries in the indices are marked as 1-37 or 2-75, where 1- or 2- refer to the 1st or 2nd volume of the "Primer", respectively, and 37, or 75, etc., indicates the page in that volume. For the reader's convenience, in the end of this book you can find Contents of Volume 2 of the Primer.

The book is based on the author's half-century-long experience of teaching mathematics at all levels, from elementary to high school, to community college, to undergraduate to graduate school. The author knows first-hand that all students have enough ability to learn elementary mathematics. I want to reiterate that the essential problem for many students is not their capability but their disposition, their desire to develop and preserve the good working attitude and persistently solve problems. The "Primer" contains as little theory as it is necessary to explain procedures and solve relevant problems. Certain properties are stated without proofs, because the latter are beyond the scope of the book.

The only exception is our treatment of geometry. We live in a physical world obeying certain geometrical laws, and the traditional neglect of geometry in remedial mathematics is detrimental for the students. Therefore, plane geometry is developed a bit more thoroughly. Because of unavoidable size limitations, three-dimensional geometry is not touched upon at all and no attempt was made to give any systematic or axiomatic treatment of the subject.

The symbol □ marks the ends of proofs or solutions of examples.

Acknowledgment

The text was set in MiKTeX and XeLaTeX dialects of LaTeX with WinEdt shell and AMS-TeX and Pstricks added packages. The author is indebted to the creators of this excellent software. Any comments, especially about possible typos and inaccuracies, are welcome at alexander.kheyfits@gmail.com

Since 1997, the author has taught at Bronx Community College of the City University of New York. The author is thankful to faculty of the BCC Department of Mathematics and Computer Science for friendly environment and help. I am grateful to Professor Robert Megginson for encouragement and to Professor Hung-Hsi Wu for useful advises. My special thanks are to Professor Peter Yom for the extremely careful reading of the manuscript.

Alexander I. Kheyfits

How to Approach and Solve Typical Problems

Nobody can give an exhausting answer to the ambitious question "How to solve a mathematical problem?" The best known answers were given by G. Polya [7]. However, in this book we solve only standard problems from the standard high-school curriculum, and certain recipes have proven to be universally useful and applicable. First of all, to solve a problem, we must understand words, that is, understand what is the question? So that, read the problem and make sure you understand the meaning of every word in it. For example, if the problem requires to find the average, you must know what "the average" is. If you forget this term, you may ask the "Primer". To this end, the "Primer" contains a traditional "Index", containing all the important terms appearing in this book. Then, if you know the words but unsure how to proceed, find a *similar problem* in the "Primer", carefully study its solution and try to emulate this solution or apply this approach to your problem. Repeat this process again and again, until you succeed.

Another very useful device to verify yourself is to design your own problem – do not think it is impossible. For instance, if you are doing a problem about the average, you can write down the costs of your last three snacks and ask your younger sister about the average of these three numbers. After a solved problem, try to compose and solve a similar problem of the same kind.

Warning. A common error is to memorize individual problems. Then, if in the problem just two sentences or two words are interchanged, the student is lost. Rather, we must study the *methods* of solving the typical problems, for instance, how to solve a quadratic equation, how to find the area of a triangle, etc. The methods are listed in the above-mentioned index "How To Do" on the sequel page.

It is also important to get used to study mathematics systematically, in particular, it is crucial to regularly do home work with a pencil (or a pen) and paper, not just "by eyes".

Thus, start reading the book and solving problems. Good Luck!

Index of Important Algorithms. How To Do This:

find the *Absolute Value* of a real number 1-57

compute the *Area of a Disc* 1-221

compute the *Area of a Quadrilateral* 1-213

compute the *Area of a Triangle* 1-214

find the *Average* 1-113

Change the Base of a logarithm 2-172

compute the *Circumference* 1-219

Compare fractions or decimals 1-111, 1-124

Complete the square 2-103

add/subtract/multiply/divide *Complex Numbers* 2-28

calculate *Compound Interest* 2-187

find *Coordinates of a Point* 2-23

change *Degree* measure to Radians 2-196

measure angles and arcs in *Degrees* 1-181

add *Digits* 1-24

find the *Distance* between two points 2-25

use the *Distributive Law* 1-69

Expand and Read integer numbers 1-46

solve *Exponential Equations* 2-174

Add/Subtract/Multiply/Divide *Fractions* 1-103

reduce a *Fraction to Lowest Terms* 1-100

change a *Fraction to a Mixed Number or to a Decimal* 1-108, 122

Graph a Linear Function 2-43

Graph a Quadratic Function 2-86

sketch the *Graph of an Exponential Function* 2-164

sketch the *Graph of Inverse Proportionality* 2-122

sketch the *Graph of a Logarithmic Function* 2-173

sketch the *Graph of a Power Function* 2-117

find the *GCF* 1-90

find the *Hypotenuse or a Leg* of a right triangle given its two other sides 1-203

Add/Subtract/Multiply *Inequalities* 1-44, 45
Solve *Inequalities* in one variable 1-146
Multiply, Divide *Whole numbers* 1-77, 79
Add/Subtract *Many-Digit Integers* 1-26, 29
find the *LCD* 1-104
find the *LCM* 1-92
Add/Subtract *Like and/or Unlike Fractions* 1-103, 104
combine *Like Terms* 1-138
solve *Linear Equations* 1-140
solve *Linear Inequalities* 1-146
solve *Logarithmic Equations* 2-177
expand/compress *Logarithmic Expressions* 2-169
compute the *Median* of a sample 1-115
change a *Mixed Number to an Improper Fraction* 1-108
find the *Mode* of a sample 1-115
find an *Opposite* of a real number 1-51
Find a Part/Percent of a number 1-132
change a *Percent* to a Fraction or a Decimal 1-132, 133
change a Fraction or a Decimal to *Percent* 1-132, 133
compute the *Perimeter of a Polygon* 1-210
compute the *Perimeter* of Triangles and Rectangles 1- 211
multiply/divide *Powers* 1-149
evaluate *Powers* of integers 1-72
Divide or Multiply by Powers of Ten 1-74
Prime-factor a natural number 1-88
solve *Proportions* 1-118
solve *Quadratic Equations* 2-96
measure angles in *Radians* 2-195
change *Radian Measure* to degrees 2-197
approximately evaluate *Radicals* 1-169
simplify *Radicals* 1-158
Rationalize the denominator 1-162
divide integers with a *Remainder* 1-81
Round Off integers and decimals 1-48, 128
write a decimal in *Scientific Notation* 1-151
Add/Subtract *Signed Numbers* 1-60
compute *Square Roots* of perfect squares 1-156
Multiply/Divide *Signed Numbers* 1-84
find sides of *Similar Triangles* 1-198
find *Simple Interest* 2-56
compute the *Slope and $y-$Intercept* 2-47
Solve a System of Two Linear Equations 2-62, 66
solve a *System of two Linear Inequalities Graphically* 2-70
compute the *Standard Deviation and the Variance of a Sample* 1-166
Transpose Terms of an equation or inequality 1-136
solve *Triangles* 2-231

determine whether two *Triangles are Similar* 1-196
compute *Trigonometric Functions* of acute angles 2-198, 202
compute *Trigonometric Functions* of arbitrary angles 2-207
solve *Trigonometric Equations* 2-224
sketch *Trigonometric Functions* 2-205, 206
prove *Trigonometric Identities* 2-214
operate with *Zero* 1-23, 34, 84

Part I

Arithmetic and Elementary Algebra

Chapter 0

Arithmetic of Whole Numbers

0.1 Addition and Subtraction of Whole Numbers

We review addition and subtraction of nonnegative integer numbers. If the reader is fluent with these operations, skip this section, go to the next one, and look back here if needed. But we included this elementary material, for it is important even in the time of calculators, and many students fail because they do not have these skills.

0.1.1 Digit-Addition Table

The ten symbols

$$0, 1, 2, 3, 4, 5, 6, 7, 8, 9$$

are called *digits*. We use the digits to write down any number, for example, 10. However, 10 is not a digit, it is a two-digit natural number. The numbers[1]

$$1, 2, 3, 4, 5, 6, 7, 8, 9, 10, 11, 12, ...$$

are called the *positive integer numbers*, or *natural numbers*, or *counting* numbers; this set of numbers is denoted by $\mathbb{N}$. Given any natural number n, we can *add* 1 to it (*increase* it by 1) and get a bigger natural number $n + 1$. Thus, 2 is *one more than* 1, 3 is *one more than* 2, etc. Therefore, the set of natural numbers is *infinite* or *unbounded* from above, that is, there is no *biggest* natural number. This set is also called the *natural series*. However, there is the *smallest* natural number, which is 1. The reader is supposed to know how to *count*, that

---

[1] By no means we intend here to built a rigorous theory, we just remind some basic terminology.

is, what integer number follows, for instance, the number 31 090 (this is 31 091), or precedes this number (this is 31 089), or any other natural number.

The natural numbers and the number 0 together make the set of *whole numbers*

$$0, 1, 2, 3, 4, 5, 6, 7, 8, 9, 10, ...,$$

denoted by $\mathbb{W}$; this set is also infinite, since even its smaller subset of the natural numbers is infinite. It is said that 1 *follows* 0, while 0 *precedes* 1; 2 follows 1, while 1 precedes 2, etc.

When any set of objects is introduced, one is interested what can be done with these objects? In the case of the whole numbers, we can perform *arithmetic operations*, namely, *addition*, *subtraction*, *multiplication*, and *division*. In this section we review the addition and subtraction of the whole numbers, leaving the multiplication and division for the next chapter.

The statement '2 follows 1' can be also expressed as '2 *is the sum of* 1 *and* 1', '3 follows 2' means '3 is the *sum* of 2 and 1', etc., '4 is the *sum* of 3 and 1', and so on. Thus, we introduced an *operation* on the whole numbers, called the *addition* and written as

$$2 = 1 + 1, \; 3 = 2 + 1, \; 4 = 3 + 1,$$

etc. If $a + b = c$, then a and b are called the *addends* and c the *sum* of these addends. Thus, in the last of the equations above, 3 and 1 are the *addends* and 4 is the *sum* of these addends.

Exercise 0.1.1 *What are the addends and the sum in the equation* $177 + 12 + 24 = 213$.

The *equality sign*, which appears in the preceding lines, is one of the most common mathematical symbols and may have different meanings. Thus, if a and b are numerical expressions, than the *equation* $a = b$ is a statement that a and b have the *same* numerical value, which may be *true*, or may be *false*. For instance, the equation $2 = 1 + 1$ is a true statement, but $2 = 1 - 1$ is false.

If a and b are algebraic expressions, containing *indeterminates*, say, indeterminate x, then the equation $a = b$ means an *equation in unknown* x, and we may have to *solve it for* x. In the sequel chapters we will discuss the latter in detail. Now we only discuss some properties of the equality sign, that were known still Euclides.

Of course, we believe and accept without any discussion, that any entity a is equal to itself, $a = a$. Other important properties of the *equality sign* "=", which we very often use without paying attention to that, are its *symmetry*: If $a = b$, then $b = a$, and its *transitivity*: If $a = b$ and $b = c$, then $a = c$.

Without going into any further details, we also accept the following features of the equality sigh:

If we add or subtract the same quantity to both sides of a valid equation, the new equation is also valid.

If we multiply both sides of a valid equation by the same quantity, the equation remains valid; and if we divide both sides of a valid equation by the same nonzero quantity, the equation remains valid.

Now we can return to the properties of arithmetic operations over natural numbers. Inserting the equation $2 = 1 + 1$ into $3 = 2 + 1$, we deduce

$$3 = 2 + 1 = (1 + 1) + 1 = 1 + 1 + 1.$$

Whence, we convince ourselves that

$$2 = 1 + 1, \ 3 = 1 + 1 + 1, \ 4 = 1 + 1 + 1 + 1, 5 = 1 + 1 + 1 + 1 + 1, \ldots,$$

that is, every natural number n can be represented as the sum of n *ones* or n *units*. In this way, we can easily compute the sum of any whole numbers, for example, $3 + 2 = (1 + 1 + 1) + (1 + 1) = 1 + 1 + 1 + 1 + 1 = 5$. However, for large numbers the procedure is very cumbersome. To make it more amenable, let us find the sums of digits. First we find the sums, which are less than 10.

Exercise 0.1.2 *Fill out the digit-addition table (Table 1) and learn it by heart.*

0+0=	1+0=	2+0=	3+0=	4+0=	5+0=	6+0=	7+0=	8+0=	9+0=
0+1=	1+1=	2+1=	3+1=	4+1=	5+1=	6+1=	7+1=	8+1=	
0+2=	1+2=	2+2=	3+2=	4+2=	5+2=	6+2=	7+2=		
0+3=	1+3=	2+3=	3+3=	4+3=	5+3=	6+3=			
0+4=	1+4=	2+4=	3+4=	4+4=	5+4=				
0+5=	1+5=	2+5=	3+5=	4+5=					
0+6=	1+6=	2+6=	3+6=						
0+7=	1+7=	2+7=							
0+8=	1+8=								
0+9=									

Table 1: Exercise 0.1.2: Digit-addition table.

The left-most column and the top-most row of Table 1 demonstrate an important property of zero 0:

$$0 + n = n + 0 = n \text{ for any number } n.$$

Because of this property, the zero 0 is called the *neutral element* of the addition.

Next we calculate the bigger sums.

Example 0.1.1 *Compute* $8 + 9$.

Solution. Instead of splitting the addends into the sums of ones as above, we notice that the sum is to be bigger than 10, since if we add 2 to 8, we already get 10. Thus, we split another addend as $9 = 2 + 7$ and now it is easy to add[2] $8 + 9 = 8 + 2 + 7 = 10 + 7 = 17$. □

---

[2]Actually we use here the associative property of addition.

Exercise 0.1.3 *Compute* $9 + 8$, $8 + 9$, $9 + 9$, $8 + 7$, $7 + 8$, $8 + 8$.

Undoubtedly, the reader has noticed that $8 + 9 = 9 + 8$. This equation is an instance of a general property of addition, called the *commutative property*:

For any two numbers,
$$a + b = b + a.$$

However, the procedure in Example 0.1.1 also is not fast enough, it is cumbersome to do this splitting in every problem again and again. The standard algorithm for adding integer numbers is based on the adding the digits. The sums of digits can be conveniently put in the chart, and it is advisable to *learn* the digit-addition table (Table 2) *by heart*.

0+0=0	1+0=1	2+0=2	3+0=3	4+0=4	5+0=5
0+1=1	1+1=2	2+1=3	3+1=4	4+1=5	5+1=6
0+2=2	1+2=3	2+2=4	3+2=5	4+2=6	5+2=7
0+3=3	1+3=4	2+3=5	3+3=6	4+3=7	5+3=8
0+4=4	1+4=5	2+4=6	3+4=7	4+4=8	5+4=9
0+5=5	1+5=6	2+5=7	3+5=8	4+5=9	5+5=10
0+6=6	1+6=7	2+6=8	3+6=9	4+6=10	5+6=11
0+7=7	1+7=8	2+7=9	3+7=10	4+7=11	5+7=12
0+8=8	1+8=9	2+8=10	3+8=11	4+8=12	5+8=13
0+9=9	1+9=10	2+9=11	3+9=12	4+9=13	5+9=14
0+10=10	1+10=11	2+10=12	3+10=13	4+10=14	5+10=15

6+0=6	7+0=7	8+0=8	9+0=9	10+0=10
6+1=7	7+1=8	8+1=9	9+1=10	10+1=11
6+2=8	7+2=9	8+2=10	9+2=11	10+2=12
6+3=9	7+3=10	8+3=11	9+3=12	10+3=13
6+4=10	7+4=11	8+4=12	9+4=13	10+4=14
6+5=11	7+5=12	8+5=13	9+5=14	10+5=15
6+6=12	7+6=13	8+6=14	9+6=15	10+6=16
6+7=13	7+7=14	8+7=15	9+7=16	10+7=17
6+8=14	7+8=15	8+8=16	9+8=17	10+8=18
6+9=15	7+9=16	8+9=17	9+9=18	10+9=19
6+10=16	7+10=17	8+10=18	9+10=19	10+10=20

Table 2: Exercise 0.1.4: The digit-addition table.

This table can be compressed as the following Table 3, where the sum of the digits k and l is shown in the cell at the crossing of the corresponding row and column.

Problem 0.1.1 *Verify, as in Example 0.1.1, that all the entries in this table are correct.*

+	0	1	2	3	4	5	6	7	8	9
0	0	1	2	3	4	5	6	7	8	9
1	1	2	3	4	5	6	7	8	9	10
2	2	3	4	5	6	7	8	9	10	11
3	3	4	5	6	7	8	9	10	11	12
4	4	5	6	7	8	9	10	11	12	13
5	5	6	7	8	9	10	11	12	13	14
6	6	7	8	9	10	11	12	13	14	15
7	7	8	9	10	11	12	13	14	15	16
8	8	9	10	11	12	13	14	15	16	17
9	9	10	11	12	13	14	15	16	17	18

Table 3: Digit-addition table.

Exercise 0.1.4 *Learn Table 3 by heart.*

We are not kidding here, we exactly mean 'learn by heart'. The readers definitely have known or will learn that to solve even simplest algebraic problems, for example to combine like terms, we must do simple arithmetic, and if one does not have the addition table "in fingertips", the solution becomes endless torture. The author and thousands of other teachers have observed for many years how the students, who were exposed to calculators from "kindergarten" and did not acquire firm and automatic arithmetic skills, have systematically failed their successive mathematical classes, up to calculus.

Exercise 0.1.5 *Fill in blanks in Table 4.*

+	10	3	6	1	4	2	8	9	0	5	7
3											
1											
9											
10											
5											
8											
6											
2											
0											
7											
4											

Table 4: The addition table for Exercise 0.1.5.

0.1.2   Addition of Positive Many-Digit Numbers

Now we can add any two positive many-digit numbers. When the second number is a single-digit number, that is, just a digit, the simplest way is linear set-up by "completing to the ten". Let us add, say, $426 + 3$. Since $6 + 3 = 9$, which is less than 10, it does not affect the digits of tens in the first addend, thus $426 + 3 = 429$. It is worth mentioning, in particular, that $a + 0 = a$ for any number a.

Now let us add $426 + 7$. We immediately see that the "distance" from 426 to the nearest multiple of 10, which is larger than 425, that is, to 430, is 4 units: $426 + 4 = 430$ and $7 > 4$. Thus, we can split the 7 as $7 = 4 + 3$ and write

$$426 + 7 = 426 + 4 + 3 = 430 + 3 = 433.$$

Exercise 0.1.6 *Add* $20 + 3$; $23 + 3$; $20 + 7$; $23 + 8$; $203 + 6$; $203 + 7$; $203 + 8$; $203 + 9$.

Of course, there is no need to write down simple problems like this one, in such detail. If we have learnt by heart the digit-addition table, we must solve such problems "by eyes". However, to add many-digit numbers, it is more convenient to use the vertical format. We demonstrate the format by the sequel simple example with small numbers.

Example 0.1.2 *Add* $25 + 7$.

Solution. We remember that $25 = 20 + 5$, thus we have to add three smaller numbers, $20 + 5 + 7$. We start up by adding the two smaller, one-digit numbers, $5 + 7 = 12$. But 12 is not a digit, $12 = 10 + 2$, that is, 12 contains 1 ten and 2 unities. Therefore, we record 2 at the place for unities and have to add two "old" tens $20 = 2 \cdot 10$ with one "new" 10, giving $20 + 10 = 30$. It is usually said that we *carry on* the number of "new" tens, that is, in this example 1 to the ten's place, and the digit 1 itself is called *carry-on*. The procedure is known as the *long addition algorithm*. It is convenient to represent it in writing as follows.

Write both addends below one another, taking care about the *vertical line-up*. This means that the digits representing unities must be in the same vertical column allocated to the unities, the digits representing tens must be in the vertical column reserved for the tens, the digits representing hundreds must be in the vertical column reserved for the hundreds, etc. In our Example 0.1.2 we write

$$
\begin{array}{r}
25 \\
+ \quad 7 \\
\hline
\end{array}
$$

The sum appears below the horizontal line, in the *sum row*. Since $5 + 7 = 10 + 2$, we put the digit of unities, 2 in the sum row, and in the corresponding column below 7, and write **the carry-on 1 (the carry-ons in all the examples are**

printed in bold) in the column for tens above 2:

$$
\begin{array}{r}
\mathbf{1} \\
25 \\
+ \quad 7 \\
\hline
2
\end{array}
$$

Now we add the digits in the *tens'* column, including the **carry-on**, $1 + 2 = 3$, and place the sum in the tens' column in the sum row:

$$
\begin{array}{r}
\not{1} \\
25 \\
+ \quad 7 \\
\hline
32
\end{array}
$$

Thus, $25 + 7 = 32$. The carry-on **1** was crossed because it represents the tens, and we added it to the digit of tens 2.

The long addition of many-digit numbers works exactly the same way, we may just need several carry-ones.

Example 0.1.3 *Compute the sum* $12\,087 + 67 + 9\,309$.

Solution. The addends must be lined up starting from the right-most column of unities as follows:

$$
\begin{array}{r}
12\,087 \\
67 \\
+ \quad 9\,309 \\
\hline
\end{array}
$$

We move from right to the left and first add the unities. Since $7 + 7 + 9 = 14 + 9 = 23$, the digit of unities in the sum is 3 and the first **carry-on** is **2**, so that we get

$$
\begin{array}{r}
\mathbf{2} \\
12\,087 \\
67 \\
+ \quad 9\,309 \\
\hline
3
\end{array}
$$

Next we add the digits of tens including the first *carry-on* **2**, $\mathbf{2} + 8 + 6 + 0 = 16$, thus the digit of tens in the sum is 6 and the second **carry-on** is **1**:

$$
\begin{array}{r}
1\!\!\not{2} \\
12\,087 \\
67 \\
+ \quad 9\,309 \\
\hline
63
\end{array}
$$

Now we take up the digits of hundreds, including the second **carry-on 1**, and have $1 + 0 + 0 + 3 = 4$, hence the digit of hundreds in the sum is 4 with zero **carry-on**:

$$
\begin{array}{r}
\mathllap{1\!\!\!/2} \\
12\,087 \\
67 \\
+ \quad 9\,309 \\
\hline
463
\end{array}
$$

At the next step we add $2 + 0 + 9 = 11$, computing the digit of thousands, 1, and the next **carry-on 1**:

$$
\begin{array}{r}
1\!\!\!/\ \ 1\!\!\!/2 \\
12\,087 \\
67 \\
+ \quad 9\,309 \\
\hline
1\,463
\end{array}
$$

And finally we find the left-most, ten-thousand digit of the sum, $1 + 1 = 2$:

$$
\begin{array}{r}
1\!\!\!/\ \ 1\!\!\!/2 \\
12\,087 \\
67 \\
+ \quad 9\,309 \\
\hline
21\,463
\end{array}
$$

□

Remark 0.1.1 *It may be convenient to write the examples like this one adding a few extra zeros, as follows:*

$$
\begin{array}{r}
12\,087 \\
00\,067 \\
+ \quad 09\,309 \\
\hline
\end{array}
$$

These zeros are insignificant in the sense of subsection 1.4.2, so that they do not change the result, but (sometimes) make writing easier.

Exercise 0.1.7 *Compute the sums. Use the long addition and do not forget to line up the addends.*

$23 + 9 =$	$983 + 7 =$
$3\,457 + 8 + 9 =$	$450\,067 + 9 =$
$456 + 8 + 6 =$	$123 + 2\,345 + 7\,008 =$
$999 + 1\,001 =$	$983 + 2\,045 + 709\,808 =$
$3\,457 + 128\,345 + 9\,909 =$	$2 + 450\,067 + 9\,801\,008 =$
$31 + 456 + 8\,709\,608 + 102\,030\,405 =$	$321 + 12 + 1\,002 + 7 + 1\,431 =$
$252 + 149 + 13 + 1\,421 + 9 =$	$6\,607 + 19 + 243 + 1\,523 =$

Exercise 0.1.8 *Design and solve two more exercises similar to the previous ones.*

0.1.3 Subtraction of Whole Numbers

Next we review the subtraction of whole numbers. We remind that the equation $a - b = c$ means that $a = b + c$; the number a in $a - b = c$ is called the *minuend*, b is called the *subtrahend*, and c the *difference* of a and b (in this order!). We start by considering only the problems, such that the minuend is bigger than the subtrahend, that is, the difference is positive. To succeed, we have to learn and memorize the differences of digits, that is, of the one-digit integer numbers.

Exercise 0.1.9 *Complete and learn by heart the subtraction table below.*

Digit Subtraction Table:

$0 - 0 = 0$

$1 - 0 = 1$ $1 - 1 = 0$

$2 - 0 =$ $2 - 1 = 1$ $2 - 2 = 0$

$3 - 0 =$ $3 - 1 = \ldots$

$4 - 0 =$ $\ldots$

$5 - 0 =$ $\ldots$

$6 - 0 =$ $\ldots$

$7 - 0 =$ $\ldots$

$8 - 0 =$ $\ldots$

$9 - 0 =$ $9 - 1 =$ $9 - 2 = \ldots$

When we add two integer numbers, the sum of digits is sometimes bigger than 10, and we must *carry* this digit to the left neighboring column. While *subtracting* integer numbers, we often have to deal with the opposite case, when we must subtract a larger digit from a smaller one. To proceed, we have to *borrow* one unit from the left neighbor of this column. Consider examples.

Example 0.1.4 *Subtract* $20 - 8$.

Solution. When a subtrahend is a one-digit number, these examples should be done as follows[3],

$$20 - 8 = (10 + 10) - 8 = 10 + (10 - 8) = 10 + 2 = 12;$$

moreover, even these computations can and should be done mentally, "by eyes". However, to subtract many-digit numbers, we must learn the technique of "borrowing".

Let us write the preceding example as

$$\begin{array}{r} 20 \\ - 8 \\ \hline \end{array}$$

---

[3]We believe that any discussion of the *associative property* at this point will be ahead of time.

We cannot subtract 8 units from 0 units here, since the result is not a digit. However, 20 consists of two 10s, and we can borrow a *ten* from these two tens, bring it over to the column of ones and there split this ten into 10 units, as

$$10 = 1 + 1 + 1 + 1 + 1 + 1 + 1 + 1 + 1 + 1.$$

Again, 10 is not a digit. Now we can subtract 8 units from 10 units, $10 - 8 = 2$, but do not forget that now we have only one ten left:

$$
\begin{array}{r}
\mathbf{10} \\
\cancel{2}0 \\
-\quad 8 \\
\hline
2
\end{array}
$$

We are done with the units and move one step to the left, to the column of tens. In the minuend we now have only one ten, **1**, while blank in the subtrahend in this column stands for 0 tens. Thus, we subtract $1 - 0 = 1$ and record this difference 1 as the left-most digit of the difference:

$$
\begin{array}{r}
\mathbf{1} \\
\cancel{2}0 \\
-\quad 8 \\
\hline
12
\end{array}
$$

$\square$

The result is not very impressive, we know that $20-8 = 12$, but this example was intended only to demonstrate the technique of *borrowing*, which allows us to subtract any numbers. Let us practice.

Example 0.1.5 *Subtract* $124 - 98$.

Solution. Many people can do this problem without writing, just by observing that $98 = 100 - 2$, hence

$$124 - 98 = 100 + 24 - 98 = 24 + 2 = 26,$$

which is a perfect solution, that can be done "by eyes.". However, to develop the computational techniques, we proceed slowly, as in the previous example, and demonstrate the detail necessary in more complicated problems. We start by representing the problem in the vertical format,

$$
\begin{array}{r}
124 \\
-\quad 98 \\
\hline
\end{array}
$$

As before, we are to borrow a 10 from $20 = 10 + 10$. Now we have $10 + 4 = 14$ unities, and we can subtract $14 - 8 = 6$, hence

$$
\begin{array}{r}
\mathbf{10} \\
1\,\cancel{2}4 \\
-\quad 98 \\
\hline
6
\end{array}
$$

Only one 10 left, and we cannot subtract 9 tens from 1 ten. Therefore, we have to make another step to the left, where there is a 1, representing a hundred. We split it into 10 tens, add the **carry-on 1**, getting 11 tens, and subtract 9, representing 9 tens in the subtrahend. Hence, the digit of tens in the difference is $11 - 9 = 2$, and the answer is

$$
\begin{array}{r}
\mathbf{11} \\
\not{1}\not{2}4 \\
- \quad 98 \\
\hline
26
\end{array}
$$

□

Example 0.1.6 *Subtract*

$$
\begin{array}{r}
103000405 \\
- \quad 90867070 \\
\hline
\end{array}
$$

Solution. The first step is easy, $5 - 0 = 5$, thus

$$
\begin{array}{r}
103000405 \\
- \quad 90867070 \\
\hline
5
\end{array}
$$

Next, to subtract 7 from 0, we borrow a hundred from the given four hundreds, and split this *borrowed* hundred into 10 tens:

$$
\begin{array}{r}
\mathbf{10} \\
103000\not{4}05 \\
- \quad 90867070 \\
\hline
5
\end{array}
$$

Thus subtracting $10 - 7$, we get

$$
\begin{array}{r}
\not{1} \ \not{0} \\
103000\not{4}05 \\
- \quad 90867070 \\
\hline
35
\end{array}
$$

Now we have to deal with the digits of hundreds, and the subtraction $3 - 0$ is immediate:

$$
\begin{array}{r}
\not{1} \ \not{0} \\
103000\not{4}05 \\
- \quad 90867070 \\
\hline
335
\end{array}
$$

Next we again have to subtract a bigger digit 7 from a smaller digit 0. To proceed, we must, as before, borrow, but the nearest available non-zero digit to the left is 3, thus we borrow 1 from the 3, leaving 2, and split this 1, representing *one million*, as $1\,000\,000 = 900\,000 + 90\,000 + 10\,000$:

$$
\begin{array}{r}
\mathbf{19910\,\cancel{1}\,0} \\
10\cancel{3}000\cancel{4}05 \\
-\quad 90867070 \\
\hline
335
\end{array}
$$

Now we do $10 - 7 = 3$,

$$
\begin{array}{r}
\mathbf{19910\,\cancel{1}\,0} \\
10\cancel{3}000\cancel{4}05 \\
-\quad 90867070 \\
\hline
3335
\end{array}
$$

Next, $9 - 6 = 3$, leading to

$$
\begin{array}{r}
\mathbf{19910\,\cancel{1}\,0} \\
10\cancel{3}000\cancel{4}05 \\
-\quad 90867070 \\
\hline
33335
\end{array}
$$

At this step we subtract $9 - 8 = 1$, so that

$$
\begin{array}{r}
\mathbf{19910\,\cancel{1}\,0} \\
10\cancel{3}000\cancel{4}05 \\
-\quad 90867070 \\
\hline
233335
\end{array}
$$

then $2 - 0 = 2$, giving

$$
\begin{array}{r}
\mathbf{1991\cancel{0}\,1\,0} \\
10\cancel{3}000\cancel{4}05 \\
-\quad 90867070 \\
\hline
2233335
\end{array}
$$

and finally, $10 - 9 = 1$, thus

$$
\begin{array}{r}
\mathbf{19910\,\cancel{1}\,0} \\
10\cancel{3}000\cancel{4}05 \\
-\quad 90867070 \\
\hline
12233335
\end{array}
$$

Hence, $103\,000\,405 - 90\,867\,070 = 12\,233\,335$. $\qquad\qquad\square$

Exercise 0.1.10 *Compute the differences.*

$23 - 9 =$	$983 - 7 =$	$3\,457 - 89 =$
$450\,067 - 9 =$	$456 - 86 =$	$232\,345 - 7\,008 =$
$999 - 101$	$3\,457 - 1\,283 =$	$983 - 245 =$
$450\,067 - 98\,010 =$	$31\,456 - 8\,709 =$	$321 - 12 =$
$252 - 149 =$	$6\,607 - 1\,523 =$	$3\,000 - 1\,999 =$

Exercise 0.1.11 *Compute. In all these examples we have to work in the natural order, from left to right. The order of operations will be discussed in detail in Section 1.6.3.*

$1\,002\,345 - 70\,908 =$	$709\,808 - 2\,045 =$
$3\,457 + 128\,345 - 9\,909 =$	$2\,450\,067 - 801\,008 =$
$38\,481 - 293 + 1\,005 =$	$8\,670 - 8\,631 + 253 =$
$1\,143 - 235 - 709 =$	$7\,599\,932 - 983\,876 =$
$31 + 870\,960 - 8\,456 =$	$123 + 679\,123 - 6\,569 =$
3 *less than* 77	*Subtract* 3 *from* 77
The difference of 77 *and* 3	3 *less than the sum of* 77 *and* 15

Exercise 0.1.12 *Design and solve two more exercises similar to the previous ones.*

0.1.4 Multiplication of Digits

It would be boring and error provoking to add $\underbrace{3 + 3 + \cdots + 3}_{23 \text{ threes}}$ 23 times. However, there is a short-cut for repeating addition, called *multiplication*. Here we review the multiplication for the one-digit integers only, and in Section 1.8 we consider multiplication of any whole numbers. The multiplication is denoted by the *central dot* as $2 \cdot 3 = 6$, or, equivalently, by the cross, as 2×3; we will systematically use the former. The numbers 2 and 3 here are called *factors* or *multipliers*, the number 6 is their *product*. If there is no ambiguity, the multiplication symbol can be omitted. For example, by agreement, the expression $a(b + c)$ is the same as $a \cdot (b + c)$ or as $a \cdot (b + c)$. But a multiplication symbol cannot be omitted in $2 \cdot 3 = 6$, for otherwise we shall read it as the two-digit number $23 \neq 6$. The products of whole numbers not exceeding 10, that is, the digits 0, 1, 2, ..., 8, 9 and the number 10, are given in the Table 5.

All the entries in table 5 can be checked by addition. Thus, $7 \cdot 4 = 7 + 7 + 7 + 7 = 14 + 7 + 7 = 21 + 7 = 28$. We observe that the table is symmetric with respect to its main diagonal. Indeed, $4 \cdot 7$ can be expanded in two different ways, either as

$$4 \cdot 7 = 4 + 4 + 4 + 4 + 4 + 4 + 4 = 8 + 4 + 4 + 4 + 4 + 4 = 28$$

·	0	1	2	3	4	5	6	7	8	9	10
0	0	0	0	0	0	0	0	0	0	0	0
1	0	1	2	3	4	5	6	7	8	9	10
2	0	2	4	6	8	10	12	14	16	18	20
3	0	3	6	9	12	15	18	21	24	27	30
4	0	4	8	12	16	20	24	28	32	36	40
5	0	5	10	15	20	25	30	35	40	45	50
6	0	6	12	18	24	30	36	42	48	54	60
7	0	7	14	21	28	35	42	49	56	63	70
8	0	8	16	24	32	40	48	56	64	72	80
9	0	9	18	27	36	45	54	63	72	81	90
10	0	10	20	30	40	50	60	70	80	90	100

Table 5: Digit Multiplication Table.

or as

$$4 \cdot 7 = 7 + 7 + 7 + 7 = 28.$$

Similarly to the addition, the multiplication is *commutative*, that is, for any a and b,

$$a \cdot b = b \cdot a.$$

Exercise 0.1.13 *Verify, as in the example above, that all the entries in Table 6 are correct and learn the multiplication table by heart – This is important for the future study, even though it looks childish. Once again, the experience shows that many students fail Calculus because they do not know arithmetic!*

Problem 0.1.2 *Why do the second from the top line and the second from the left column contain only zeros? What property of the zero shows up here?*

This property says that the product of any number and zero, in any order, is always zero:

$$a \cdot 0 = 0 \cdot a = 0 \cdot 0 = 0.$$

□

Next, we observe that the third row from top is identical to the upper-most row, and the third column from the left is identical to the left-most column. This is not a coincidence and exhibits a simple fact, that the 1 is the so-called *identity* or *neutral* element for multiplication, meaning that for any number a,

$$a \cdot 1 = 1 \cdot a = a.$$

Exercise 0.1.14 *Fill in Table 6 and learn it by heart.*

$0 \cdot 0 =$	$1 \cdot 0 =$	$2 \cdot 0 =$	$3 \cdot 0 =$	$4 \cdot 0 =$	$5 \cdot 0 =$
$0 \cdot 1 =$	$1 \cdot 1 =$	$2 \cdot 1 =$	$3 \cdot 1 =$	$4 \cdot 1 =$	$5 \cdot 1 =$
$0 \cdot 2 =$	$1 \cdot 2 =$	$2 \cdot 2 =$	$3 \cdot 2 =$	$4 \cdot 2 =$	$5 \cdot 2 =$
$0 \cdot 3 =$	$1 \cdot 3 =$	$2 \cdot 3 =$	$3 \cdot 3 =$	$4 \cdot 3 =$	$5 \cdot 3 =$
$0 \cdot 4 =$	$1 \cdot 4 =$	$2 \cdot 4 =$	$3 \cdot 4 =$	$4 \cdot 4 =$	$5 \cdot 4 =$
$0 \cdot 5 =$	$1 \cdot 5 =$	$2 \cdot 5 =$	$3 \cdot 5 =$	$4 \cdot 5 =$	$5 \cdot 5 =$
$0 \cdot 6 =$	$1 \cdot 6 =$	$2 \cdot 6 =$	$3 \cdot 6 =$	$4 \cdot 6 =$	$5 \cdot 6 =$
$0 \cdot 7 =$	$1 \cdot 7 =$	$2 \cdot 7 =$	$3 \cdot 7 =$	$4 \cdot 7 =$	$5 \cdot 7 =$
$0 \cdot 8 =$	$1 \cdot 8 =$	$2 \cdot 8 =$	$3 \cdot 8 =$	$4 \cdot 8 =$	$5 \cdot 8 =$
$0 \cdot 9 =$	$1 \cdot 9 =$	$2 \cdot 9 =$	$3 \cdot 9 =$	$4 \cdot 9 =$	$5 \cdot 9 =$
$0 \cdot 10 =$	$1 \cdot 10 =$	$2 \cdot 10 =$	$3 \cdot 10 =$	$4 \cdot 10 =$	$5 \cdot 10 =$

$6 \cdot 0 =$	$7 \cdot 0 =$	$8 \cdot 0 =$	$9 \cdot 0 =$	$10 \cdot 0 =$
$6 \cdot 1 =$	$7 \cdot 1 =$	$8 \cdot 1 =$	$9 \cdot 1 =$	$10 \cdot 1 =$
$6 \cdot 2 =$	$7 \cdot 2 =$	$8 \cdot 2 =$	$9 \cdot 2 =$	$10 \cdot 2 =$
$6 \cdot 3 =$	$7 \cdot 3 =$	$8 \cdot 3 =$	$9 \cdot 3 =$	$10 \cdot 3 =$
$6 \cdot 4 =$	$7 \cdot 4 =$	$8 \cdot 4 =$	$9 \cdot 4 =$	$10 \cdot 4 =$
$6 \cdot 5 =$	$7 \cdot 5 =$	$8 \cdot 5 =$	$9 \cdot 5 =$	$10 \cdot 5 =$
$6 \cdot 6 =$	$7 \cdot 6 =$	$8 \cdot 6 =$	$9 \cdot 6 =$	$10 \cdot 6 =$
$6 \cdot 7 =$	$7 \cdot 7 =$	$8 \cdot 7 =$	$9 \cdot 7 =$	$10 \cdot 7 =$
$6 \cdot 8 =$	$7 \cdot 8 =$	$8 \cdot 8 =$	$9 \cdot 8 =$	$10 \cdot 8 =$
$6 \cdot 9 =$	$7 \cdot 9 =$	$8 \cdot 9 =$	$9 \cdot 9 =$	$10 \cdot 9 =$
$6 \cdot 10 =$	$7 \cdot 10 =$	$8 \cdot 10 =$	$9 \cdot 10 =$	$10 \cdot 10 =$

Table 6: The expanded digit multiplication table (Exercise 0.1.14).

Answers 0.1

Exercise 0.1.1. 177, 12 24 are the addends, 213 is the sum.

Exercise 0.1.3. 17; 17; 18; 15; 15; 16.

Exercise 0.1.5. See Table 7 on P. 37.

Exercise 0.1.6. 209; 210; 211.

Exercise 0.1.7. $23 + 9 = 32$; $983 + 7 = 990$; $3\,457 + 8 + 9 = 3\,474$; $450\,067 + 9 = 450\,076$; $456 + 8 + 6 = 470$; $123 + 2\,345 + 7\,008 = 9\,476$; $999 + 1\,001 = 2\,000$; $983 + 2\,045 + 709\,808 = 712\,836$; $3\,457 + 128\,345 + 9\,909 = 141\,711$; $2 + 450\,067 + 9\,801\,008 = 10\,251\,077$; $31 + 456 + 8\,709\,608 + 102\,030\,405 = 110\,740\,500$; $321 + 12 + 1\,002 + 7 + 1\,431 = 2\,773$; $252 + 149 + 13 + 1\,421 + 9 = 1\,844$; $6\,607 + 19 + 243 + 1\,523 = 8\,392$

+	10	3	6	1	4	2	8	9	0	5	7
3	13	6	9	4	7	5	11	12	3	8	10
1	11	4	7	2	5	3	9	10	1	6	8
9	19	12	15	10	13	11	17	18	9	14	16
10	20	13	16	11	14	12	18	19	10	15	17
5	15	8	11	6	9	7	13	14	5	10	12
8	18	11	14	9	12	10	16	17	8	13	15
6	16	9	12	7	10	8	14	15	6	11	13
2	12	5	8	3	6	4	10	11	2	7	9
0	10	3	6	1	4	2	8	9	0	5	7
7	17	10	13	8	11	9	15	16	7	12	14
4	14	7	10	5	8	6	12	13	4	9	11

Table 7: Exercise 0.1.5

Exercise 0.1.9.

$0 - 0 = 0$;
$1 - 0 = 1$; $1 - 1 = 0$;
$2 - 0 = 2$; $2 - 1 = 1$; $2 - 2 = 0$;
$3 - 0 = 3$; $3 - 1 = 2$; $3 - 2 = 1$; $3 - 3 = 0$;
$4 - 0 = 4$; $4 - 1 = 3$; $4 - 2 = 2$; $4 - 3 = 1$; $4 - 4 = 0$;
$5 - 0 = 5$; $5 - 1 = 4$; $5 - 2 = 3$; $5 - 3 = 2$; $5 - 4 = 1$; $5 - 5 = 0$;
$6 - 0 = 6$; $6 - 1 = 5$; $6 - 2 = 4$; $6 - 3 = 3$; $6 - 4 = 2$; $6 - 5 = 1$;
$7 - 0 = 7$; $7 - 1 = 6$; $7 - 2 = 5$; $7 - 3 = 4$; $7 - 4 = 3$; $7 - 5 = 2$;
$8 - 0 = 8$; $8 - 1 = 7$; $8 - 2 = 6$; $8 - 3 = 5$; $8 - 4 = 4$; $8 - 5 = 3$;
$9 - 0 = 9$; $9 - 1 = 8$; $9 - 2 = 7$; $9 - 3 = 6$; $9 - 4 = 5$; $9 - 5 = 4$;

$6 - 6 = 0$;
$7 - 6 = 1$; $7 - 7 = 0$;
$8 - 6 = 2$; $8 - 7 = 1$; $8 - 8 = 0$;
$9 - 6 = 3$; $9 - 7 = 2$; $9 - 8 = 1$; $9 - 9 = 0$

Exercise 0.1.10.

$23 - 9 = 14$ $983 - 7 = 976$
$3\,457 - 89 = 3\,368$ $450\,067 - 9 = 450\,058$
$456 - 86 = 370$ $232\,345 - 7\,008 = 225\,337$
$999 - 101 = 898$ $3\,457 - 1\,283 = 2\,174$
$983 - 245 = 738$ $450\,067 - 98\,010 = 352\,057$
$31\,456 - 8\,709 = 22\,747$ $321 - 12 = 309$
$252 - 149 = 103$ $6\,607 - 1\,523 = 5\,084$
$3\,000 - 1\,999 = 1\,001$

Exercise 0.1.11.

$1\,002\,345 - 70\,908 = 931\,437$

$3\,457 + 128\,345 - 9\,909 = 121\,893$

$38\,481 - 293 + 1\,005 = 39\,193$

$1\,143 - 235 - 709 = 199$

$31 + 870\,960 - 8\,456 = 862\,535$

74

74

$709\,808 - 2\,045 = 707\,763$

$2\,450\,067 - 801\,008 = 1\,649\,059$

$8\,670 - 8\,631 + 253 = 292$

$7\,599\,932 - 983\,876 = 6\,616\,056$

$123 + 679\,123 - 6\,569 = 672\,677$

74

$89.$

Chapter 1

The Integers

Here, assuming the firm knowledge of the introductory chapter 0, we systematically review the four arithmetic operations: addition, subtraction, multiplication and division of the signed integer numbers.

1.1 Terminology

Every mathematical text consists of statements (narrative sentences), called *theorems, lemmas, propositions*, etc. Traditionally, by lemma we understand simple, auxiliary statement, and by theorem more important result. The choice of the terminology, though, is not very crucial and depends upon the writer; sometimes you can see *Claims* or *Assertions*. It is more important that to develop a rigorous mathematical theory, we must separate several initial *primary* statements, which we accept for granted, as obvious, while all the other statements must be *proved* in some precise mathematical sense. The *primary* statements, which we accept without proofs, are called *axioms* or *postulates*.

A classical example of an axiom is *Euclides' Fifth Postulate* or the *Parallel Lines axiom*:

Given a line in a plane and a point outside of the line, there is one and only line, going through the given point and parallel to the give line.

For more than two thousands years people tried tried to prove that this statement is a theorem, that is, to derive this claim from other axioms. And only half-a-century ago it was proved that we can develop *two* independent geometries: one where this axiom is valid, and another one, where, given a line and a point beyond this line, there are infinitely many parallel lines through this point. and both geometries describe important portions of our Universe, both have important applications. This example shows that mathematics is alive and has many open problems.

1.2   Natural Numbers

Everyone is familiar with the *positive integer numbers*, called also *natural* or *counting* numbers; this *number set* is traditionally denoted by $\mathbb{N}$:

$$\mathbb{N} = \{1, 2, 3, 4, 5, 6, 7, 8, 9, 10, 11, ...\}. \tag{1.2.1}$$

We learn these numbers, at least a few smaller among them, in the early childhood without any visible effort, while talking and playing with parents and friends, and *naturally* call them *natural numbers*. They are also called counting numbers, because we use them to *count* objects, say *one* child, *two* parents, *three* toys, etc.

Collections of similar things (items, entities) are called in mathematics *sets* and are denoted by (curly) braces, as in formula (1.2.1) above. These things are called *elements* of the set. If a is an element of the set X, this is written as $a \in X$, otherwise $a \notin X$. For example, we can write $1 \in \mathbb{N}$ but New York $\notin \mathbb{N}$.

Most sets that we deal with in our lives, are *finite*, meaning we can count all their elements in finite time. For example, a week consists of *seven* days, most people have *twenty* fingers, nobody has more than 999 999 siblings, etc. However, since any number can be increased by 1, there is no biggest natural number; we say that the set $\mathbb{N}$ does not have the *largest* element, it is an *infinite set*,; this infiniteness is indicated in formula (1.2.1) by the three lower dots ..., called *ellipsis*.

What about the opposite, left direction? It was a huge intellectual leap, which took people several centuries, to introduce a special number *zero* to denote "nothing", and the set containing no element, called *empty set* and denoted by $\emptyset$. The natural numbers and zero[1] are called the *whole numbers*; this set is denoted as $\mathbb{W}$:

$$\mathbb{W} = \{0, 1, 2, 3, 4, 5, 6, 7, 8, 9, 10, ...\}.$$

Exercise 1.2.1 *Are the empty set $\emptyset$ and the set of whole numbers $\mathbb{W}$ finite or infinite?*

If we increase a whole number n by one, the resulting number is denoted by $n + 1$ and is said to (immediately) *follow* n. In turn, n *precedes* $n + 1$. For instance, 4 follows 3, 1 follows 0, 99 follows 98, 0 precedes 1, and 99 precedes 100.

Exercise 1.2.2 *What natural number follows 0? 1? 9? 1 234 567 890?*

Exercise 1.2.3 *What whole number precedes 9? 1 234 567 890? 2? 1? 0?*

Exercise 1.2.4 *List all whole numbers (1) between 3 and 13 inclusive, that is, including the numbers 3 and 13; (2) between 3 and 13 exclusive, that is, excluding the numbers 3 and 13; (3) between 999 and 1001 exclusive; (4) between 12 and 13 inclusive; (5) between 12 and 13 exclusive?*

---

[1] The designation of zero as a whole but not natural number is a matter of agreement, many people think it is *natural* to consider zero also as a natural number, but we follow another tradition and do not designate 0 as a natural number.

Exercise 1.2.5 *Design and solve two more exercises similar to the previous one.*

Fig. 1.1 visualizes some whole numbers as points of the *number line*. The x here is the *generic* symbol denoting numbers populating the number line.

Figure 1.1: The positive part of the number line.

We see that so far the number line is populated very sparsely, with the whole numbers only; gradually we assign a (real) number to every point of the line.

Most measurements in real life have certain *units* (units of measurements!) attached, like 3 dollars, 4 pounds, 100 miles. However, in the following examples we consider, for the most part, *dimensionless* numbers, that is, numbers with no unit of measurement attached.

Answers 1.2

Exercise 1.2.1. $\emptyset$ is finite; the set $\mathbb{W}$ of whole numbers is infinite.
Exercise 1.2.2. 1; 2; 10; 1 234 567 891.
Exercise 1.2.3. 8; 1 234 567 889; 1; 0; No whole number precedes 0.
Exercise 1.2.4 (1) 3,4,5,6,7,8,9,10,11; (2) 4,5,6,7,8,9,10; (3) 1000;
(4) 12, 13; (5) None, this is the empty set.

1.3 Inequalities

The number line determines the natural ordering of numbers. By the long-standing tradition, if a number a is located on the number line to the left of a number b, it is said that a is *smaller* (or *less*) than b; in turn, b is said to be *bigger* (or *larger*, or *greater*) than a. There is a useful mnemonics to memorize that relation: *Left – Less*. These relations are expressed by special *inequality* symbol:

$$a < b.$$

The same relationship between the two quantities a and b can be equivalently written as

$$b > a.$$

For example, the inequality $2 < 3$ and its equivalent inequality $3 > 2$ are valid, these statements are true. Zero is less than any positive number a, $0 < a$, and vice versa, any positive number a is greater than zero, $a > 0$. However, the inequalities $2 < 2$ and $4 > 4$ are false. The arrow in Fig. 1.1 indicates the traditional direction of growth on the number line – from left to right.

Any number, *which is bigger than* 0, is called a *positive number.* for example, all natural numbers are positive. Later on, we learn that there are many non-integer positive numbers. However, to solve many problems, people need much broader set of numbers. Numbers *smaller than* 0 are called *negative numbers*; they will be introduced in section 1.5. The positive numbers and zero are called *nonnegative* numbers; the negative numbers and zero are called *nonpositive* numbers.

For example, the inequality $x > 0$ means that x is a positive number, and $x < 0$ says that x is a negative number.

The inequalities $a < b$ and $c < d$ are said to be *of the same sense*, meaning that both are 'less than'; the inequalities $a > b$ and $c > d$ also have *the same sense 'bigger than'*. The inequalities $a < b$ and $c > d$ have the *opposite sense*, because one is 'less than' and the other is 'greater than'.

Any inequality can be read from *left to right* and from *right to left*, for instance, $10 > 9$ can be read "10 is bigger than 9" or "9 is less than 10", and can be written in an equivalent way as $9 < 10$. The tip of the inequality symbol always points to the smaller quantity and the wider opening to the bigger quantity. The three other kinds of inequalities are also useful:

$$a \leq b,$$

which is read "a is *less than or equal to* b"; this inequality is equivalent to "a does not exceed b" or "a is no more than b", and is equivalent to the double statement "$a < b$ or $a = b$". The inequality

$$a \geq b$$

is read "a is *greater than or equal to* b", which can also be said "a is no less than b", and is equivalent to the double statement "$a > b$ or $a = b$". The inequality

$$a \neq b$$

is read "a *is not equal to* b" and means precisely this, that is, "a and b are *different* quantities".

We repeat that the inequality $0 \leq a$ is valid for every nonnegative number a, and $b \leq 0$ for every nonpositive number b.

For example, all the inequalities $2 < 3$, $3 > 2$, $0 < 1$, $2 \leq 2$, $2 \geq 2$, $4 \geq 4$, $2 \leq 3$, $3 \geq 1$, $2 \neq 4$ are true. On the other hand, $0 \leq -1$ and $3 \neq 3$ fail to be true, these two inequalities are false.

Exercise 1.3.1 *In the following expressions, replace the symbol ? with an appropriate inequality symbol from the list $\{<, >, \leq, \geq, \neq\}$ to make the expression true. Sometimes several options are possible: for example, instead of $5\ ?\ 6$ we can write $5 < 6$, or $5 \leq 6$, or $5 \neq 6$; all these inequalities are true. However, we cannot replace $5\ ?\ 6$ with $5 > 6$ or $5 \geq 6$, because they are both false.*

$$0 \ ? \ 6 \qquad 6 \ ? \ 0 \qquad \tfrac{2}{3} \ ? \ 100 \qquad 5 \ ? \ \tfrac{3}{4} \qquad 15 \ ? \ 64$$

$$55 \ ? \ 6 \qquad 50 \ ? \ 26 \qquad 100 \ ? \ 885 \qquad 105 \ ? \ 605 \qquad 5 \ ? \ 4$$

Exercise 1.3.2 *Some of the following inequalities are false, the others are true. Correct errors, that is, replace the inequality symbol in false statements with a right one. It might be that more than one symbol can be used. For example, $3 > 4$ is false, but the following three inequalities are true, $3 < 4$, or $3 \neq 4$, or $3 \leq 4$.*

$$3 > 0 \qquad 3 < 2 \qquad 4 \geq 4 \qquad 9 < 8 \qquad 15 \geq 10$$

$$8 \leq 8 \qquad 0 \geq 11 \qquad 100 > 99 \qquad 998 < 997 \qquad 5 \leq 4$$

Consider three pairwise different numbers a, b, c, such that $a < b$ and $b < c$; that is, on the number line b is situated to the right of a and c to the right of b. We say in this case that b is *between* a and c. For example, 2 is between 1 and 3, but 3 is not between 1 and 2.

Exercise 1.3.3 *Write down three different integer numbers between 1 and 205. Write down three different numbers between 1 and 205. How many integers are between 1 and 3, inclusive? Exclusive? Between 1 and 2?*

Exercise 1.3.4 *Design and solve two more exercises similar to the previous one.*

Again, consider three numbers a, b, c, such that $a < b$ and $b < c$. It is obvious now that c is located to the right of a, $a < c$. This is an important conclusion.

Theorem 1.3.1 *Transitive Property of Inequalities*

For any real numbers a, b, c, if $a < b$ and $b < c$, then

$$a < c.$$

Of course, if $a > b$ and $b > c$, then $a > c$. □

Exercise 1.3.5 *For any real numbers a, b, c, if $a \leq b$ and $b \leq c$, then $a \leq c$. What is the conclusion, if $a < b$, but $b \leq c$?*

Every mathematical statement contains one or more precisely formulated conditions, called *premises*, and the resulting *conclusion*, which must follow from the premises through some logical rules. In the theorem above, the premises are the inequalities $a < b$ and $b < c$, and the assumption that a, b, and c are real numbers; the conclusion is the inequality $a < c$.

Consider an obvious inequality $3 < 4$, and add any number, say, 13 to both sides of this inequality; we get $3 + 13 < 4 + 13$, that is, $16 < 17$, which is, evidently, also true. If we subtract a positive number, which is the same as to add a negative one, for example, $3 - 2 < 4 - 2$, that is, $1 < 2$, we again get a valid inequality. This simple observation is a special case of the following important claim.

Theorem 1.3.2 *Additive Property of Inequalities*

If we add the same positive quantity to both sides of an inequality, then a valid inequality remains valid and invalid remains invalid: for any $c \geq 0$,

$$a < b \Rightarrow a + c < b + c.$$

□

Remark 1.3.1 *The symbol $\Rightarrow$ here means "implies" or "if...then". Thus, the formula $a < b \Rightarrow a + c < b + c$ above reads* If $a < b$, then $a + c < b + c$.

Since c can be negative, we can write $a - c < b - c$. Reversing these inequalities we have the following properties: For any c,

$$a > b \Rightarrow a + c > b + c$$

$$a < b \Rightarrow a - c < b - c$$

$$a > b \Rightarrow a - c > b - c.$$

We can also add inequalities. Namely, given two inequalities, $a < b$ and $c < d$, by *adding* them we mean that we add their left-hand sides, separately add their right-hand sides, and connect these two sums by the same inequality sign; that is, we get $a+c < b+d$. For instance, after adding the valid inequalities $2 < 7$ and $3 < 8$ we get $2 + 3 < 7 + 8$, that is, $5 < 15$, which is also valid.

Warning: *Only inequalities of the same sense can be added. Addition of the inequalities of opposite sense leads to errors.* Indeed, if we try to add two correct inequalities $1 < 2$ and $19 > 3$, we would get a clearly false statement $20 = 1 + 19 < 5 = 2 + 3$.

However, the inequalities of *opposite sense* can be *subtracted*. For example, subtracting the inequality $1 < 2$ from $19 > 3$, we get a valid statement $19 - 1 > 3 - 2$ or $18 > 1$.

Exercise 1.3.6 *Can the following inequalities be added?*

$$(1) \quad 0 < 6 \quad and \quad 6 < 8 \qquad (2) \quad 6 < 60 \quad and \quad 4 > 14$$

Can we subtract them?

Exercise 1.3.7 *Add or subtract, whichever is possible, the following inequalities pairwise.*

$$(1) \quad 0 < 6 \quad and \quad 6 > 0 \qquad (2) \quad 3 > 0 \quad and \quad 0 \geq 0;$$

$$(3) \quad 2 < 100 \quad and \quad 1 < 2 \qquad (4) \quad 15 > 6 \quad and \quad 55 > 6$$

$$(5) \quad 50 > 26 \quad and \quad 10 < 88 \qquad (6) \quad 105 > 65 \quad and \quad 5 > 4$$

If a is positive and $a < b$, then by the addition property we get $a + a < b + a$, thus $2a < a + b$. Similarly, $a + b < 2b$. Hence by the transitive property of inequalities, $2a < 2b$. It is possible to prove that this property preserves for any *positive* quantity c, leading to the

Theorem 1.3.3 *Multiplicative Property of Inequalities*.

*If we multiply both sides of an inequality by the same **positive** quantity, then the sense of the inequality is preserved, that is, for any positive $c > 0$,*

$$a < b \Rightarrow ca < cb$$

and

$$a > b \Rightarrow ca > cb.$$

$\square$

Exercise 1.3.8 *Can we restate the theorem with $<$ or $>$ signs replaced by $\leq$ or $\geq$?*

Answers 1.3

Exercise 1.3.1. $0 < 6; 6 > 0; \frac{2}{3} < 100; 5 > 3/4; 15 < 64; 55 > 6; 50 > 26;$
   $100 < 885; 105 < 605; 5 > 4.$
Exercise 1.3.2. $3 > 2; 9 > 8; 0 < 11; 998 > 997; 5 > 4.6;$ the other inequalities are correct.
Exercise 1.3.3. For example, $1 < 2 < 31 < 202 < 205.$
   For example, $1 < 2 < 7/2 < 31/2 < 205.$
Exercise 1.3.6. (1) We can add but not subtract, because both have the same sense. (2) We can subtract but not add, because both have the opposite sense.
Exercise 1.3.7. (1) We can subtract and get $-6 < 6$. (2) We can add and get $3 > 0$. (3) We can add and get $3 < 102$. (4) We can add and get $70 > 12$. (5) We can subtract and get $40 > -62$. (6) We can add and get $110 > 69$.

1.4   Decimal Place-Value System

1.4.1   Place-Value Systems

The well-known symbols for the first *ten* whole numbers, namely

$$0,\ 1,\ 2,\ 3,\ 4,\ 5,\ 6,\ 7,\ 8,\ 9$$

are called *digits*. Every digit represents the corresponding *one-digit whole number*. To represent many-digit numbers, we usually use the *decimal place-value system*. There are also non place-value number systems, for example, *Roman numerals*, but they are less convenient for computations. A place-value system is determined by its *base*. Human beings have ten fingers on hands, and due to this reason we use decimal place-value system with the base of 10, containing 10 digits shown above. Current computers use the *binary place-value system* with the base of 2; it has only two digits, 0 and 1.

Exercise 1.4.1 *Among the following, which are digits and which are not?*

$$1, 11, 2, 10, 101, 9, 99, -1, 0$$

Exercise 1.4.2 *Is the set of digits finite or infinite? How many elements does it contain?*

The right-most digit in a positive integer number 123 represents the number of units in the number, its left neighbor represents the number of tens in the number, the next, third digit, if counting from right to the left, gives the number of hundreds; the next positions, to the left, represent thousands, then ten-thousands, hundred-thousands, millions, ten-millions, hundred-millions, billions, etc.

In a place-value system, the same digit may have different *values*, depending upon its *place* (position) in a number. For example, the number 111 is written by making use of the digit 1 repeated three times, but the right-most 1 represents one *unity* or just a *one*, the middle 1 represents a *ten*, that is, 10 unities, and the left-most 1 represents a *hundred*, that is, 10 tens or 100 unities. Thus, the number 111 is an abbreviation of the sum $100 + 10 + 1$.

In the same way, we can expand the number 51 034 as

$$51\,034 = 50\,000 + 1\,000 + 30 + 4,$$

which can be represented as in Table 1.1.

Whole Number	Digit of Ten-Thousands	Digit of Thousands	Digit of Hundreds	Digit of Tens	Digit of Unities
51 034	5	1	0	3	4
51 034 =	$5 \cdot 10\,000$	$+1 \cdot 1\,000$	$+0 \cdot 100$	$+3 \cdot 10$	$+4 \cdot 1$

Table 1.1: Decimal expansion of 51 034.

Let us notice that the digit of hundreds here is zero, and if we omit the zero, we get another, smaller number $5\,134 = 5\,000 + 100 + 30 + 4$, shown in Table 1.2.

Whole Number	Digit of Thousands	Digit of Hundreds	Digit of Tens	Digit of Unities
5 134	5	1	3	4
5 134 =	$5 \cdot 1\,000$	$+1 \cdot 100$	$+3 \cdot 10$	$+4 \cdot 1$

Table 1.2: Decimal expansion of 5 134.

We notice that when we move along a number to the left, the *value* of each digit, "its *weight*", *increases ten-fold* at each step. When we move in the opposite direction, to the right, this value *decreases ten-fold*. Thus, in 222, the middle 2 represents 20, that is, ten times the right-most 2, and the left-most 2 represents 200, that is, it is ten times *heavier* than the middle 2. This is the precise meaning of the term 'place-value system.'

1.4.2 Significant and Insignificant Digits

Let us compare the numbers 123, 0123 and 1230. If we expand them in decimal system (base 10), we have

$$123 = 100 + 20 + 3 = 1 \cdot 100 + 2 \cdot 10 + 3 \cdot 1,$$
$$0123 = 0 \cdot 1000 + 100 + 20 + 3,$$
$$1230 = 1000 + 200 + 30 + 0,$$

hence, the first two numbers are the same, $123 = 0123$, but the third one is ten times the former, $1230 = 123 \cdot 10$. Moreover, the number $1023 = 1000 + 20 + 3$ is bigger than 123 but less than 1230. Thus, zeros in decimal numbers can play quite different roles. The zeros located to *the left* of all the non-zero digits are called *insignificant* (non-significant) *zeros*, while zeros located to the *right* of any non-zero digit, including the zeros between two non-zero digits, are called *significant*. Insignificant zeros can be omitted, it is just a matter of convenience whether to write them or not. However, if we delete a significant zero, the value of the number will change. For instance, $090 = 90$, but $90 \neq 9$.

Exercise 1.4.3 *Expand the following numbers as the sums of unities, tens, hundreds, thousands, etc.*

$$300\,450 = \qquad 1\,001\,200 = \qquad 1\,000\,000 =$$
$$1\,500\,050 = \qquad 908\,657\,002 = \qquad 2\,132\,435\,465 =$$

Exercise 1.4.4 *In the following numbers, which zeros are significant and which are insignificant?*

100	010	015	5050
50	10	105	05004060

Exercise 1.4.5 *Design and solve two more exercises similar to the previous ones.*

Exercise 1.4.6 *Are the zeros, used in the car license plates, significant or not? The same question regarding the lottery tickets?*

1.4.3 Rounding

Writing down many-digit numbers like $1\,309\,658\,003$ is cumbersome and may involve errors. Moreover, in many problems several right-most digits are all but useless, they provide very little information – indeed, what is \$3 comparing to a billion? In such problems it is convenient to *round off* the number, that is, to find an approximate value of the number by replacing a few right-most digits of the number by zeros. How many digits are to be replaced by zeros, depends on a problem we are solving – the problem must specify, to what place we have to round the number. A problem usually spells out like this: "Round off to the nearest *unity*, or to the nearest *ten*, or to the nearest *hundred*, etc.

Example 1.4.1 *Round off to the nearest ten the following ten two-digit numbers,*

$$10, 11, 12, 13, 14, 15, 16, 17, 18, 19.$$

Solution. *These numbers are between* 10 *(inclusive) and* 20 *(exclusive). We observe that* $14 - 10 = 4$, *which is less than* $20 - 14 = 6$, *therefore, it is reasonable to assume that* 14 *is closer to* 10 *than to* 20; *this is even more true for* $10, 11, 12, 13$. *On the other hand,* $20 - 16 = 4$ *is less than* $16 - 10 = 6$, *and the same is true for* $17, 18, 19$. *Thus, if we have to round an integer from the set*

$$10, 11, 12, 13, 14, 15, 16, 17, 18, 19$$

to the nearest ten, *the closest "ten" for the numbers* $10, 11, 12, 13, 14$ *is* 10, *while for* $16, 17, 18, 19$ *the nearest is* 20; *the middle number* 15 *by definition is attached to the second set, thus,* 15, *rounded to the nearest ten, is* 20.   □

Surely, the same reasoning is valid for the integers with any number of digits, and we state the general rule for the rounding.

To round off a given whole number to the specified position:

Locate the digit D *at the place we want the number to be rounded off to.*

If the digit, which is the immediate right neighbor of D *is less than* 5 *(that is, it is* $0, 1, 2, 3$ *or* 4*) preserve* D *and replace all the digits to the right of* D *by zeros.*

On the other hand, if the digit, which is the immediate right neighbor of D *is* 5 *or more than* 5 *(that is, it is* $5, 6, 7, 8$ *or* 9*) increase* D *by* 1 *and replace all the digits to the right of* D *by zeros.*

Example 1.4.2 *Round off* 13 *to the nearest ten.*

Solution. The digit of tens in the number is 1. Since the digit of units (its right neighbor) is 3, and $3 < 5$, we must preserve 1 and replace 3 with 0. The answer is $13 \approx 10$. Similarly, 126, rounded to the nearest ten, is $126 \approx 130$; 115, rounded to the nearest ten, is $115 \approx 120$; and 140, rounded to the nearest ten, is $140 \approx 140$.   □

Example 1.4.3 *Round off the number* 1 309 648 038 *to the nearest ten.*

Solution. The digit of tens in the number is 3 and its right number, that is the digit of units is $8 > 5$. Thus, we change 3 by 4, replace the 8 with 0, and get

$$1\,309\,648\,038 \approx 1\,309\,648\,040.$$

□

If we have to round off the same number 1 309 648 038 to the nearest *hundred*, we see that the digit of hundreds is 0 and its right neighbor in the original number is 3, which is less than 5, hence

$$1\,309\,648\,038 \approx 1\,309\,648\,000.$$

If we depart from the rounded number 1 309 648 040, the result is the same. Now let us round off the same number 1 309 648 038 to the nearest *thousand*. The digit of thousands is 8 and its right neighbor is $0 < 5$, hence after rounding we get

$$1\,309\,648\,038 \approx 1\,309\,650\,000.$$

However, if we have to round off the same number 1 309 648 038 to the nearest *ten-thousand*, we see that the digit of ten-thousands is 4 and its right neighbor is $8 > 5$. Whence by the rule, we replace 4 by $4 + 1 = 5$ and get

$$1\,309\,648\,038 \approx 1\,309\,650\,000.$$

If we want to continue and round off the same number 1 309 648 038 to the digit of *hundred-thousands*, which is 6, the right neighbor of this 6 is $5 \geq 5$, so that we increase the 6 by 1 and replace all the digits to the right by zeros:

$$1\,309\,648\,038 \approx 1\,309\,700\,000.$$

Finally, to round off the same number

$$1\,309\,648\,038$$

to the digit of *millions*, we must increase the current 9 by 1, for the right neighbor of 9 is $6 > 5$. But $9 + 1 = 10$, which *is not* a digit, thus we replace 9 by 0 AND increase its *left neighbor* by 1, resulting in

$$1\,309\,648\,038 \approx 1\,310\,000\,000.$$

Exercise 1.4.7 *Round off each of the following numbers to the nearest ten, hundred, thousand, etc., whichever is appropriate. For example, $123 \approx 120$ to the nearest ten, $123 \approx 100$ to the nearest hundred, $123 \approx 0$ to the nearest thousand.*

$1\,207 \approx$	$7\,008 \approx$	$2\,345 \approx$	$983 \approx$
$909 \approx$	$3\,457 \approx$	$128\,345 \approx$	$9\,999 \approx$

$$709\,808 \approx$$

Exercise 1.4.8 *Design and solve two more exercises similar to the previous one.*

Answers 1.4

Exercise 1.4.1. Only $1, 2, 9$ and 0 are digits

Exercise 1.4.2. The set of digits is finite, it contains 10 elements

Exercise 1.4.3. $300\,450 = 3 \cdot 100\,000 + 0 \cdot 10\,000 + 0 \cdot 1\,000 + 4 \cdot 100 + 5 \cdot 10 + 0 \cdot 1$
$1\,001\,200 = 1 \cdot 1\,000\,000 + 1 \cdot 1\,000 + 2 \cdot 100; \; 1\,000\,000 = 1 \cdot 1\,000\,000$

Exercise 1.4.4. The insignificant zeros are only the left-most zeros in 010, in 015, and in 05 004 060; all the other zeros are significant.

Exercise 1.4.7. $1\,207 \approx 1\,210 \approx 1\,200 \approx 1\,000$; $7\,008 \approx 7\,010 \approx 7\,000$;

$$2\,345 \approx 2\,350 \approx 2\,400 \approx 2\,000; \qquad 983 \approx 980 \approx 1\,000;$$
$$909 \approx 910 \approx 900 \approx 1\,000; \qquad 3\,457 \approx 3\,460 \approx 3\,500;$$
$$128\,345 \approx 128\,350 \approx 128\,300 \approx 128\,000; \qquad 9\,999 \approx 10\,000;$$
$$709\,808 \approx 709\,810 \approx 709\,800 \approx 710\,000 \approx 700\,000 \approx 1\,000\,000.$$

1.5   Negative Numbers

If we start at any natural number, say, 4, and count back with the unit steps, 4, 3, 2, 1, we eventually exhaust all the natural numbers, and the next step "down", that is, to the left leads us to 0. But the next unit step from this point to the left along the number line brings us into the unchartered land beyond the zero, and a natural label for this point is -1. Now we can introduce the negative numbers.

When we add any two positive numbers or a positive number and the number zero, the result is always positive, however, the difference of two positive numbers does not have to be positive. If $a > b$, then the difference $a - b > 0$, but if $a < b$, our common sense tells us that the difference $a - b$ cannot be positive. If $a < b$, thus $b - a$ is positive, the difference $a - b$ is called the *negative number* $-(b - a)$ *opposite* to the positive number $b - a$. For example, $2 - 3 = -(3 - 2) = -1$, $9 - 10 = -(10 - 9) = -1$, $6 - 13 = -(13 - 6) = -7$, etc.

We observe in passing, that exactly as a positive number can appear as the sum of several pairs of addends ($6 = 1 + 5$, and $6 = 2 + 4$, and $6 = 3 + 3$, etc.), a negative number can occur as the difference of various pairs of numbers, for instance,

$$-1 = 2 - 3 = 3 - 4 = 4 - 5 = \cdots = 101 - 102 = 0 - 1 = \cdots$$

Figure 1.2: Number line.

The negative numbers, defined in section 1.4, occupy the left part of the number line, to the left of 0 – Fig. 1.2. The well-known 'real-life' example is a thermometer (placed horizontally). The numbers -1, -2, -3 , -4, ... are called the *negative integer numbers*. The whole (nonnegative integer) numbers and the negative integer numbers together are called the *integer numbers* or just the *integers*; this set is traditionally denoted by

$$\mathbb{Z} = \{\ldots - 4,\ -3,\ -2,\ -1,\ 0,\ 1,\ 2,\ 3,\ \ldots\}.$$

Exactly as the natural numbers are unbounded from above, the negative integer numbers are unbounded from below, that is, there is no smallest integer number; for any integer n there exists a smaller integer, for instance, $n - 1$.

If we depart from zero on the number line, the negative numbers and the positive numbers are located in *opposite* directions, therefore, we call number -3 *opposite* to 3; and vice versa, 3 is *opposite* to -3; number 5 is *opposite* to -5; and vice versa, -5 is *opposite* to 5, etc. In general, for any non-zero number x, the numbers x and $-x$ are called *additive opposite* to one another. Numbers written "without" a sign, like 5, are *positive* by default, that is, $5 = +5$, etc. Whence, to find the opposite to a number, we have only to change its sign for the opposite sign, " $+$ " for " $-$ " or " $-$ " for " $+$ ".

To repeat, the opposite of a positive number is always negative, and the opposite of a negative number is always positive. Thus, the opposite of 6 is $-(6) = -6$, and the opposite of -7 is $-(-7) = 7$. The only exception is 0, which is equal to its opposite, $-0 = 0$; there is only one zero in our world, the zero is *unique*. The pairwise opposite numbers are called the *additive inverses* to each other.

If we look back at the examples in the preceding paragraphs, we have $6 + (-6) = 0$, and $(-7) + (7) = 0$. This is a general fact:

The sum of any real number, positive, negative, or zero, and its (additive) opposite number is zero, that is, for any a

$$a + (-a) = (-a) + a = 0.$$

Example 1.5.1 *Compute* $-(-(-(-5)))$.

Solution. We start from inside and first of all find $-(-5)$, that is, we look for the opposite of the negative number. Since the opposite of a negative number -5 is a positive number, we have $-(-5) = 5$. At the next step we get $-(-(-5)) = -5$, and finally, $-(-(-(-5))) = -(-5) = 5$. However, if the problem would ask to find the opposite of the number $-(-(-(-5)))$, the answer would be $-(-(-(-5)))) = -5$. □

Remark 1.5.1 *It is worthy to pay attention to the parity of how many negative signs " $-$ " are in the expressions like above: If this sign occurs an even number of times, then the result is positive; otherwise the result is negative; compare Example 1.5.1 above.*

Exercise 1.5.1 *Find the additive inverses (opposites) of the following numbers and check that the sum of a number and its inverse is always zero.*

-123	$7\,008$	$-(-2\,345)$	$-(-(-(709\,808)))$
$(-(-(-(-3\,457))))$	0	-0	(-0)
$-(-0)$	$-(-(-0))$	1	-1
(-1)	$-(-1)$	$-(1)$	$-(-(-1))$

The integers 1 and 2 are called *consecutive* integers, since $2 = 1 + 1$ and there is no integer number between 1 and 2. However, 1 and 3 are not consecutive, 3 does not follow 1, for another integer, namely 2, is between them, $1 < 2 < 3$. We can consider *three consecutive integers*, for example, $2, 3, 4$, or six, $-5, -4, -3, -2, -1, 0$. The three consecutive integers with the smallest -7 are $-7, -6, -5$; the three consecutive integers with the middle -7 are $-8, -7, -6$; the three consecutive integers with the largest -7 are $-9, -8, -7$. Four consecutive integers with the smallest -7 are $-7, -6, -5, -4$, and four consecutive integers with the biggest 1 are $-2, -1, 0, 1$.

Positive and negative numbers together are called *signed* numbers. Zero does not have a sign, $0 = +0 = -0$.

Exercise 1.5.2 (1) *What integer immediately precedes* 0? -1? -3? -31? -899? -1001? *What integer follows* 0? -1? -3? -31? -100? -999?
(2) *Between what two integers is* -13 *located?* 0? -101? -70? 1 000 000? (3) *Between what two closest integers is* -13 *located?* 0? -101? -70? 1 000 000?

Exercise 1.5.3 *Design and solve two more exercises similar to the previous ones.*

Answers 1.5

Exercise 1.5.1. The opposite of -123 is $-[-123] = 123$; $-7\,008$; $-[-(-2\,345)] = -2\,345$;
$-[-(-(-(709\,808)))] = 709\,808$; $-[-(-(-(-3\,457)))] = -3\,457$;
$-[0] = 0$; $-[-0] = 0$; $-[(-0)] = 0$; $-[-(-(-0))] = 0$; $-[1] = -1$;
$-[-1] = 1$; $-[(-1)] = 1$; $-[-(-1)] = -1$; $-[-(1)] = 1$; $-[-(-(-1))] = 1$.
Exercise 1.5.2. (1) 0 is preceded by -1; -2 precedes -1; -3 is preceded by -4; -31 is preceded by -32; -899 is preceded by -900; -1001 is preceded by -1002; 1 follows 0, 0 follows -1, -2 follows -3, -30 follows -31, -99 follows -100, -998 follows -999.
(2) -13 is located, for example, between -141 and -10 or between -100 and 1.
(3) -13 is located between -14 and -12, 0 is located between -1 and 1, -101 is located between -102 and -100, -70 is located between -71 and -69, $-1\,000\,000$ is located between $-1\,000\,001$ and $-999\,999$.

1.6   Addition of Signed Numbers

In this section we review addition of positive and negative integer numbers

1.6.1   Properties of Addition

The Digit Addition Table 3 on p. 27 is *symmetric* with respect to its main diagonal. For instance, $2 + 3 = 3 + 2$. We observe from here, that the sum of any two numbers does not depend upon their order. This property is called the *commutative property of addition*:

For any numbers a and b,

$$a + b = b + a.$$

Another essential feature of the addition is called the *associative property*: *For any numbers a, b, and c,*

$$(a + b) + c = a + (b + c).$$

Due to this property, if we have to add three or more numbers, we can do addition in an arbitrary order and we often write such addition problems without parentheses at all, for example, $3 + 9 + 7 = (3 + 9) + 7 = 3 + (9 + 7)$. Hence for computations we can choose the most convenient order. For instance, combining the commutative and associative laws, we get

$$3 + 9 + 7 = (3 + 9) + 7 = (9 + 3) + 7 = 9 + (3 + 7) = 9 + 10 = 19.$$

Of course, in practice most of these intermediate steps are not shown explicitly, but we do them, maybe subconsciously, "by eyes".

The number (digit) 0 plays a special role for the addition. The digit addition table 2 on p. 23 shows that for any digit d, $0 + d = d + 0 = d$, and the same property is true for any number; 0 is called the *neutral element for addition*, that is,

For any number n,
$$0 + n = n + 0 = n.$$

Exercise 1.6.1 *Evaluate without using a calculator.*

$$147 + 18 + 53 \qquad 3 + 50 + 90 + 850 + 7 \qquad 191 + 253 + 19 + 17$$

Exercise 1.6.2 *Compute the sums. Use the long addition and do not forget to line up the addends.*

$123 + 2\,345 + 7\,008 =$	$983 + 2\,045 + 709\,808 =$
$3\,457 + 128\,345 + 9\,909 =$	$2 + 450\,067 + 9\,801\,008 =$
$31 + 456 + 8\,709\,608 + 102\,030\,405\,060 =$	$321 + 12 + 1\,002 + 7 + 1\,431 =$
$252 + 149 + 13 + 1\,421 + 9 =$	$6\,607 + 19 + 243 + 1\,523 =$

Exercise 1.6.3 *Design and solve two more exercises similar to the previous one.*

Answers 1.6

Exercise 1.6.1. 218;   1 000;   480.
Exercise 1.6.2. 9 476; 712 836; 141 711; 10 251 077; 102 039 115 155; 2 773; 1 844; 8 392.

1.7   Inverse Operations I. Subtraction

Each arithmetic operation has its *inverse operation*, meaning the operation which "undoes" the initial one. The inverse of the addition is *subtraction*. For instance, $4 + 3 = 7$, then, $7 - 3 = 4$, thus, the inverse operation for the addition is the subtraction.

The subtraction is defined as follows. Since, for instance, $2 + 3 = 5$, we define the difference $5 - 3 = 2$ or $5 - 2 = 3$. In general, if

$$a + b = c$$

then we define the difference

$$c - b = a \quad \text{and} \quad c - a = b.$$

We remind that if a, b, and c are related by the equation $c - b = a$, then c is called the *minuend*, b the *subtrahend* and a the *difference* of c and b. There are several other ways to mention the difference $c - b$, for example, one can say "subtract b from c" or "b less than c". Indeed, 10 is 5 less than 15, $15 - 5 = 10$.

Vice versa, addition is the inverse operation to subtraction. Indeed, if $15 - 9 = 6$, then $9 + 6 = 15$, and if $9 - 15 = -6$, then $15 + (-6) = 9$.

From this point on, the symbol " $-$ " is *overloaded*, it has at least two meanings.

First, *if the sign "-" applies to a number, the sign means the additive opposite, or additive inverse of the number: thus, -5 is the opposite of 5, and $-(-(5)) = 5$. The " $--$ " sign in this meaning is sometimes written slightly above the middle line, as in* $^-5$.

Second, *if the "$--$" sign separates two terms of an algebraic expression, it means the subtraction: thus, $3 - 7$ means the difference of 3 and 7, which is $3 - 7 = -4$. Therefore, in the latter expression the " $-$ " sign plays different roles on the left, where it denotes the operation of subtraction, and on the right, where it means the additive opposite of a number. This should not lead to any misunderstanding.*

Unlike addition, the subtraction is *not commutative*, it does not possess the commutative property; indeed, $4 - 3 = 1 > 0$, but $3 - 4$ cannot be positive since we subtract a bigger number from a smaller. As a matter of fact, the differences $a - b$ and $b - a$ have opposite signs, these two numbers are the *additive inverses* to one another. We always have $a - b \neq b - a$, unless $a = b$, rather

$$a - b = -(b - a).$$

If $b = a$, then both differences vanish, $a - b = a - a = b - b = 0$.

Exercise 1.7.1 *Compute. In every case explain whether the " $-$ " sign denotes the opposite number or the subtraction.*

$0 - 0 =$	$0 + 0 =$	$0 - (-0) =$	$0 + (-0) =$
$1 - 1 =$	$1 + (-1) =$	$1 - (-1) =$	$1 - (-(-1)) =$

$$1 - (-(-(-1))) =$$
$$123456789 - (-(-(-(-123456789)))) =$$
$$1 - (-(-(-(-1)))) =$$
$$123456789 + (-(-(-(-123456789)))) =$$

We have already seen that many problems include expressions in parentheses, and we have to "drop" the parentheses (or brackets, or braces) that is, to write an equal expression *without* these separators. Analyzing the previous examples, we arrive at the simple rule.

Theorem 1.7.1 *If a part of an expression is embraced into parentheses or a pair of other separators, and we have to rewrite the expression without the separators, then*

If there is a "+" sign in front of the opening parenthesis, we can just drop the parentheses and get an equal expression.

If there is a "−" sign in front of the opening parenthesis, then to drop the parentheses and get an equal expression, we must change every sign inside the parentheses, that is, replace each "+" sign inside the separator with the "−" sign and replace each "−" sign with the "+" sign. □

For example, $3 + (a - b) = 3 + a - b$, and $3 - (a - b) = 3 - a + b$. Keep in mind that no sign means by default the "+" sign. For instance, $(5 - 9 - a + b) - c = 5 - 9 - a + b - c$, $2 + (5 - 9 - a + b) - c = 2 + 5 - 9 - a + b - c$, while $2 - (5 - 9 - a + b) - c = 2 - 5 + 9 + a - b - c$.

Exercise 1.7.2 *An item priced initially at \$450, was marked down by \$75. What is its sale price?*

Exercise 1.7.3 *An item priced initially at \$450, was marked down by \$75 and 50 cents. What is its sale price?*

Exercise 1.7.4 *An item priced initially at \$450 and 25 cents, was marked down by \$75. What is its sale price?*

Exercise 1.7.5 *An item priced initially at \$450 and 25 cents, was marked down by \$75 and 50 cents. What is its sale price?*

Exercise 1.7.6 *Design and solve two more exercises similar to the previous ones.*

Remark 1.7.1 *The addition has the neutral element 0, that is, $x + 0 = 0 + x = x$ for any x. The subtraction does not have such an element, indeed, $x - 0 = x$ but $0 - x = -x \neq x$ unless $x = 0$.*

1.7.1 Addition of Signed Numbers

When we add two signed numbers, $a + b$, each of them can be either positive (non-negative) or negative (non-positive), therefore, we have $2 \cdot 2 = 4$ combinations of signs. We have learnt, however, that for any number a,

$$a + 0 = a - 0 = 0 + a = a,$$

thus we can neglect the cases $a = 0$ or $b = 0$ and consider the following four possibilities:

(1) Both a and b are (strictly) positive, $a > 0$, $b > 0$

(2) Both a and b are negative, $a < 0$, $b < 0$

(3) a is positive and b is negative, $a > 0$, $b < 0$

(4) a is negative and b is positive, $a < 0$, $b > 0$.

We have already developed the addition of positive numbers, that is, case (1), hence we have to learn how to add two negative numbers, case (2), and a positive and a negative number, cases (3) and (4). First we study how to find the sum of two negative numbers. It is convenient to think money. Indeed, if someone has a loan, say borrowed $2 000, and has to take another loan, this time of $1 000, in real life these two loans cannot annihilate one another, they *increase the debt*; now the person owes $2 000 + $1 000 = $3 000. Whence, it is natural to define the sum of negative numbers as follows.

To add several negative numbers, we have to add their additive inverses or, which is the same, their absolute values, that is, to add **positive** *numbers and negate this positive number.*

Example 1.7.1 *Add* $(-2) + (-5) + (-13)$.

Solution. The additive opposites of the addends are $-(-2) = 2$, $-(-5) = 5$, and $-(-13) = 13$, respectively; therefore, we add these opposites, which are positive numbers, and change the sign:

$$(-2) + (-5) + (-13) = -(2 + 5 + 13) = -20.$$

Similarly, if the temperature was $-2°$, then *dropped* by $5°$, and then again *dropped* by $13°$, then the final temperature is $(-2) + (-5) + (-13) = -20°$. $\square$

Remark 1.7.2 (1) *Since a sum of positive numbers is positive, we see that any sum of negative numbers is itself negative.*

(2) *Due to this property, the sum of negative numbers can be written using only "−" signs; for example,*

$$(-2) + (-5) + (-13) = -2 - 5 - 13,$$

and the "−" sign can be "factored out" as

$$-2 - 5 - 13 = -(2 + 5 + 13) = -20.$$

Warning. The students sometimes confuse the rules pertinent to different operations. Many students remember that "the product of two negative numbers is positive". However, the rule above refers to the *addition* of negative numbers, not to their *multiplication* – the addition and the multiplication are subject to different rules.

To formalize these definitions, we use a technical notion mentioned above, convenient here and in many other instances.

Definition 1.7.1 *The absolute value of a real number x is the number x itself if this number is nonnegative, that is, if $x \geq 0$, and the additive inverse of the number x if the number x is negative, $x \leq 0$. Denoting the absolute value of a number x by two vertical bars as $|x|$, this definition can be written in the following succinct form:*

$$|x| = \begin{cases} x \ \text{if} \ x \geq 0 \\ -x \ \text{if} \ x \leq 0 \end{cases}.$$

For instance, $|3| = 3$ because we ask for the absolute value of the positive number 3 and $|-3| = 3$ as well, because now we want the absolute value of a negative number $x = -3$, thus we have to apply the second line of the definition above, and we compute $|-3| = -(-3) = 3$. We see that the absolute value is never negative and it is zero only if $x = 0$. Of course, this definition equally applies to any real number, either integers, fractions, or decimals; for example, $|-\frac{1}{2}| = \frac{1}{2}$ and $|-102.0067| = 102.0067$.

The definition can be also expressed in geometrical terms. The absolute value of x is the distance along the number line from the point corresponding to the number x to the origin. We note that in the Euclidean geometry all distances are positive or zero.

Example 1.7.2 *Compute $-|-|-33||$.*

Solution. This example emphasizes the difference between the absolute value and parentheses – it is impossible to move the external "-" sign inside the vertical bars, and we must start deep inside. Thus, $|-33| = 33$, so that

$$-|-|-33|| = -|-33|.$$

Again, we have $|-33| = 33$, therefore, $-|-|-33|| = -|-33| = -33$. □

Exercise 1.7.7 *Find the absolute values.*

$|123 + 2\,345 + 7\,008| =$	$|-709\,808| =$
$|128\,345 + |-9\,909|| =$	$-|-|-8\,709\,608|| =$
$|35 + |-35|| =$	$|-|-8\,709\,608|| =$
$|-243| - |-245| =$	$|-243| + |-245| =$
$|2 + 450\,067 + |-98\,010|| =$	$|35 - |-35|| =$

Exercise 1.7.8 *Sketch the points on the number line that satisfy the inequalities $x = 2$, $x > 2$, $x \geq 2$, $x < 2$, $x \leq 2$, $x \neq 2$, $|x| > 2$, $|x| < 2$, $|x| \geq 2$, $|x| \leq 2$, $|x| \neq 2$, $2 < x < 3$, $2 < x \leq 3$, $2 \leq x < 3$, $2 \leq x \leq 3$, $3 < x < 2$.*

Exercise 1.7.9 *Design and solve two more exercises similar to the previous one.*

Theorem 1.7.2 *To add two negative numbers, we must add their absolute values and negate this sum. In symbols, if $x < 0$ and $y < 0$, then*

$$x + y = -(|x| + |y|).$$

For example, $(-3)+(-5) = -(3+5) = -8$. The procedure can be thought of as if we pull ('factor out') the "$-$" sign out of the expression. In this and similar examples, the first pair of parentheses can be omitted without any ambiguity:

$$(-3) + (-5) = -3 + (-5) = -(3 + 5) = -8.$$

But the second pair of parentheses cannot be dropped, since without them we would get improperly written expression $+ - 5$; such expressions are ambiguous and must be avoided. ▢

It should be remarked that the notion of the absolute value allowed us to define the addition of new objects (the negative numbers) through the operation, we have already studied - the addition of positive numbers. This is not an uncommon situation, all the definitions in this chapter were designed so that we either add positive numbers or subtract a smaller positive number from a larger one, so that the difference is positive.

Exercise 1.7.10 *Add negative numbers.*

$(-123) + (-2\,345) + (-7\,008) =$ $(-123) + (-7\,008) =$

$-3\,457 + (-128\,345) + (-9\,909) =$ $-983 + (-709\,808) =$

$-2 + (-450\,067) + (-9\,801\,008) =$ $(-456) + (-8\,709\,608) =$

$-641 + (-2\,390) =$ $-4\,290 + (-621) + (-329) =$

Exercise 1.7.11 *Rewrite without grouping symbols.*

$-[-123 - 7\,008] =$ $-(-q - w + b - h) - (-t - y - d) =$

$-983 - (-709\,808) =$ $-3\,457 + (-128\,345 + v - 9\,909) =$

$-2 - \{-45\,006 + (-p - 8 + k)\} =$ $-\{-[x + (-456) + (-8\,709\,608)] - n\} =$

Exercise 1.7.12 *Design and solve two more exercises similar to the previous ones.*

Now we take up cases (3) and (4) above, that is, we study how to add two numbers of opposite signs, a positive and a negative number. Since the addition is commutative, $a + b = b + a$, we can always set the first addend to be negative; for example, to add $5 + (-7)$, we can instead calculate $(-7) + 5$. Before we give formal rules for adding signed numbers, let us consider an illuminating example with temperature.

Example 1.7.3 (1) *The temperature in NYC was* $3°F$, *degrees* Fahrenheit. *Then it fell* $2°F$ *down. What is the current temperature?*

(2) *The temperature in NYC was* $-3°F$. *Then it fell* $2°F$ *down. What is the current temperature?*

(3) *The temperature in NYC was* $-3°F$. *Then it* rose *by* $2°F$. *What is the current temperature?*

(4) *The temperature in NYC was* $-3°F$. *Then it* rose *by* $2°F$ *and after that it fell* $4°F$ *down. What is the current temperature?*

(5) *The temperature in NYC was* $-3°F$. *Then it fell* $4°F$ *down and after that it* rose *by* $2°F$. *What is the current temperature?*

Solution. (1) Intuitively clear that the current temperature is $3 - 2 = 1°F$. The equation is a *mathematical model* of the problem. This is a typical model, to compute the *change* in any quantity, one must *subtract the terminal value of the quantity from the initial value.*

(2) Similarly to the first part of the problem, we subtract $-3 - 2$, however, now we have to subtract a positive number from a negative number. Again, it is intuitively clear that the temperature *drops*, becomes smaller, thus we compute the result as $-3 - 2 = (-3) + (-2) = -(3 + 2) = -5°F$.

(3) Since the temperature is rising, we now have to add, $-3 + 2 = -1°F$.

(4) As before, the temperature becomes $-3 + 2 - 4 = -1 - 4 = -5°F$.

(5) Now we have $-3 - 4 + 2 = -5°F$. □

Using these examples as motivation, we consider the addition problem $a + b$, where $a < 0$ and $b > 0$. We remember that while adding a positive number b to any number a, we actually increase this number, that is, we must move from the point a on the number line to the right. Now we see that there are two possibilities. If b is not big enough, namely, if b is smaller than the distance from the point a to 0, then after traveling the distance b from a, we cannot cover the entire distance from a to 0 and remain to the left of the origin, in the negative domain.

For example, let us calculate $-3 + 2$, that is, $a = -3$ and $b = 2$. The distance from -3 to 0 is the (additive) opposite of -3, that is, 3, and adding 2 we "use" only 2 units of this distance, thus we arrive at the point located at the distance $3 - 2 = 1$ from zero, but in the negative domain; therefore, $-3 + 2 = -1$. This result is obvious, but we need to see all these small details to develop machinery necessary to deal with big numbers. As an example, let us find $-133 + 65$. Comparing with the previous example, we see that departing from the point -133, we move 65 to the right and arrive at the point $-(133 - 65) = -68$.

Suppose now that b is big enough, namely, b is bigger than the distance from the point a to 0. Now, after reaching 0 we still have to travel the difference between b and the distance from a to 0. The latter difference is b minus the opposite of $a < 0$, that is, the difference is $b - (-a) = b + a$. For instance, $-3 + 4 = 4 - 3 = 1$, since here $a = -3$ and $-a = -(-3) = 3$. As one more example, $-133 + 345 = 345 - 133 = 212$.

Whence, if both k and l are positive numbers, then $-k + l = -(k - l)$ if $k \geq l$, and $-k + l = l - k$ if $k \leq l$. These formulas reduce the task of adding a positive and a negative number to subtracting a *smaller* positive number from a bigger also positive number.

Exercise 1.7.13 *Compute.*

$81 + (-100) =$ $-100 + 81 =$

$100 + (-81) =$ $345 + (-346) =$

$128\,345 + (-9\,909) =$ $-8\,709\,608 + 897\,056 =$

$35 + (-35) =$ $-8\,709\,608 + 10\,000\,000 =$

$-123 + 2\,345 =$ $347 + (-709\,808) =$

$450\,067 + (-98\,010) =$ $(-346) + (345) =$

Exercise 1.7.14 *Design and solve two more exercises similar to the previous one.*

1.7.2   Addition and Subtraction of Signed Numbers

Now we are ready to define the addition and subtraction of numbers of any sign. As we have already noticed, all these definitions reduce new problems, involving the negative numbers, to the old ones, but dealing with positive numbers. We begin by finding the sum of a positive and a negative number. To motivate the rule, we start out with a simple example $4 + 3 = 7$ and consider its graphical model on the number line:

Figure 1.3: $4 + 3 = 7$

We see that adding a positive number 3 shifts the first addend, 4, *three* steps to the right. It is natural now that the addition of a negative number must shift the first addend to the left. It may be also useful to think this over in terms of money. Indeed, if we have some balance and make a withdrawal, the balance is decreasing, hence the withdrawal can be considered as addition (deposit) of a negative amount.

It should be remarked that this reasoning does not depend on the sign of the first addend – in both cases, whether the first number is positive or negative, the sum becomes smaller, the sum shifts along the number line to the left.

Compare now the sums $4 + (-3)$ and $4 + (-5)$, where the second addends in both cases are negative. In the first case we must move point 4 three steps to the left, and since the point 4 is four units to the right from 0, the sum stays to the right of 0, that is, the sum is positive, $4 + (-3) = 1$. In the second example, we must make five steps to the left, thus overstepping 0 and arriving at the negative part of the number line; the sum is negative, $4 + (-5) = -1$.

We illustrate these examples as follows:

$$+4 = (+1) + (+1) + (+1) + (+1),$$

while

$$-3 = (-1) + (-1) + (-1).$$

If we add the right-hand sums column-wise, the first three columns result in $1 + (-1) = 0$ each, and we are left with one positive 1 in the upper row, thus $4 - 3 = 1$. However, to compute $4 + (-5)$, we add

$$4 = 1 + 1 + 1 + 1$$

with

$$-5 = (-1) + (-1) + (-1) + (-1) + (-1),$$

and now we are left with an extra -1, thus, $4 + (-5) = -1$.

Based on these remarks, we state the following rule for adding positive and negative numbers.

Theorem 1.7.3 *To compute the sum $a + b$, where $a > 0$ and $b < 0$, we compute the absolute values $|a| = a$ and $|b| = -b$, (pay attention that b itself is negative!) compare the numbers $|a|$ and $|b|$ and subtract the smaller absolute value from the bigger one. Finally, we apply the sign of the number with larger absolute value to this difference.*

Let us look again at the example $4 + (-3)$. Here $|4| = 4$, $|-3| = 3$; considering the inequality $3 < 4$, we must subtract $4 - 3 = 1$, and since the bigger absolute value, 4 comes from a positive number, the result is positive, whence $4 + (-3) = +1$. In the second example $4 + (-5)$, $|4| = 4$, $|-5| = 5$, and we must subtract $5 - 4 = 1$. But now the bigger absolute value, 5 comes from a negative number -5, thus the result must be negative, $4 + (-5) = -1$.

These examples are trivial, usually we do such problems "by eyes", without explicitly applying the formal rule above. However, there are many problems, especially with big numbers, where the students systematically commit errors unless the rules are used. That is why we need these rules and have to learn them by heart and practice.

We reiterate that in the procedure we always subtract a smaller positive number from another positive *but bigger* positive number, since the absolute value of any number is never negative. Thus this difference is positive (or maybe zero if $|a| = |b|$). After that we have to touch up this difference and the final sum may be negative.

Example 1.7.4 *Add* $-123 + 45$.

Solution. Since the expression contains no parentheses, the "−" sign applies to 123 only, it signifies the opposite of 123, and we have to add a negative and a positive number. The absolute values of the addends are $|-123| = 123$ and $|45| = 45$, thus we find the difference $123 - 45 = 78$. Since the bigger absolute value, 123, is the absolute value of a negative number -123, while the smaller absolute value, 45, is the absolute value of a positive number 45, the result must be negative, thus $-123 + 45 = -78$.   □

In problems like this, it is often convenient to remember that the negative sign can be thought of as -1, to "factor it out", and transform the problem as follows:

$$-123 + 45 = -(123 - 45) = -78.$$

This problem and alike can be visualized as follows:

$$-123 = \overbrace{-1 - 1 - \cdots - 1 - 1 \cdots - 1}^{123\ (-1)s}$$

$$45 = \underbrace{+1 + 1 + \cdots + 1}_{45\ (+1)s}.$$

We immediately observe that there are more negative than positive unities, specifically, there are $123 - 45 = 78$ more negative than positive unities.

Example 1.7.5 *Calculate* $(-223) + 457 + (-145)$.

Solution. We have to add three numbers, and first we add $(-223) + 457$. Here it is convenient to use the commutative property of addition, thus the problem boils down to subtracting a smaller positive number from a larger one:

$$(-223) + 457 = 457 + (-223) = 457 - 223 = 234.$$

Now, the example ends as follows

$$(-223) + 457 + (-145) = 234 + (-145) = 234 - 145 = 89.$$ □

Just to repeat, the sum of positive numbers is always positive, the sum of negative numbers is always negative, the sum of a positive and a negative number may be either positive or negative, depending upon the sign of a number with the *bigger* absolute value.

Exercise 1.7.15 *Calculate.*

$1\,002\,345 + (-70\,908) =$	$-1\,002\,345 + (-70\,908) =$
$709\,808 + (-2\,045) =$	$3\,457 + 128\,345 + (-9\,909) =$
$-3\,457 + 128\,345 + (-9\,909) =$	$2\,450\,067 + (-801\,008) =$
$-2\,450\,067 + (-801\,008) =$	$31 + 870\,960 + (-8\,456) =$
$31 + (-870\,960) + (-8\,456) =$	$(-31) + 870\,960 + (-8\,456) =$

Exercise 1.7.16 *Design and solve two more exercises similar to the previous one.*

Next we study how to subtract signed numbers. As in the case of addition, we consider separately several cases. We know that if the subtrahend is positive, the difference is less than the minuend. If we depict this problem on the number line, we see that the difference is located to the left of a. We want to preserve this picture for the case, when the subtrahend is negative. Thus, if we subtract a negative number, the difference must be larger than the minuend. For example, $13-(-5)$ is the number, which is 5 more than 13, that is, $13-(-5) = 13+5 = 18$.

All these examples show that to subtract a number, whether it is positive or negative, we have to add the opposite of this subtrahend to the minuend. If the subtrahend is positive, this rule also works, but it may complicate the solution. Indeed, $13 - 5 = 13 + (-5)$, but it is simpler to do directly, $13 - 5 = 8$. However, in the case $5 - (-13)$, since the opposite of the subtrahend, $-(-13) = 13$ is positive, we have immediately $5 - (-13) = 5 + 13 = 18$.

We repeat the simple idea behind the following rules is that if we subtract a positive number, that is, the *subtrahend is positive*, then the difference must be smaller than the minuend, while if we subtract a negative number, that is, the *subtrahend is negative*, then the difference must become larger than the minuend. It is also worth repeating that we reduce new problems to the old ones, which have already been solved; namely, we introduce the subtraction through the *addition*.

Theorem 1.7.4 *For any a and b, the difference $a - b$ is the sum*

$$a - b = a + (-b),$$

where $-b$ is the additive inverse (opposite) of b.

Example 1.7.6 *Compute.* (1) $-5 - 4 = -5 + (-4) = -(5+4) = -9$.
(2) $17 - 31 = 17 + (-31) = -(|-31| - |17|) = -(31 - 17) = -14$. □

Remark 1.7.3 *In simple problems with small numbers, like in this example, after small practice, we must compute the answer immediately, "by eyes". But we still must know and practice general formal algorithms as above to solve more complicated problems with large numbers. The important step is to 'see' the sign of the difference, whether it is positive or negative.*

Remark 1.7.4 *It is always useful to verify our calculations. We computed the difference $7 - 4 = 3$. To check this, we can add $4 + 3 = 7$. In general, if $a - b = c$, then it must be $b + c = a$ and also $a - c = b$. For instance, please check, as in the example above, that if $17 - 31 = -14$, then also $31 - 14 = 17$ and $17 - (-14) = 31$.*

Exercise 1.7.17 *Compute.*

$$1\,002\,345 - (-70\,908) =$$

$$-709\,808 - (-2\,045) =$$

$$-3\,457 + 128\,345 - (-9\,909) =$$

$$-2\,450\,067 - (-801\,008) =$$

$$(-870\,960) - (-8\,456) =$$

$$-1\,002\,345 - (-70\,908) =$$

$$3\,457 + 128\,345 - (-9\,909) =$$

$$2\,450\,067 - (-801\,008) =$$

$$870\,960 - (-8\,456) =$$

$$(-31) + 870\,960 - (-8\,456) =$$

Exercise 1.7.18 *The temperature on a winter night was $-15°F$. At 12 p.m. the same day the temperature reached a high of $-1°F$. Then the temperature fell down by $-15°F$.*

(1) *By how many degrees Fahrenheit did the temperature increase from the night to the midday?*

(2) *When was the temperature higher, at the beginning or at the end of this period?*

Exercise 1.7.19 *A climber went down from the summit at $8\,093$ ft to the camp at $4\,833$ ft. What was the change in his altitude?*

Exercise 1.7.20 *Design and solve two more exercises similar to the previous ones.*

1.7.3   Order of Operations I

We often have to perform long calculations containing only additions and subtractions, like $13 - 8 + 4 - 2 - 1 + 6$. In these cases, the addition has no preference, we proceed *FROM LEFT TO RIGHT*, unless there are parentheses or other *grouping symbols* (separators) like brackets, (curly) braces, fraction lines, radicals, etc. Thus, in the previous example, we start by subtracting $13 - 8 = 5$ and then move from left to the right, as

$$13-8+4-2-1+6 = 5+4-2-1+6 = 9-2-1+6 = 7-1+6 = 6+6 = 12.$$

To override this standard *order of operations*, one must use *parentheses* or some other *grouping symbols*. Calculations within the grouping symbols (separators) *must be done first.*

Example 1.7.7 *Compute $13 - (8 + 4) - (2 - 1) + 6$.*

Solution. We first work inside parentheses,

$$13-(8+4)-(2-1)+6 = 13-12-(2-1)+6 = 13-12-1+6 = 1-1+6 = 0+6 = 6.$$

Here both parentheses are independent upon one another and can be done simultaneously:

$$13 - (8 + 4) - (2 - 1) + 6 = 13 - 12 - 1 + 6 = 1 - 1 + 6 = 0 + 6 = 6.$$

In the following example, we have *nested separators*,

$$13 - [(8 + 4) - (2 - 1)] + 6,$$

and we have to work from inside out, that is,

$$13 - [(8 + 4) - (2 - 1)] + 6 = 13 - [12 - 1] + 6 = 13 - 11 + 6 = 2 + 6 = 8.$$

$\square$

Exercise 1.7.21 *Calculate.*

$$3 + (-128 - 9) = \qquad\qquad -2 - 801 + 608 =$$

$$(-2 - 801) + 608 = \qquad\qquad -2 - (801 + 608) =$$

$$1\,345 - 7\,908 + 78 = \qquad\qquad 808 - 2\,045 - 33 =$$

$$3\,457 + (8\,345 - 9\,909) = \qquad\qquad 2\,450 - 8 - 5\,608 =$$

$$2\,450 - (801 - 506) = \qquad\qquad 31 + [870\,960 - (8\,456 + 123)] =$$

Exercise 1.7.22 *Design and solve two more exercises similar to the previous one.*

Now, after introducing the negative numbers and operations with them, we can extend Theorem 1.3.2.

Theorem 1.7.5 *Additive Property of Inequalities*

If we add the same positive or negative quantity to both sides of an inequality, then a valid inequality remains valid and invalid remains invalid: for any c,

$$a < b \implies a + c < b + c \ and \ a < b \implies a - c < b - c.$$

Reversing this inequality, we get for any, positive or negative c,

$$a > b \implies a + c > b + c$$

$$a < b \implies a - c < b - c$$

$$a > b \implies a - c > b - c.$$

$\square$

Answers 1.7

Exercise 1.7.1. 0; 0; 0; 0; 0; 0; 2; 0; 2; 0; 0; 246913578.
Exercise 1.7.2. \$375.
Exercise 1.7.3. \$374.50.
Exercise 1.7.5. \$375.25.
Exercise 1.7.6. \$374.75.
Exercise 1.7.7. $-9\,476$; $-7\,131$; $-141\,711$; $-710\,791$; $-10\,251\,077$; $-8\,710\,064$;
   $-3\,031$; $-5\,240$.
Exercise 1.7.10. $7\,131$; $q + w - b + h + t + y + d - k$; $v - 141\,711$; $708\,825$; $p - k + 45\,012$;
   $n + x - 8\,710\,064$.
Exercise 1.7.11. -19; -19; 19; -1; $118\,436$; $-7\,812\,552$; 0; $1\,290\,392$; 2; 222; $-709\,461$;
$352\,057$; -1.

Exercise 1.7.13. 9 476; 709 808; 138 254; −8 709 608; 70; 8 709 608; −2; 488; 548 079; 0.

Exercise 1.7.15. 931 437; −1 073 253; 707 763; 121 893; 114 979; 1 649 059; −3 251 075; 862 535; −879 385; 862 473.

Exercise 1.7.17. 1 073 253; −931 437; −707 763; 141 711; 134 797; 3 251 075; −1 649 059; 879 416; −862 504; 879 385.

Exercise 1.7.19. −134; −195; −195; −1 411; −6 485; −1 270; 1 893; −3 166; 2 155; 862 412.

1.8   Multiplication and its Properties

1.8.1   "If And Only If" Statement

The phrase "*Condition **A** is valid If And Only If condition **B** is valid*" occurs often in mathematical texts. It means that if we know that the condition **A** is valid, we can claim, without any reservation, that the condition **B** is valid too, and vice versa, if the condition **B** holds good, we can safely claim the condition **A**. For example,

"A natural number is a multiple of 10 if and only if its last digit is 0".

Exercise 1.8.1 *Prove this statement.*

A synonym of the "if and only if" statement is the phrase "necessary and sufficient". It is said that the condition "A" is necessary and sufficient for the condition "B" if they are equivalent, that is, when "A" holds if and only if "B" holds.

1.8.2   Odd and Even Numbers

It is said that an integer number k *divides* an integer number l if $l = k \cdot n$, where n is another integer. Thus, when we divide l over k (or k into l, which is the same), the remainder is 0. Usually we consider these properties for whole numbers only. In many problems it is important to know whether one number divides another number. First of all, we study divisibility by 2.

Definition 1.8.1 *A whole number is called* even, *if it can be evenly, that is, with zero remainder, divided by* 2. *Otherwise, a whole number is called odd.*

For instance, the numbers $0, 2, 14, 128$ are even, while $1, 5, 111$ are odd numbers.

Exercise 1.8.2 *In the following list, which numbers are even and which are odd?*

872, 8, 1 002 225, 2 002 432, 908, 80, 709 615, 2 045, 0, 128 817, 3, 9 909.

Analyzing these examples, we state the following properties.

Proposition 1.8.1 *A whole number is even if and only if its last digit is either* 0, *or* 2, *or* 4, *or* 6, *or* 8.

A whole number is odd if and only if its last digit is either 1, *or* 3, *or* 5, *or* 7, *or* 9. □

It is worth repeating that each part of the claim connects two statements, say, the first part compares the property of a whole number to be even with the property of a whole number to have the last digit of its decimal representation either 0, or 2, or 4, or 6, or 8. The assertion is that these two properties can occur only *simultaneously*, they are *equivalent*.

Exercise 1.8.3 *Give two examples of three consecutive even, and three consecutive odd numbers.*

Problem 1.8.1 *Prove that any two consecutive integers have different* parity, *that is, one of them is* odd *and the other is* even.

Exercise 1.8.4 *Verify that each of the numbers* 36, 306, 3 708, 812 112 *is a multiple of 3, while the numbers* 37, 38, 407 *are not.*

Exercise 1.8.5 *Design and solve two more exercises similar to the previous one.*

Such *divisibility* properties are crucial in the current applications of mathematics to security issues, such as designing reliable computer codes, safe passwords, etc.

Problem 1.8.2 *Analyze the numbers in Exercise 1.8.4 and prove that*

(1) *A whole number is divisible by 5 if and only if its last digit is either* 0 *or* 5.

(2) *A whole number is divisible by 10 if and only if its last digit is* 0 .

(3) *A whole number is divisible by 3 if and only if the sum of its digits is divisible by 3.*

(4) *A whole number is divisible by 9 if and only if the sum of its digits is divisible by 9.*

(5) *A whole number is divisible by 6 if and only if it is divisible by both 2 and 3.*

(6) *A whole number is divisible by 4 if and only if the two right-most digits make a number divisible by 4. For example, 34512 is a multiple of 4, because 12 is, while 34513 is not a multiple of 4, because 13 is not a multiple of 4,*

1.8.3 Properties of Multiplication

In Section 0.1.4 we observed some properties of multiplication of digits, in particular, we know that the multiplication of digits is *commutative*. When we review (or study anew) multiplication of many-digit numbers, we will see that it is also commutative, for it is based on the multiplication of digits, that is, of single-valued integer numbers.

Two other important features of the multiplication are its *associative* property and *distributive* property. For instance, if we want to multiply $2 \cdot 3 \cdot 4$, we can proceed as $(2 \cdot 3) \cdot 4 = 6 \cdot 4 = 24$, *associating* first 2 with 3.

Or we can do $2 \cdot (3 \cdot 4) = 2 \cdot 12 = 24$, *associating* first 3 and 4. In both cases the result is the same; this is a particular instance of the *associative property of multiplication* claiming that this is always the case. Symbolically, for any numbers a, b, c,

$$(a \cdot b) \cdot c = a \cdot (b \cdot c)$$

.

Due to this property we can write

$$(a \cdot b) \cdot c = (a \cdot b) \cdot c = a \cdot b \cdot c$$

without parentheses at all and compute the products in the most convenient way. For example, to multiply $13 \cdot 5 \cdot 2$, we can proceed as

$$(13 \cdot 5) \cdot 2 = 65 \cdot 2 = 130,$$

or we can do

$$13 \cdot (5 \cdot 2) = 13 \cdot 10 = 130;$$

in the second calculation all the multiplications are done "by eyes", without using a calculator.

The *distributive property* connects addition and multiplication; it states that for any numbers a, b, c,

$$c \cdot (a + b) = c \cdot a + c \cdot b. \tag{1.8.1}$$

Of course, since b can be both positive and negative, a similar property holds for the subtraction as well,

$$c \cdot (a - b) = c \cdot a - c \cdot b.$$

Moreover, due to the commutativity of multiplication, we have also

$$(a + b) \cdot c = a \cdot c + b \cdot c, \tag{1.8.2}$$

and due to the associativity, the same distributive property holds good also for several addends,

$$c \cdot (a - b + d) = c \cdot a - c \cdot b + c \cdot d. \tag{1.8.3}$$

Example 1.8.1 *Compute* $3 \cdot (12 - 9 - 18 + 15)$.

Solution. We can first calculate the expression in parentheses, $12 - 9 - 18 + 15 = 3 - 18 + 15 = -15 + 15 = 0$, and then multiply, $3 \cdot 0 = 0$, or we can distribute and multiply as $3 \cdot 12 = 36$, $3 \cdot 9 = 27$, $3 \cdot 18 = 54$, $3 \cdot 15 = 45$, and then finish the job by computing

$$36 - 27 - 54 + 45 = 9 - 54 + 45 = -45 + 45 = 0,$$

surely, with the same result 0. Which way is simpler, depends upon the problem.

Exercise 1.8.6 *Compute in two different ways:*

$$3(17 - 4 + 11) =$$

$$205(31 - 40 + 90) =$$

$$(19 + 14 + 31 + 6)10 =$$

Now we extend the distributive property for products of sums each containing several addends.

Example 1.8.2 *Multiply* $(p + q) \cdot (a + b)$.

Solution. Let us denote $c = p + q$, then the problem is exactly as the left-hand side of (1.8.1), $c \cdot (a + b)$, and by this equation we have

$$c \cdot (a + b) = c \cdot a + c \cdot b.$$

Now we replace here c by its equal expression $p + q$ and deduce the equation

$$(p + q) \cdot (a + b) = (p + q) \cdot a + (p + q) \cdot b.$$

Applying twice distributive law (1.8.2), we derive the equation

$$(p + q) \cdot (a + b) = p \cdot a + q \cdot a + p \cdot b + q \cdot b.$$

$\square$

We observe that the right-hand side of the latter contains $4 = 2 \cdot 2$ terms, containing pair-wise products of each term of the first sum $p + q$ by every term of the second sum $a + b$. We can plausibly guess now, and this guess can be rigorously *proved*, the following property.

Theorem 1.8.1 *To multiply two sums containing any number of addends each, we must multiply every addend of the first sum by every addend of the second sum and add all these pair-wise products.* $\square$

Example 1.8.3 *Multiply* $(p + q + r + s)(a + b + c)$.

Solution. We remind that by default, since there is no operation symbol between the parentheses in the example, it is the multiplication, that is, this example can be rewritten as

$$(p + q + r + s)(a + b + c) = (p + q + r + s) \cdot (a + b + c).$$

Applying the distributive rule as above, we get the following $4 \cdot 3 = 12$ pair-wise products,

$$(p + q + r + s) \cdot (a + b + c)$$

$$= (p + q + r + s) \cdot a + (p + q + r + s) \cdot b + (p + q + r + s) \cdot c$$

$$= p \cdot a + q \cdot a + r \cdot a + s \cdot a + p \cdot b + q \cdot b + r \cdot b + s \cdot b + p \cdot c + q \cdot c + r \cdot c + s \cdot c,$$

exactly 12 pair-wise products, as we have expected. In double products $p \cdot a$, etc., a symbol for the multiplication is shown to avoid any confusion with a two-digit integer pa. To describe this procedure we sometimes say that we *open parentheses* in the expression given.   □

Example 1.8.4 *Multiply* $(p - q + r)(a - b - c)$.

Solution. We immediately write down $3 \cdot 3 = 9$ pair-wise products (pay attention to the signs!)

$$(p - q + r)(a - b - c)$$

$$p \cdot a - p \cdot b - p \cdot c - q \cdot a + q \cdot b + q \cdot c + r \cdot a - r \cdot b - r \cdot c.$$

□

Exercise 1.8.7 *Multiply.*

$$(2 - a + g)(b - t + 50) =$$

$$(-d - f - h - j)(a - 6) =$$

$$(2a + v + 4)(3 - d) =$$

Exercise 1.8.8 *Design and solve two more exercises similar to the previous one.*

Example 1.8.5 *Compute the sum* $1 + 2 + \cdots + 10$.

Solution. The ellipsis symbol $\cdots$ indicates that we skip a few numbers in the middle, and the addends must follow the pattern clear from the presented numbers. In the example, the first two numbers represent the first two natural numbers, thus we infer that the given sum must contain all the natural numbers from 1 to 10 *inclusive*. Reinstating the missing numbers, we have to find the sum

$$1 + 2 + 3 + 4 + 5 + 6 + 7 + 8 + 9 + 10.$$

It is not too difficult to compute this sum straightforwardly, indeed,

$$1 + 2 + 3 + 4 + 5 + 6 + 7 + 8 + 9 + 10 = 3 + 3 + 4 + 5 + 6 + 7 + 8 + 9 + 10$$

$$= 6 + 4 + 5 + 6 + 7 + 8 + 9 + 10 = 10 + 5 + 6 + 7 + 8 + 9 + 10 = \cdots = 55.$$

However, if the sum consists of many addends, this addition quickly becomes tedious and impractical. There is, nonetheless, an elegant trick, attributed to 5-year-old Gauss, that allows almost instant computation of such sums. It is clear due to the properties of addition, that if we calculate the same sum in inverse order, starting from the last number and moving to the left, the value is the same; let us denote the sum by S. Using this observation, we write these two sums one under another,

$$S = 1 + 2 + 3 + 4 + 5 + 6 + 7 + 8 + 9 + 10$$
$$S = 10 + 9 + 8 + 7 + 6 + 5 + 4 + 3 + 2 + 1$$

and observe that there are 10 columns to the right of the equality signs, and the sum of the two numbers in each column is 11:

$$1 + 10 = 2 + 9 = 3 + 8 = \cdots = 10 + 1 = 11.$$

Since there are 10 columns and we found the sum S twice, we have $2S = 11 \cdot 10 = 110$, or $S = \frac{110}{2} = 55$. □

Example 1.8.6 *Compute the sum* $3 + 4 + \cdots + 10 + 11$.

Solution. If we analyze the solution of the previous example, we notice that the two numbers in every column are equidistant from the ends of the initial sum. Indeed, in the first column we add $1 + 10$, that is, the very first and the very last terms of the sum, in the second column we add $2 + 9$, that is, the second and the penultimate terms of the sum, etc. Let us try to use this observation, employing (implicitly) the commutative and associative properties of addition, and without writing the sum twice; in this problem we write down all the terms explicitly,

$$3 + 4 + 5 + 6 + 7 + 8 + 9 + 10 + 11 = (3 + 11) + (4 + 10) + (5 + 9) + (6 + 8) + 7$$
$$= 14 + 14 + 14 + 14 + 7,$$

where the last number, 7, remained without the match. This is because the initial sum consists of $(11 - 3) + 1 = 9$ terms, that is of *odd* number of terms. Now we can easily compute the result,

$$3 + 4 + 5 + 6 + 7 + 8 + 9 + 10 + 11 = 4 \cdot 14 + 7 = 63.$$

□

Exercise 1.8.9 *Evaluate the sums.*

$$1 + 2 + \cdots + 23$$
$$3 + 4 + \cdots + 7$$
$$191 + 253 + 19 + 17$$
$$1 + 2 + 3 + \ldots + 99$$
$$29 + 28 + 27 + \cdots + 2 + 1$$
$$2 + 4 + 6 \cdots + 28 + 30$$

Answers 1.8

Exercise 1.8.2. Even numbers 872, 8, $2\,002\,432$, 908, 80, 0. Odd Numbers $1\,002\,225$, $709\,615$, $2\,045$, $128\,817$, 3.

Exercise 1.8.3. For example, $(0,2,4)$, $(96,98,100)$, $(1,3,5)$, $(999,1001,1003)$.

Exercise 1.8.4. $36 = 3 \cdot 12$; $306 = 3 \cdot 102$; $3\,708 = 3 \cdot 1\,236$; $812\,112 = 3 \cdot 270\,704$; $37 = 3 \cdot 12 + 1$; $38 = 3 \cdot 12 + 2$; $407 = 3 \cdot 135 + 2$.

Exercise 1.8.6. $3(17 - 4 + 11) = 3 \cdot 24 = 72$ or $3(17 - 4 + 11) = 3 \cdot 17 - 3 \cdot 4 + 3 \cdot 11 = 51 - 12 + 33 = 72$; $205(31 - 40 + 90) = 205 \cdot 81 = 16\,605$ or $205(31 - 40 + 90) = 205 \cdot 31 - 205 \cdot 40 + 205 \cdot 90 = 6\,355 - 8\,200 + 18\,450 = 16\,605$; $(19 + 14 + 31 + 6)10 = (50 + 20)10 = 700$, or $(19 + 14 + 31 + 6)10 = 19 \cdot 10 + 14 \cdot 10 + 31 \cdot 10 + 6 \cdot 10 = 190 + 140 + 310 + 60 = 500 + 200 = 700$.

Exercise 1.7.7. $(2 - a + g)(b - t + 50) = 2b - a \cdot b + b \cdot g - 2t + a \cdot t - g \cdot t + 100 - 50a + 50g$; $(-d - f - h - j)(a - 6) = -a \cdot d - a \cdot f - a \cdot h - a \cdot j + 6d + 6f + 6h + 6j$; $(2a + v + 4)(3 - d) = 6a + 3v + 12 - 2a \cdot d - v \cdot d - 4d$.

Exercise 1.8.9. $1 + 2 + \cdots + 23 = (1 + 23) \cdot 23 \div 2 = 276$; $3 + 4 + \cdots + 7 = (3 + 7) \cdot 5 \div 2 = 25$ or $1 + 2 + 3 + 4 + \cdots + 7 - (1 + 2) = 8 \cdot 7 \div 2 - 3 = 28 - 3 = 25$; $191 + 253 + 19 + 17 = 210 + 270 = 480$; $1 + 2 + 3 + \ldots + 99 = = 100 \cdot 99 \div 2 = 4950$; $29 + 28 + 27 + \cdots + 2 + 1 = (29 + 1) \cdot 29 \div 2 = 435$; $2 + 4 + 6 + \cdots + 28 + 30 = 2(1 + 2 + 3 + \cdot + 15) = 2 \cdot 16 \cdot 15 \div 2 = 240$.

1.9   Powers

1.9.1   Basic Properties of Powers

Multiplication of whole numbers is a shortcut for addition: it is easier to multiply $12 \cdot 13$ (If we know how to do that!) than to add 12 or 13 identical addends. Similarly, powers can be considered as a shortcut for multiplication. First we consider only powers with whole exponents.

Definition 1.9.1 *Given a number a and a positive integer k, the product of k equal factors a is called the kth power (or sometimes k^{th} index) of a and is denoted by a^k:*

$$a^k = \underbrace{a \cdot a \cdot \cdots \cdot a}_{k \ times}.$$

Here a is called the base and k the exponent.

For instance, $3^2 = 3 \cdot 3 = 9$, while $2^3 = 2 \cdot 2 \cdot 2 = 8$, thus we see from this example that exponentiation is not commutative.

Consider now the following sequence of powers (Please check the computations!):

$$3^1 = 3$$

$$3^2 = 9$$

$$3^3 = 27$$

$$3^4 = 81$$

$$3^5 = 243$$

$$3^6 = 729$$

We can easily move on, for example, $3^7 = 729 \cdot 3 = 2\,187$, $3^8 = 2\,187 \cdot 3 = 6\,561$, etc. Now, what about the opposite direction, that is, where the exponents are decreasing; what is 3^0? We can easily imagine a product consisting of just one factor, like $3 = 3^1$, but what about a product with *no* terms? Let us compare the right-hand sides of these equations. Then we observe that $81 = \frac{243}{3}$, $27 = \frac{81}{3}$, $9 = \frac{27}{3}$ and $3 = \frac{9}{3}$.

To preserve the pattern and due to certain other reasons, we have to *define* $3^0 = \frac{3}{3} = 1$.

Definition 1.9.2 *For any non-zero number $a \neq 0$,*

$$a^0 = 1.$$

The symbol 0^0 is undefined.

Exercise 1.9.1 *Rewrite using power notation. For example,*

$$3 \cdot 3 \cdot 3 \cdot 3 \cdot 5 \cdot 5 = 3^4 \cdot 5^2 = 81 \cdot 25 = 2025.$$

$7 \cdot 7 \cdot 3 \cdot 3 \cdot 3 =$	$2 \cdot 2 \cdot 2 \cdot 2 \cdot 2 \cdot 6 =$
$5 \cdot 5 \cdot 5 \cdot 2 \cdot 2 \cdot 2 =$	$10 \cdot 10 \cdot 10 \cdot 10 \cdot 10 =$
$1 \cdot 1 \cdot 1 \cdot 1 =$	$10 \cdot 10 \cdot 0 \cdot 10 \cdot 10 \cdot 10 =$

Exercise 1.9.2 *Compute the following powers. Based on these examples, what is the difference between odd and even powers of positive and negative numbers?*

$10^2 =$	$10^1 =$	$10^0 =$	$10^3 =$
$10^4 =$	$(-10)^2 =$	$(-10)^1 =$	$(-10)^0 =$
$(-10)^3 =$	$(-10)^4 =$	$1^2 =$	$1^0 =$
$(-1)^0 =$	$(-5)^3 =$	$12^2 =$	$2^2 =$
$-(-1)^0 =$	$-5^3 =$	$-5^2 =$	$-2^2 =$
$2^{10} =$	$4^5 =$	$7^3 =$	$2^{10} \div 2^4 =$
$-2^{10} =$	$1^{1000} =$	$0^{10} =$	$200^0 =$

Exercise 1.9.3 *Design and solve two more exercises similar to the previous ones.*

Analyzing these examples, we claim the following property.

Proposition 1.9.1 *An even power of both positive and negative numbers is positive; an odd power of positive numbers is positive. However, an odd power of negative numbers is negative.*

1.9.2   Powers of Ten

The powers of 10 are easiest to compute. Indeed, we have

$$10^2 = 10 \cdot 10 = 100,$$

$$10^3 = 10 \cdot 10 \cdot 10 = 1\,000,$$

$$10^4 = 10 \cdot 10 \cdot 10 \cdot 10 = 10\,000,$$

etc. The pattern here is clear, the natural power of 10 contains exactly as many zeros as the exponent. In the opposite direction,

$$10^1 = 10 \qquad \text{and} \qquad 10^0 = 1.$$

The negative powers will be considered in the next chapter.

Now we study how to multiply by the powers of 10. We know that $10^2 = 10 \cdot 10 = 100$. We can continue and compute

$$10^3 = 1\,000, \ 10^4 = 10\,000, \ 10^5 = 100\,000, \ 10^6 = 1\,000\,000,$$

that is a million, etc.

Analyzing these examples, we immediately notice that any natural power of 10 is the digit 1 with as many following zeros as is the exponent of the power.

Exercise 1.9.4 *Compute. For example,* $10^3 \cdot 10^5 = 1\,000 \cdot 100\,000 = 100\,000\,000,$ *that is, one thousand times one hundred thousands is one hundred millions.*

$10^2 \cdot 10 =$	$10^2 \cdot 10^0 =$	$10^{12} \cdot 10^6 =$
$(-10)^2 \cdot 10^3 =$	$-10^2 \cdot 10^2 =$	$10^2 \cdot (-10)^4 =$
$10^3 \cdot 10^9 =$	$10 \cdot 10^5 =$	$10^6 \cdot 10^4 =$

Exercise 1.9.5 *Design and solve two more exercises similar to the previous one.*

Moreover, when we multiply any whole number k by 10, the value of each of its digits is increased *ten-fold* .

Example 1.9.1 *Multiply* $3 \cdot 10^2$.

Solution. The product is $3 \cdot 10^2 = 10^2 \cdot 3 = 300$, *three hundreds*. Extending our analysis above, we see that we just have to attach the two zeros to the first factor. In the same way, $34 \cdot 10^2 = 3\,400$, $3 \cdot 10^3 = 3\,000$, and $54 \cdot 10^6 = 54\,000\,000$. □

Therefore, to multiply any whole number x by an nth-power of 10, that is, by 10^n, it is enough to append n zeros on the right of the x:

$$x \cdot 10^n = x \underbrace{0...0}_{n \ zeros} .$$

For example, $4\,567 \cdot 10^3 = 4\,567\,000.$

Exercise 1.9.6 *Compute.*

$$10^2 \cdot 10 = \qquad\qquad 45 \cdot 10^0 = \qquad\qquad 120 \cdot 10^6 =$$

$$1\,225 \cdot 10^3 = \qquad\qquad 527\,809 \cdot 10^2 = \qquad\qquad 1\,092 \cdot 10^4 =$$

$$10\,308 \cdot 10^6 = \qquad\qquad 156 \cdot 10^5 = \qquad\qquad 16 \cdot 10^4 =$$

Answers 1.9

Exercise 1.9.1. $7 \cdot 7 \cdot 3 \cdot 3 \cdot 3 = 7^2 \cdot 3^3 = 1323$, $2 \cdot 2 \cdot 2 \cdot 2 \cdot 2 \cdot 6 = 2^5 \cdot 6 = 192$, $5 \cdot 5 \cdot 5 \cdot 2 \cdot 2 \cdot 2 = 5^3 \cdot 2^3 = 1\,000$, $10 \cdot 10 \cdot 10 \cdot 10 \cdot 10 = 10^5 = 100\,000$, $1 \cdot 1 \cdot 1 \cdot 1 = 1^4 = 1$, $10 \cdot 10 \cdot 0 \cdot 10 \cdot 10 \cdot 10 = 10^5 \cdot 0 = 0$

Exercise 1.9.2.

$10^2 = 100$	$10^1 = 10$	$10^0 = 1$	$10^3 = 1\,000$
$10^4 = 10\,000$	$(-10)^2 = 100$	$(-10)^1 = -10$	$(-10)^0 = 1$
$(-10)^3 = -1\,000$	$(-10)^4 = 10\,000$	$1^2 = 1$	$1^0 = 1$
$(-1)^0 = 1$	$(-5)^3 = -125$	$12^2 = 144$	$2^2 = 4$
$-(-1)^0 = -1$	$-5^3 = -125$	$-5^2 = -25$	$-2^2 = -4$
$2^{10} = 1\,024$	$4^5 = 1\,024$	$7^3 = 343$	$2^{10} \div 2^4 = 2^6 = 64$
$-2^{10} = -1\,024$	$1^{1000} = 1$	$0^{10} = 0$	$200^0 = 1$

Exercise 1.9.4.

$$10^2 \cdot 10 = 1\,000 \qquad\qquad 10^2 \cdot 10^0 = 100$$

$$10^{12} \cdot 10^6 = 10^{18} \qquad\qquad (-10)^2 \cdot 10^3 = 10^5 = 100\,000$$

$$-10^2 \cdot 10^2 = -10^4 = -10\,000 \qquad\qquad 10^2 \cdot (-10)^4 = 10^6 = 1\,000\,000$$

$$10^3 \cdot 10^9 = 10^{12} \qquad\qquad 10 \cdot 10^5 = 10^6 = 1\,000\,000$$

$$10^6 \cdot 10^4 = 10^{10} = 10\,000\,000\,000$$

Exercise 1.9.6. $10^2 \cdot 10 = 1\,000$, $45 \cdot 10^0 = 45$, $120 \cdot 10^6 = 120\,000\,000$, $1\,225 \cdot 10^3 = 1\,225\,000$, $527\,809 \cdot 10^2 = 52\,780\,900$, $1\,092 \cdot 10^4 = 10\,920\,000$, $10308 \cdot 10^6 = 10\,308\,000\,000$, $156 \cdot 10^5 = 15\,600\,000$, $16 \cdot 10^4 = 160\,000$

1.10   Long Multiplication

1.10.1   Multiplication of a Many-Digit Number by a One-Digit Number

Example 1.10.1 *Multiply* $3\,024 \cdot 9$.

Solution. Expanding into the powers of 10,

$$3\,024 = 3 \cdot 10^3 + 0 \cdot 10^2 + 2 \cdot 10 + 4,$$

and employing the distributive law, we see that we must multiply out these four addends by 9. The procedure can be conveniently written down as follows.

$$3024 \cdot 9 = (3 \cdot 1\,000 + 2 \cdot 10 + 4) \cdot 9 = 3 \cdot 1\,000 \cdot 9 + 2 \cdot 10 \cdot 9 + 4 \cdot 9$$

$$= 27 \cdot 1\,000 + 18 \cdot 10 + 36 = 27\,216.$$

□

Keeping in mind the next step, namely, the multiplication of two many-digit numbers by making use of the so-called *long multiplication*, we expose the same example, $3\,024 \cdot 9$, in vertical format. In the case of a one-digit factor, it looks cumbersome, and it is so, but in the general case of many-digit numbers, this format is convenient and should be studied if one wants to understand how calculators and computers do arithmetic. We write

$$
\begin{array}{r}
3\,024 \\
\cdot \quad 9 \\
\hline
\end{array}
$$

Since $4 \cdot 9 = 36 = 3 \cdot 10 + 6$, which is not a digit, we record the digit of unities, 6, in the column of unities and move the *carry-on* **3** to the tens column, that is, to the left:

$$
\begin{array}{r}
...\mathbf{3} \\
3\,024 \\
\cdot \quad 9 \\
\hline
.....6
\end{array}
$$

Now we multiply the next digit of the first factor, 2, by 9 and add the carry-on **3**, $2 \cdot 9 + 3 = 21$, thus computing the digit of tens, 1, of the product and a new carry-on, **2**:

$$
\begin{array}{r}
..\mathbf{2}\cancel{\mathbf{3}} \\
3\,024 \\
\cdot \quad 9 \\
\hline
....16
\end{array}
$$

We crossed the first carry-on, 3, just to avoid any confusion with the next step and the next carry-on. At this step we have $0 \cdot 9 + 2 = 2$, thus we get the sequel digit, 2, of the product with the **0** carry-on:

$$
\begin{array}{r}
..\mathbf{0}\cancel{\mathbf{2}}\cancel{\mathbf{3}} \\
3\,024 \\
\cdot \quad 9 \\
\hline
...216
\end{array}
$$

Finally, $3 \cdot 9 = 27$, and we have completed the product:

$$
\begin{array}{r}
..\mathbf{0}\cancel{\mathbf{2}}\cancel{\mathbf{3}} \\
3\,024 \\
\cdot \quad 9 \\
\hline
27\,216
\end{array}
$$

thus, $3\,024 \cdot 9 = 27\,216$.   □

Example 1.10.2 *Multiply* $1\,002\,345 \cdot 8$.

Solution. In this example we show the same approach but proceed faster and do not write down some intermediate steps. Again, we first multiply the right-most digit, 5, of the first factor by the second factor, $5 \cdot 8 = 40$, thus we record 0 as the first digit of the product, and the first carry-on is **4**. Then we repeat the procedure, $4 \cdot 8 + 4 = 36$, therefore, the second digit of the product is 6 and the second carry-on is **3**. Next. $3 \cdot 8 + 3 = 27$, hence the third carry-on is **2**, etc. The final result is

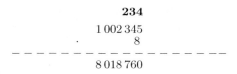

Exercise **1.10.1** *Multiply.*

$1\,002\,345 \cdot 8 =$ $709\,808 \cdot 5 =$

$3\,457 \cdot 9 =$ $2\,450\,067 \cdot 8 \cdot 5 =$

$2\,450\,067 \cdot 7 \cdot 3 =$ $31 \cdot 6 \cdot 5 =$

Exercise **1.10.2** *Design and solve two more exercises similar to the previous one.*

]

1.10.2 Multiplication of Many-Digit Whole Numbers

Now we can multiply any whole numbers.

Example **1.10.3** *Multiply* $124 \cdot 305$.

Solution. We expand $305 = 3 \cdot 100 + 0 \cdot 10 + 5$, thus by the distributive law,

$$124 \cdot 305 = 124 \cdot (3 \cdot 100 + 0 \cdot 10 + 5) = 124 \cdot 3 \cdot 100 + 124 \cdot 0 \cdot 10 + 124 \cdot 5.$$

Therefore, we must perform three multiplications and add the results, which can be conveniently written as follows.

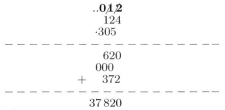

The appearance of the powers of 10 explains why we must shift every next product one step to the *left*. This procedure, called the *long multiplication*, can be conveniently written down as follows. If the second factor has, as in this example, a significant 0, the result contains a line of 0s. In such a case, it is convenient to skip this row of 0s and shift the next line one extra position to the left, so that the "2" in 372 occurs beneath the "6" in 620.

Hence, we write this example as

$$..0\!\!\!/\,1\!\!\!/\,2$$
$$124$$
$$\cdot 305$$

$$620$$
$$+372$$

$$37\,820$$

$\square$

Example 1.10.4 *Multiply* $3\,024 \cdot 809$.

Solution. Expanding both factors into the powers of 10, we get
$$3\,024 = 3 \cdot 10^3 + 2 \cdot 10 + 4 \text{ and } 809 = 8 \cdot 10^2 + 9,$$
thus we must multiply out
$$\left(3 \cdot 10^3 + 2 \cdot 10 + 4\right) \cdot \left(8 \cdot 10^2 + 9\right).$$
Again, we must multiply pair-wise all these addends.

$$3\,024$$
$$\times \quad 809$$

The product $3\,024 \cdot 9 = 27\,216$ was computed in example 1.10.1:

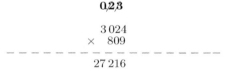

$$0\!\!\!/\,2\!\!\!/\,3$$
$$3\,024$$
$$\times \quad 809$$

$$27\,216$$

Multiplication by 0 gives only 0, therefore, next we multiply $3\,024$ by 8. However, the 8 is the digit of hundreds, thus we put the new product in the line below the first product and line it with the digit of hundreds in the latter, that is, with the middle 2:

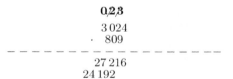

$$0\!\!\!/\,2\!\!\!/\,3$$
$$3\,024$$
$$\cdot \quad 809$$

$$27\,216$$
$$24\,192$$

Pay attention that the right-most 2 in the last row is in the column exactly beneath the 8 in the second factor. Finally (remember the distributive law!) we have to add these two products, resulting in the product we sought for:

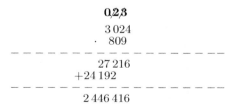

$$0\!\!\!/\,2\!\!\!/\,3$$
$$3\,024$$
$$\cdot \quad 809$$

$$27\,216$$
$$+24\,192$$

$$2\,446\,416$$

$\square$

Remark 1.10.1 *As we have already mentioned, it is not an error to insert a line of zeros, ...0000..., but it is just a distraction and should be avoided.*

Let us practice.

Exercise 1.10.3 *Multiply.*

$$341 \cdot 120 = \qquad 2\,095 \cdot 203 = \qquad 1\,002\,345 \cdot 7 =$$

$$808 \cdot 2\,045 = \qquad 3\,457 \cdot 909 = \qquad 2\,045 \cdot 88 =$$

Exercise 1.10.4 *Design and solve two more exercises similar to the previous one.*

Answers 1.10
Exercise 1.10.1.

$$1\,002\,345 \cdot 8 = 8\,018\,760 \qquad 709\,808 \cdot 5 = 3\,549\,040 \qquad 3\,457 \cdot 9 = 31\,113$$

$$2\,450\,067 \cdot 8 \cdot 5 = 98\,002\,680 \quad 2\,450\,067 \cdot 7 \cdot 3 = 51\,451\,407 \quad 31 \cdot 6 \cdot 5 = 930$$

Exercise 1.10.3.

$$341 \cdot 120 = 40\,920 \qquad 2\,095 \cdot 203 = 425\,285 \qquad 1\,002\,345 \cdot 7 = 7\,016\,415$$

$$808 \cdot 2\,045 = 1\,652\,360 \quad 3\,457 \cdot 909 = 3\,142\,413 \quad 2\,045 \cdot 88 = 179\,960$$

1.11 Inverse Operations II. Division of Whole Numbers

1.11.1 Long Division of Natural Numbers

Division is the inverse operation to multiplication. We define c to be a *quotient* of a and $b \neq 0$ and write $a \div b = c$ if $a = b \cdot c$; here a is called the *dividend* and b the *divisor*. For example, $5 \cdot 7 = 35$, therefore, $35 \div 7 = 5$, where 35 is the dividend, 7 the divisor, and 5 the quotient. Since multiplication is commutative, we also have $7 \cdot 5 = 35$, thus $35 \div 5 = 7$; now 5 is the divisor and 7 the quotient. There is a convenient verbal expression for division problems, we say that 5 *goes* 7 *times into* 35, or vice versa, that 7 *goes* 5 *times into* 35; indeed,

$$35 = 5 + 5 + 5 + 5 + 5 + 5 + 5 = 7 + 7 + 7 + 7 + 7.$$

In the same fashion, 7 goes 4 times into 28, for $28 = 4 \cdot 7$. However, since $28 < 29 < 35$, no such a representation is possible for 29, 29 cannot be written as a product of whole numbers. The ratio $29 \div 7$ is not an integer, it is a *rational number*.

Since $6 \div 3 = 2$, we say that 3 *divides* 6 *evenly* or with *zero remainder*. However, in most cases the remainder is not zero. A procedure for finding the quotient and the remainder for any two natural numbers is called the *long division*. It is reversal of the long multiplication. First we demonstrate the *long division algorithm* if the remainder is zero.

Example 1.11.1 *Divide* $60 \div 4$.

Solution. If we compute consecutive multiples of the divisor 4, namely $4 \cdot 1 = 4$, $4 \cdot 2 = 8$, $4 \cdot 3 = 12$,... we eventually get $4 \cdot 15 = 60$, thus $60 \div 4 = 15$. It is, however, cumbersome and may be time-consuming to divide by consecutive trials, but the procedure can be conveniently arranged as follows. Let us recall that to *multiply* 4 by 15, we first multiply $4 \cdot 5 = 20$, getting 0 as the right-most digit of the product and the carry-on 2. Then we multiply $4 \cdot 1$ and add the carry-on, getting the second digit of the product, $4 \cdot 1 + 2 = 6$. To divide, we reverse all these steps.

We begin by writing

$$4 \overline{\smash{\big)}\ 60}$$

and separate the shortest possible left part of the dividend 60, such that the divisor 4 can be divided into this part – in this example this part is just one digit 6. Since $4 \cdot 1 = 4 < 6$ but $4 \cdot 2 = 8 > 6$, we see that 4 goes into 6 just once. We record this (incomplete) quotient 1 above the dividend, as

$$4 \overline{\smash{\big)}\ \overset{1}{60}}$$

Next we multiply the divisor by this first "incomplete quotient", $4 \cdot 1 = 4$, place this product below the 6:

$$\begin{array}{r} \overset{1}{} \\ 4 \overline{\smash{\big)}\ 60} \\ 4 \end{array}$$

and subtract 4 from 6:

$$\begin{array}{r} \overset{1}{} \\ 4 \overline{\smash{\big)}\ 60} \\ \underline{-4} \\ 2 \end{array}$$

In the dividend 6 is the digit of tens. Hence, the 1 on the top is the digit of tens in the quotient, and we placed it in the column with the digit of tens 6 in the dividend.

We have described here the loop in the long division algorithm –

Divide, Multiply, Subtract

which repeats again and again in every use of the long division algorithm.

To continue, we notice that we have used only the first digit 6 of the dividend and have not used yet the second digit, 0. Now we bring the latter down and attach to the intermediate difference 2, thus deriving an intermediate dividend 20,

$$\begin{array}{r} \overset{1}{} \\ 4 \overline{\smash{\big)}\ 60} \\ \underline{-4} \\ 20 \end{array}$$

This number 20 is bigger than the divisor 4, hence we can continue and start the second loop of the long division algorithm. Since 4 goes 5 times into 20, we divide 4 into 20, get a 5, and record this 5 on the top, next to 1:

$$\begin{array}{r} \overset{15}{} \\ 4 \overline{\smash{\big)}\ 60} \\ \underline{-4} \\ 20 \end{array}$$

At the next step we multiply the divisor 4 by the previous (incomplete) quotient 5, $4 \cdot 5 = 20$, and subtract this product from the previous intermediate dividend 20:

$$
\begin{array}{r}
15 \\
4\ )\overline{60} \\
-4 \\
\hline
20 \\
-20 \\
\hline
0
\end{array}
$$

Since the difference is 0 and we have used all the digits of the dividend, the division is finished and we found that $60 \div 4 = 15$ or $60 = 4 \cdot 15$. □

Exercise 1.11.1 *Divide; in all these problems the answers are integer numbers, that is, with zero remainder.*

$872 \div 8 =$	$1\,002\,432 \div 908 =$	$99\,840 \div 80 =$
$709\,615 \div 2\,045 =$	$128\,817 \div 9\,909 =$	$870\,968 \div 8\,456 =$
$2\,452\,064 \div 8 =$	$2\,450\,259 \div 801 =$	$870\,975 \div 45 =$

Exercise 1.11.2 *Design and solve two more exercises similar to the previous one.*

Now we consider an example of long division with a *remainder*.

Example 1.11.2 *Divide* $60 \div 13$.

Solution. When we multiply two integers, we compute the digits of the product starting from the right. Now, division is the inverse operation to multiplication, so that we compute the digits of the quotient from the left, one after another. We compute consecutive multiples of the divisor 13, namely $13 \cdot 1 = 13$, $13 \cdot 2 = 26$, $13 \cdot 3 = 39$, $13 \cdot 4 = 52$, and $13 \cdot 5 = 65$, we observe that $13 \cdot 5 = 65 > 60$, thus 13 goes 4 times into 60, and we still have the (non-zero) remainder $60 - 52 = 8$, or $60 = 13 \cdot 4 + 8$. Now we apply the long division algorithm. We again write

$$13\ )\overline{60}$$

and since we calculated that 13 goes four times into 60, we record this (incomplete) quotient above the dividend, such that the 4 must be lined up with 0, for we divided 13 into 60:

$$
\begin{array}{r}
4 \\
13\ )\overline{60}
\end{array}
$$

Next we multiply $13 \cdot 4 = 52$ and place this product below 60:

$$
\begin{array}{r}
4 \\
13\ )\overline{60} \\
52
\end{array}
$$

Finally, we subtract 52 from 60:

$$
\begin{array}{r}
4 \\
13\ )\overline{60} \\
-\ 52 \\
\hline
8
\end{array}
$$

This is the same loop in the long division algorithm – *Divide, Multiply, Subtract*. To finish the job, we notice that the remainder 8 is less than the divisor 13, thus the division is completed. Here 8 is the remainder and 4 the (incomplete) quotient; as before, we have $60 = 13 \cdot 4 + 8$. The result can be written as $60 \div 13 = 4(R\ 8)$. □

Example 1.11.3 *Divide* $1\,203 \div 14$.

Solution. To find the first, left-most digit of the quotient, we start by dividing 14 into a certain left part of the dividend 1203. 14 cannot be divided into 1, nor into 12; thus we start by dividing 14 into 120. If we multiply 14 by the biggest digit, the product $14 \cdot 9 = 126$ is larger than 120 – we overshoot and want to try smaller digits. Now, if we try 7 instead of 9, then $14 \cdot 7 = 98$, which is smaller than 120, but the difference (Remember the loop: Divide, Multiply, Subtract) $120 - 98 = 22$ is bigger than the divisor 14, thus 7 also is not good; now we undershoot. Whence, the only choice for the first digit of the quotient is 8. Since we divide 14 into 120, we must write 8 in the column where the right-most digit of 120 is, that is, above the 0:

$$14 \ )\overline{\overset{\displaystyle 8}{1203}}$$

This is important: if we place that 8 above the right-most digit 3, which often happens, such bad writing immediately leads to the error!

The 0 is the digit of *tens* in the dividend and 8 is the digit of *tens* in the quotient. According to the long division algorithm, now we multiply $14 \cdot 8 = 112$, put this product beneath 120 and subtract it from the latter number:

$$
\begin{array}{r}
\overset{\displaystyle 8}{} \\
14 \ )\overline{1203} \\
-\,112 \\
\hline
8
\end{array}
$$

To proceed, we bring down the next digit of the dividend, that is, 3:

$$
\begin{array}{r}
\overset{\displaystyle 8}{} \\
14 \ )\overline{1203} \\
-\,112 \\
\hline
83
\end{array}
$$

Now we divide 14 into 83 and by trial find the next digit, 5, of the quotient:

$$
\begin{array}{r}
\overset{\displaystyle 8\,5}{} \\
14 \ )\overline{1203} \\
-\,112 \\
\hline
83
\end{array}
$$

The last loop in the example, $14 \cdot 5 = 70$ and $83 - 70 = 13$, gives the remainder 13:

$$
\begin{array}{r}
\overset{\displaystyle 8\,5}{} \\
14 \ )\overline{1203} \\
-\,112 \\
\hline
83 \\
-70 \\
\hline
13
\end{array}
$$

The result can be written as $1203 = 14 \cdot 85 + 13$.   □

Now we consider an example exhibiting some less obvious features of the long division algorithm.

Example 1.11.4 *Divide* $1\,001$ *over* 5.

Solution. To initiate the long division algorithm, we write

$$5 \overline{)\ 1001}.$$

5 cannot be divided into 1, thus we must attach the next digit to 1 and divide 5 into 10. The result, 2, is to be written above 10 in the dividend, vertically aligned:

$$
\begin{array}{r}
2 \\
5 \overline{)\ 1001}
\end{array}
$$

We do the same loop – after dividing we multiply 5 by 2 and subtract the product $5 \cdot 2 = 10$ from the first intermediate dividend, that is, from 10:

$$
\begin{array}{r}
2 \\
5 \overline{)\ 1001} \\
-\ 10 \\
\hline
0
\end{array}
$$

The difference is 0 and we are to bring down the next digit of the dividend, which is also 0:

$$
\begin{array}{r}
2 \\
5 \overline{)\ 1001} \\
-\ 10 \\
\hline
00
\end{array}
$$

Next we must divide 5 into 0 resulting, of course, in 0. The important and often missed step is *writing down* this 0 at the appropriate place in the quotient above the dividend:

$$
\begin{array}{r}
2\,0 \\
5 \overline{)\ 1001} \\
-\ 10 \\
\hline
00
\end{array}
$$

To find the next digit of the result, we are to bring down the last digit of the dividend, 1:

$$
\begin{array}{r}
2\,0 \\
5 \overline{)\ 1001} \\
-\ 10 \\
\hline
001
\end{array}
$$

and then divide 5 into $001 = 1$; therefore, the next digit of the quotient is again 0:

$$
\begin{array}{r}
2\,0\,0 \\
5 \overline{)\ 1001} \\
-\ 10 \\
\hline
001
\end{array}
$$

Multiplying 5 by 0 and subtracting from 1, we find the remainder, 1, since all the digits of the dividend are now used:

$$
\begin{array}{r}
2\,0\,0 \\
5 \overline{)\ 1001} \\
-\ 10 \\
\hline
001 \\
-\ 000 \\
\hline
1
\end{array}
$$

Whence, $1\,001 = 5 \cdot 200 + 1$, which can be immediately checked by multiplication and addition. $\quad\square$

Exercise 1.11.3 *Divide with a remainder. Write the answers as $a = b \cdot Q + R$, where Q and R are integers, Q is the incomplete quotient, R is the remainder.*

$$870 \div 8 = \qquad\qquad 1\,002\,345 \div 908 =$$

$$1\,002\,345 \div 70 = \qquad\qquad 9\,809 \div 2\,045 =$$

$$128\,345 \div 128\,199 = \qquad\qquad 2\,450\,067 \div 8 =$$

Problem 1.11.1 *Sasha's gross annual salary is $37 440. What is her weekly, by-weekly, semi-monthly, and monthly gross income? For the payroll office, a year consists of 52 weeks, 26 by-weekly periods, 24 semi-monthly periods, and 12 months.*

Exercise 1.11.4 *Design and solve two more exercises similar to the previous ones.*

1.11.2   Multiplication and Division Involving Zero

It is a good point here to refresh operations with zero.

A product including at least one zero factor is itself zero. For example, $999 \cdot 0 \cdot 888 = 0$.

If the denominator of a rational expression is zero or is a product containing zero factor, the whole expression is undefined. The latter means that there is no reasonable way to assign a numerical value to this expression. For example,

$$\frac{17}{3 \cdot 0 \cdot 71} \text{ is undefined}$$

and

$$\frac{2(3^2 - 9)}{25 - 5^2} \text{ is undefined.}$$

1.11.3   Multiplication and Division of Signed Numbers

When we multiply or divide positive numbers, the result is positive. Now we have to learn how to multiply or divide any signed numbers, positive and negative. First of all, let us recall that the multiplication is an abbreviation for addition, for instance, $3 \cdot 5 = 5 + 5 + 5 = 15$, so that it should be $3 \cdot (-5) = (-5) + (-5) + (-5) = -15$. Thus, the product of a *positive* number 3 and a *negative* number -5 is *negative*, $3 \cdot (-5) = -15$. Of course, it is not a property of the particular numbers 3 and -5. In general, it can be proved that this property is valid for all numbers. Since the multiplication is commutative, the same must be valid if the first factor is negative while the second positive.

Theorem 1.11.1 *The product of any positive number and any negative number, in either order, is a negative number, and this rule applies to any numbers, integers, fractions, decimals,... .* $\square$

Since $-15 = (-1) \cdot 15$, we can write the example above as

$$3 \cdot (-5) = 3 \cdot (-1) \cdot 5 = -(3 \cdot 5).$$

In other words, the product of a negative and a positive number, in either order, is the *opposite* of the product of their *absolute values*.

Next, let us multiply two negative numbers, say $(-3) \cdot (-5)$. Since $-3 = (-1) \cdot 3$, and the multiplication is associative, the problem can be written as $(-3) \cdot (-5) = (-1) \cdot [3 \cdot (-5)]$, and by the previous rule, we must find the opposite of the *negative* product $3 \cdot (-5) = -15$. Because the opposite of a negative number is positive, we have $(-3) \cdot (-5) = -(-15) = 15$. Again, the following statement can be proved in general.

Theorem 1.11.2 *The product of any two negative numbers is a positive number, namely, it is the product of the absolute values of the factors.* □

Now we can easily learn how to divide signed numbers. Indeed, let us consider a positive number $a > 0$ and a negative number $b < 0$, and let $a \div b = c$. By the definition of division, this means $a = b \cdot c$, and if c were positive, then a must have been negative; however, a is positive. The same reasoning implies that the ratio of two negative numbers must be positive, and we state the following result.

Theorem 1.11.3 *When we divide a positive number over a negative number, or a negative number over a positive number, the quotient is negative.*
The ratio of two negative numbers is positive. □

These rules can be conveniently combined in one.

Theorem 1.11.3' *The product or the quotient of two numbers of opposite signs, one positive and another negative, is a negative number.*
The product or the quotient of two numbers of the same sign is positive. □

For example, $(-4) \cdot 3 = -12$. We remark that this example, and all the similar problems, can be written without the first pair of parentheses as $-4 \cdot 3 = -12$.
However, the expression $4 \cdot -3$ is not good, since two consecutive symbols, $\cdot -$ can lead to errors and misunderstanding, and *must* be separated by parentheses, like $4 \cdot (-3) = -12$.
Analyzing the 'rules of signs' above, we observe that if a problem involves *only multiplication and division*, it is convenient first to determine the sign of the result, and then "forget" about the signs and operate the absolute values of the given numbers.

Example 1.11.5 *Compute* $\frac{(-3) \cdot 6 \cdot (-1)}{(-1) \cdot (-7) \cdot (-5)}$.

Solution. The product or quotient of two negative numbers is positive, therefore, every pair of negative signs 'cancels out' each other. Since the expression contains an odd number (five) of the negative signs, one " $-$ " sign remains without a pair, thus, the result is negative. Hence,

$$\frac{(-3) \cdot 6 \cdot (-1)}{(-1) \cdot (-7) \cdot (-5)} = -\frac{3 \cdot 6 \cdot 1}{1 \cdot 7 \cdot 5} = -\frac{18}{35}.$$

□

Remark 1.11.1 *In fractions, the " $-$ " sign can be placed at three different places with the same result, for example,*

$$\frac{-15}{3} = \frac{15}{-3} = -\frac{15}{3} = -5.$$

Compare with

$$\frac{-15}{-3} = \frac{15}{3} = 5.$$

Exercise 1.11.5 *Compute.*

$$1\,002 \cdot (-78) = \qquad\qquad -9\,808 \cdot 45 =$$

$$(-241) \cdot (-1\,008) = \qquad\qquad -14 \cdot 12 \cdot (-101) \cdot (-5) =$$

Exercise 1.11.6 *Identify the dividend, divisor, and quotient in each of the examples and exercises in this section.*

Exercise 1.11.7 *Design and solve two more exercises similar to the previous one.*

1.11.4   Order of Operations II

We started discussing the order of operations in Section 1.7.3, where we dealt with addition and subtraction only. Now we have learnt multiplication, division and powers, and we must include these operations in the scheme. Our procedures follow two simple and logical rules:

First, work inside the most deeply nested separators.

Second, always work from more advanced to less advanced operations.

The latter means that since the addition and subtraction are mutually inverse, we treat them as the operations of the same level, addition does not have any advantage over subtraction. On the other hand, the multiplication is the abbreviation for addition, so that multiplication and division are more advanced than addition and subtraction, and must be executed before the latter. By the same logic, since powers (the exponentiation) mean abbreviation for multiplication, we place them (and later the radicals as the inverse of powers) above the multiplication and division and execute them before the latter.

Example 1.11.6 *Compute* $32 \div 8 \cdot 5 - 6$.

Solution. The expression has no parentheses or other separators, and contains three arithmetic operations, $\div$, $\cdot$, $-$, in order from left to right. Since the subtraction is of the lowest rank here, it will be done in the end, and we must first compute $32 \div 8 \cdot 5$. In this part we have two operations of the same level, $\div$ and $\cdot$, which are to be done in order as they go, *from left to right*. Hence, we compute $(32 \div 8) \cdot 5 = 4 \cdot 5 = 20$, and the original problem reduces to $32 \div 8 \cdot 5 - 6 = 4 \cdot 5 - 6 = 20 - 6 = 14$. $\qquad\square$

Example 1.11.7 *Compute* $32 \div 8 \cdot 5 - 6 \cdot 3$.

Solution. Unlike the previous example, this one includes another multiplication, which also must be executed before the subtraction. Hence, the whole expression is split into two parts, each of which must be done before the subtraction. Since these parts are independent, they can be worked on *simultaneously.*

Therefore, as before, we compute $32 \div 8 \cdot 5 = 20$, then we multiply $6 \cdot 3 = 18$, and then we finish the job by subtracting $32 \div 8 \cdot 5 - 6 \cdot 3 = 20 - 18 = 2$. $\square$

Example 1.11.8 *Compute* $32 \div 8 \cdot (5 - 6 \cdot 3)$.

Solution. Now the parentheses force us to compute first $5 - 6 \cdot 3 = 5 - 18 = -13$, and then $32 \div 8 \cdot (-13) = 4 \cdot (-13) = -52$. $\square$

Example 1.11.9 *Compute* $32 \div 8 \cdot [(5 - 6) \cdot 3]$.

Solution. Here we have to deal with nested separators, therefore, first of all we do $(5 - 6) \cdot 3 = -1 \cdot 3 = -3$. Then $32 \div 8 \cdot (-3) = 4 \cdot (-3) = -12$. $\square$

Exercise 1.11.8

$$3 + 45 \div (-9) = \qquad\qquad 3 - 2 \cdot (-8) \div 4 =$$

$$-2\,450 + (-80 \div 8) = \qquad\qquad 310 \div (-10) \cdot (-8) =$$

$$2\,450 + (80 \div (-8)) = \qquad\qquad -310 \div (-10) \cdot (-8) =$$

Exercise 1.11.9 *Design and solve two more exercises similar to the previous one.*

Answers 1.11

Exercise 1.11.1.

$$872 \div 8 = 109 \qquad 1\,002\,432 \div 908 = 1\,104 \qquad 99\,840 \div 80 = 1\,248$$

$$709\,615 \div 2\,045 = 347 \qquad 128\,817 \div 9\,909 = 13 \qquad 870\,968 \div 8\,456 = 103$$

$$2\,452\,064 \div 8 = 306\,508 \qquad 2\,450\,259 \div 801 = 3\,059 \qquad 870\,975 \div 45 = 19\,355$$

Exercise 1.11.3.

$$870 = 8 \cdot 108 + 6 \qquad\qquad 1\,002\,345 = 908 \cdot 1\,103 + 821$$

$$1\,002\,345 = 70 \cdot 14\,319 + 15 \qquad 9\,809 = 2\,045 \cdot 4 + 1\,629$$

$$128\,345 = 128\,199 \cdot 1 + 146 \qquad 2\,450\,067 = 8 \cdot 306\,258 + 3$$

Exercise 1.11.5.

$$1\,002 \cdot (-78) = -78\,156; \qquad\qquad -9\,808 \cdot 45 = -441\,360;$$

$$(-241) \cdot (-1\,008) = 242\,928; \qquad -14 \cdot 12 \cdot (-101) \cdot (-5) = -84\,840.$$

Exercise 1.11.8.

$$3 + 45 \div (-9) = -2; \qquad\qquad 3 - 2 \cdot (-8) \div 4 = 7;$$

$$-2\,450 + (-80 \div 8) = -2\,460; \qquad 310 \div (-10) \cdot (-8) = 248;$$

$$2\,450 + (80 \div (-8)) = 2\,440; \qquad -310 \div (-10) \cdot (-8) = -248.$$

1.12   Prime Numbers. Prime Factorization

Every mathematical equation is a "two-way street" – we can read and use it from left to right and from right to left, whichever is necessary for our problem. When we read distributive law (1.8.1) from left to right,

$$c \cdot a + c \cdot b = c \cdot (a + b),$$

we do what is called *factorization*, we *factor out* the *common factor* c and represent the *sum* $c \cdot a + c \cdot b$ as the product

$$c \cdot (a + b)$$

of two factors c and $a+b$. If the factors are simpler than the initial expression, then the factorization can be useful. In particular, it may be essential to represent an integer number as a product of smaller integers.

Compare two numbers 6 and 7. The former can be *factored* in two different ways, $6 = 2 \cdot 3$ and $6 = 1 \cdot 6$, while the latter can be factored only as $7 = 1 \cdot 7$. The integer numbers, similar to 7 are called *prime numbers*.

Definition 1.12.1 *A positive integer number, which is bigger than 1, is called prime if it does not have integer factors, distinct from 1 and itself, that is, factors which are greater than 1 and smaller than the number itself; such factors are called proper factors. All the other whole numbers, which are larger than 1, are called composite numbers. By agreement, the 1 is neither a prime nor composite.*

The prime numbers smaller than 100, are listed here,

$$2, \ 3, \ 5, \ 7, \ 11, \ 13, \ 17, \ 19, \ 23, \ 29, \ 31, \ 37, \ 41, \ 43, \ 47,$$

$$53, \ 59, \ 61, \ 67, \ 71, \ 73, \ 79, \ 83, \ 89, \ 97,$$

while a first few composite numbers are

$$4, \ 6, \ 8, \ 9, \ 10, \ 12, 14, \ 15, \ldots .$$

The only even prime number is 2, since if a number $p > 2$ is even, than 2 is its *proper* factor, hence p has a proper factor smaller than itself and cannot be prime.

Consider, for example, a number 159. Since its last digit 9 is odd, the number itself is odd and cannot be divided by 2. However we can directly see for ourselves that the next prime, 3, divides 159 evenly, $159 \div 3 = 53$, or $3 \cdot 53 = 159$. In the same way, we can straightforwardly check that none other prime number, smaller than 53, divides the latter, thus 53 is also prime, however, 159 is composite since $159 = 3 \cdot 53$. This representation is called the *prime factorization* of 159. The prime factorization is unique if we fix the order of the prime factors, for instance, from smallest to largest. The algorithm described above can be conveniently displayed as follows.

Example 1.12.1 *Find the prime factorization of* 96.

Solution. Since the last digit is 6, this number is even, that is, the 2 is its factor, $96 \div 2 = 48$. The factorization problems can be visualized by the diagram

$$2\Big|\ \begin{array}{l} 96 \\ 48 \end{array}$$

Next, 48 is also even, thus we can divide it by 2, $48 \div 2 = 24$, and extend the diagram down as

$$
\begin{array}{c|c}
2 & 96 \\
2 & 48 \\
  & 24 \\
\end{array}
$$

We continue the same way,

$$
\begin{array}{c|c}
2 & 96 \\
2 & 48 \\
2 & 24 \\
  & 12 \\
\end{array}
$$

then

$$
\begin{array}{c|c}
2 & 96 \\
2 & 48 \\
2 & 24 \\
2 & 12 \\
  & 6 \\
\end{array}
$$

and

$$
\begin{array}{c|c}
2 & 96 \\
2 & 48 \\
2 & 24 \\
2 & 12 \\
2 & 6 \\
  & 3 \\
\end{array}
$$

The last quotient, 3, is prime and we can divide it only by itself:

$$
\begin{array}{c|c}
2 & 96 \\
2 & 48 \\
2 & 24 \\
2 & 12 \\
2 & 6 \\
3 & 3 \\
  & 1 \\
\end{array}
$$

The numbers occurring in the left column, 2, 2, 2, 2, 2, 3, are all the prime factors of 96, and we see that 2 occurs here five times. Thus,

$$96 = 2 \cdot 2 \cdot 2 \cdot 2 \cdot 2 \cdot 3 = 2^5 \cdot 3.$$

With small numbers, we can generate the prime factorization straightforwardly, without resorting to the long columns above. For example,

$$80 = 2 \cdot 40 = 2 \cdot 2 \cdot 20 = 2 \cdot 2 \cdot 2 \cdot 10 = 2 \cdot 2 \cdot 2 \cdot 2 \cdot 5 = 2^4 \cdot 5.$$

$\square$

The exponents 5 or 4 above are called the *multiplicity* of the factor 2; The multiplicity of 3 or of 5 is 1. As another example, we can check that $2^3 \cdot 3^2 \cdot 5 = 360$, thus, the multiplicities of $2, 3$ and 5 in the prime factorization of 360 are $3, 2$ and 1, respectively.

Of course, the prime factorization of a prime number consists of the only factor – the number itself, like $13 = 13$.

Exercise 1.12.1 *Find the prime factorizations of the following integers. Write the repeating prime factors as powers and indicate their multiplicities.*

$78 =$	$90 =$	$345 =$	$1\,002 =$	$709 =$
$808 =$	$45 =$	$33 =$	$457 =$	$128 =$
$354 =$	$909 =$	$2 =$	$450 =$	$69 =$
$50 =$	$608 =$	$31 =$	$870 =$	$960 =$

Exercise 1.12.2 *Design and solve two more exercises similar to the previous one.*

Answers 1.12

Exercise 1.12.1.

$$78 = 2 \cdot 3 \cdot 13; \quad 90 = 2 \cdot 3^2 \cdot 5; \quad 345 = 3 \cdot 5 \cdot 23; \quad 1\,002 = 2 \cdot 3 \cdot 167;$$
$$709 = 1 \cdot 709; \quad 808 = 2^3 \cdot 101; \quad 45 = 3^2 \cdot 5; \quad 33 = 3 \cdot 11;$$
$$457 = 1 \cdot 457; \quad 128 = 2^7; \quad 354 = 2 \cdot 177; \quad 909 = 3^2 \cdot 101;$$
$$2 = 1 \cdot 2; \quad 450 = 2 \cdot 3^2 \cdot 5^2; \quad 69 = 3 \cdot 23; \quad 50 = 2 \cdot 5^2;$$
$$608 = 2^5 \cdot 19; \quad 31 = 1 \cdot 31; \quad 870 = 2 \cdot 3 \cdot 5 \cdot 29; \quad 960 = 2^6 \cdot 3 \cdot 5.$$

1.13   GCF and LCM

Let us compare the prime factorizations of 12 and 18, which are $12 = 2 \cdot 2 \cdot 3$ and $18 = 2 \cdot 3 \cdot 3$. We observe, that the numbers 12 and 18 have two common prime factors, 2 and 3; therefore, the product of these factors, $2 \cdot 3 = 6$ also is their common factor. Moreover, 12 and 18 clearly have no common factor bigger than 6. This *largest* common factor is called the *Greatest Common Factor* (**GCF**) and is denoted by $GCF(12, 18)$. Thus, $GCF(12, 18) = 6$. In general, the $GCF(a, b, ..., d)$ of the natural numbers $a, b, ...d$ is the largest natural number, which divides evenly (with zero remainder) each of the numbers $a, b, ..., d$.

The *algorithm* for computing the $GCF(a, b, ..., d)$ is now straightforward: find the prime factorizations of all the numbers $a, b, ...d$, select and multiply their *common factors*, and use each of the latter with the *smallest multiplicity* among the given numbers. For if a number k has a factor $2^2 = 4$, but not $2^3 = 8$, and another number l has a factor 2^3, then the latter cannot be a common factor since it does not divide the k.

Example 1.13.1 *Find the $GCF(20, 50)$.*

Solution. As before,

$$
\begin{array}{r|r}
2 & 20 \\
2 & 10 \\
5 & 5 \\
  & 1
\end{array}
\qquad \text{and} \qquad
\begin{array}{r|r}
2 & 50 \\
5 & 25 \\
5 & 5 \\
  & 1
\end{array}
$$

Thus, $GCF(20, 50) = 2 \cdot 5 = 10$. We can also immediately find $20 = 2^2 \cdot 5$ and $50 = 2 \cdot 5^2$, thus both 2 and 5 are common factors. However, the multiplicity of 2 in 20 is 2, while that in 50 is 1, therefore, $2^2 = 4$ cannot enter as a factor into the $GCF(20, 50)$, since 4 is not a factor of 50, and we must use $2^1 = 2$, where the exponent 1 is the multiplicity of the 2 in 20. In the same fashion, since the smallest of the multiplicities of 5 in 20 and 50 is $\min(1, 2) = 1$, only one $5 = 5^1$ is a common factor of 20 and 50. Again, $GCF(20, 50) = 2 \cdot 5 = 10$. $\qquad\square$

Another algorithm for computing the GCF of two numbers, called the *Euclidean algorithm*, requires only consecutive divisions of integer numbers. We demonstrate it on the previous example.

Example 1.13.2 *Use the Euclidean algorithm to find the $GCF(20, 50)$.*

Solution. The algorithm starts by dividing the bigger given number over the smaller. Thus, we divide $50 \div 20$ and find $50 = 2 \cdot 20 + 10$, where 10 is the remainder. This equation shows that any common factor of 50 and 20 necessarily must also be a common factor of the remainder, 10 and a smaller number.

Therefore, at the next we again divide, this time $20 \div 10$, that is, the previous divisor over the remainder, and get $20 = 2 \cdot 10 + 0$. When we got the zero remainder, that shows that the last non-zero remainder is the GCF in the problem, that is, $GCF(20, 50) = 10$, as in the first solution. $\qquad\square$

Example 1.13.3 *Find the $GCF(3, 10)$.*

Solution. Since $10 = 2 \cdot 5$, and the prime number 3 is not among the factors of 10, we conclude that $GCF(3, 10) = 1$. If we employ the Euclidean algorithm, we get first $10 = 3 \cdot 3 + 1$, and next $3 = 3 \cdot 1 + 0$, hence again, $GCF(3, 10) = 1$. $\qquad\square$

Such numbers, whose GCF is 1, are called *mutually prime*, even though one or all of them can be composite numbers.

Exercise 1.13.1 *Compute the GCFs using both methods, the Euclidean algorithm and prime factorization.*

$GCF(20, 78) =$	$GCF(2, 10, 50) =$	$GCF(20, 5) =$
$GCF(1\,002, 12, 24) =$	$GCF(280, 80) =$	$GCF(20, 45) =$
$GCF(25, 50) =$	$GCF(25, 45) =$	$GCF(25, 345) =$
$GCF(50, 90, 25) =$	$GCF(25, 55) =$	$GCF(25, 350) =$

Exercise 1.13.2 (1) *Compare both algorithms – do you observe any advantage of either of them?*

(2) *Try to prove that the Euclidean algorithm always returns the GCF of two numbers.*

(3) *How to find the GCF of three or more numbers by making use of the Euclidean algorithm?*

Exercise 1.13.3 *Design and solve two more exercises similar to the previous one.*

The GCF is a factor of several given numbers. In many problems we have to look in another direction and find a number such that it can be *divided over* every of the given natural numbers. To put it another way, we want to find an integer number such that every given number is its factor. For example, given the numbers 5 and 6, we observe that 5 is a factor of the 5 itself, a factor of $10 = 2 \cdot 5$, a factor of $15 = 3 \cdot 5$, a factor of $20 = 4 \cdot 5$, etc. These numbers, $5, 10, 15, 20, 25, 30, 35, \ldots$, are called *multiples* of the 5; this sequence is, obviously, infinite together with the sequence of the natural numbers, thus every integer number has infinitely many integer multiples.

In the same way, the multiples of 6 are $6, 12, 18, 24, 30, 36, \ldots$. We observe that if we extend these sequences far enough, we find in them (infinitely many) common terms, namely, $30, 60, 90, \ldots$. These numbers are called the *common multiples* of 5 and 6, and since all these numbers are positive, among them there must be the smallest number, called the *Least Common Multiple* (**LCM**).

Thus, we found that $LCM(5, 6) = 30$.

An algorithm for computing the LCM was shown in the example above. Now we state the algorithm in general.

To find the LCM($a, ..., d$) of several numbers:

Start with the largest number, say a (it may be shorter than if we start with a smaller one), compute a few consecutive multiples of this number, that is, $a, 2a, 3a, 4a, \ldots$, and for each of these multiples verify whether it is a multiple of all the other numbers $b, ..., d$ – the first multiple of a with this property is the $LCM(a, \ldots, d)$.

In the example above, if we start with 6, we compute consecutively the multiples of 6, that is, $6 = 6 \cdot 1, 12 = 6 \cdot 2, 18 = 6 \cdot 3, 24 = 6 \cdot 4$, and neither of these four numbers is a multiple of 5. However, the next multiple, $30 = 6 \cdot 5$, is also a multiple of 5, thus, the $LCM(5, 6) = 30$.

Another algorithm for computing the LCM, similar to the first algorithm for computing the GCF, is the following: Prime factor all the given numbers, collect all prime factors, which appear in at least one of the given numbers, and include it as a factor in the LCM with the *largest multiplicity* for this factor among the given numbers. In the example above with $LCM(5, 6)$, 5 is prime and $6 = 2 \cdot 3$, thus we get the three prime factors, 2,3, and 5, each with the multiplicity of 1, hence the $LCM(5, 6) = 2 \cdot 3 \cdot 5 = 30$.

Example 1.13.4 *Find the $LCM(24, 90)$.*

Solution. Since $24 = 2^3 \cdot 3$ and $90 = 2 \cdot 3^2 \cdot 5$, the prime factors appeared are 2 with the largest multiplicity of 3, 3 with the largest multiplicity of 2, and 5 with the largest multiplicity of 1, therefore, is the $LCM(24, 90) = 2^3 \cdot 3^2 \cdot 5 = 360$.

We can directly check out that among the first four multiples of 90, namely, 90, 180, 270, and 360, the latter is the smallest, which is also a multiple of 24 and, therefore, a multiple of 12. $\qquad\qquad\Box$

Example 1.13.5 *Find the $LCM(1002, 24, 12)$.*

Solution. We start by prime factoring 1002,

$$
\begin{array}{r|r}
2 & 1002 \\
3 & 501 \\
167 & 167 \\
& 1
\end{array}
$$

Next we factor $24 = 2^3 \cdot 3$ and $12 = 2^2 \cdot 3$. The prime factors occurring here are 2 with the largest multiplicity of 3, 3 with the largest multiplicity of 1, and a simple (that is, with the multiplicity 1) factor 167, therefore, the $LCM(1002, 24, 12) = 2^3 \cdot 3 \cdot 167 = 4008$. □

Exercise 1.13.4 *Compute the LCMs.*

$LCM(20, 78) =$	$LCM(2, 10, 50) =$	$LCM(20, 5) =$
$LCM(102, 12, 24) =$	$LCM(280, 80) =$	$LCM(20, 45) =$
$LCM(25, 50) =$	$LCM(25, 45) =$	$LCM(25, 345) =$
$LCM(50, 90, 25) =$	$LCM(25, 55) =$	$LCM(25, 350) =$

Exercise 1.13.5 *Use the long division algorithm to check whether 17 divides 143; whether 17 divides 153.*

Exercise 1.13.6 *Design and solve two more exercises similar to the previous ones.*

Answers 1.13

Exercise 1.13.1.

$GCF(20, 78) = 2;$	$GCF(2, 10, 50) = 2;$	$GCF(20, 5) = 5;$
$GCF(1\,002, 12, 24) = 6;$	$GCF(280, 80) = 40;$	$GCF(20, 45) = 5;$
$GCF(25, 50) = 25;$	$GCF(25, 45) = 5;$	$GCF(25, 345) = 5;$
$GCF(50, 90, 25) = 5;$	$GCF(25, 55) = 5;$	$GCF(25, 350) = 25.$

Exercise 1.13.4.

$LCM(20, 78) = 780;$	$LCM(2, 10, 50) = 50;$	$LCM(20, 5) = 20;$
$LCM(102, 12, 24) = 408;$	$LCM(280, 80) = 560;$	$LCM(20, 45) = 180;$
$LCM(25, 50) = 50;$	$LCM(25, 45) = 450;$	$LCM(25, 345) = 1\,725;$
$LCM(50, 90, 25) = 450;$	$LCM(25, 55) = 275;$	$LCM(25, 350) = 350.$

Exercise 1.13.5. No; Yes.

Chapter 2

Rational Numbers

The sum, difference, and product of integer numbers is always an integer; however, the quotient of two integers does not have to be an integer. For example, if we want to divide 1 into two equal parts, the result, likely, is to be positive and less than 1. but there is no positive integer number between 0 and 1, therefore, this quotient cannot be an integer. To solve such problems, we must extend the world of numbers beyond the integers and introduce quantities of a new nature, *non-integer* numbers. In this chapter we study the set of *rational numbers*. This set includes the integers, but it is wider and contains also non-integer elements.

2.1 Introduction to Rational Numbers

Question 2.1.1 *On the number line, see Fig. 2.1, are there any numbers between the points 0 and 1? 1 and 2?*

Figure 2.1: Are there any numbers between the points 0 and 1? 1 and 2?

To *count* several things, say, students in the classroom, it is sufficient to know the natural (*counting*) numbers. However, if we have to measure lengths, weights, etc., we need *quantities* representing parts of the whole things, in this case parts of integer numbers. Suppose we want to assign a number to the point of the number line exactly half-way between 0 and 1. Thus, it cannot be 0, nor any positive integer. This number is naturally called *one-half* or *a half*.

As another example, suppose we measured the length of box to be 3 inches and we have to express the length in feet. We know that one foot is equal to 12 inches, therefore, 1 inch represents *one-twelfth* part of a foot, and three inches represent *three-twelfths* of a foot. These quantities, one-half, one-twelfth, three-twelfths, etc., represent parts of other quantities. To use these quantities with no regard to the initial objects, like the length, cost, etc., we now introduce *numbers* of new nature, *rational numbers*, called so because they are used, in particular, to measure *ratios* (*quotients*) of certain quantities.

Remark 2.1.1 *We have no doubts that we can cut a pie into two or three or four pieces. We also have no doubts that there are quantities – rational numbers that measure these pieces as parts of the whole pie. For the justification of this statement we refer the interested reader to special literature, for example, [2].*

Suppose we want to divide a certain quantity into several parts – think about cutting a pizza pie into equal slices. Now, when we considered the natural numbers $\{1, 2, 3, \ldots\}$, we did not have special symbols for pies, other special symbols for knives, etc., we have introduced *abstract, ideal* objects, called *natural numbers* and suitable for counting objects of *any nature*[1].

By the same token, we do not have special numbers for slices of a pizza pie, other special quantities for parts of anything else, etc. Like the integers, the rational numbers are abstract objects, measuring *parts* of the unity. The power of *mathematics*, its successful applications in numerous human activities are based on this *abstract* nature of mathematical results.

The rational numbers appear as results of dividing of an integer number over another integer number. In writing, exactly as the integers are represented by digits, the rational numbers are represented by pairs of integer numbers. These ordered pairs are called *fractions*. The fractions are written as

$$\frac{p}{q}$$

where p and q are two integer numbers[2]. The top number, p is called the *numerator* and q is called the *denominator* of the fraction; they are separated by the horizontal fraction bar or *fraction line*. Sometimes it is more convenient to denote fractions by a slash, as

$$\frac{p}{q} \equiv p/q.$$

The symbol $\equiv$ in $a \equiv b$ means that the two expressions a and b are equal *identically*, in all cases under consideration.

Let us say once and for all, that the denominator of any fraction *cannot* be 0. Indeed, if q were to be zero, $q = 0$, and we try to define the quotient $c = p/q$, we must have some number $c = p \div 0$. Let us try, for instance, the value $c = 1$. Then, since the division is inverse of multiplication, we would have $p = q \cdot c$, or $1 = 0 \cdot 1$. But the product of 0 by any number is 0, while $0 \cdot 1 = 0$; thus we immediately arrive at the obviously false statement, or the *contradiction* $1 = 0$. It is clear that the contradiction, $1 = 0$, does not depend on our choice of the value $c = 1$, any other choice of value for c would lead to a similar contradiction.

If, however, $p = q = 0$, then the equation $0/0 = c$, rewritten as $0 = c \cdot 0$, has infinitely many solutions for c, so that we again have no justifiable choice for c. That is why there is no reasonable way to assign a value to a fraction with the zero denominator, and everyone knows a short expressions of this fact:

---

[1]We should not confuse these abstract, ideal objects, called sometimes mental images, – namely, the counting numbers, with the symbols – digits, representing these objects.

[2]Later on, we will encounter fractions whose terms are not necessarily integer numbers, but such a fraction can represent a non-rational number.

Division by zero is impossible

or

A fraction with zero denominator is **undefined**.

On the other hand, it is intuitively clear that it does not matter into how many parts we divide *zero* – any part must be zero as well. Therefore, a fraction with zero numerator is zero,

$$\frac{0}{a} = 0,$$

unless $a = 0$, in which case the fraction $\frac{0}{0}$ is *undefined*.

2.2 Fractions and Mixed Numbers

2.2.1 Meaning of Fractions

In this section we study the rational numbers in more detail. These numbers are of more general nature than the integers and were introduced to measure parts of various entities. To write down the rational numbers, people invented special symbols, called fractions. To make numbers "visible", we introduced in Sect. 1.1 , see Fig. 1.1, a special graph, called *number line*. Initially we labeled only integer numbers (integer points) on the line, leaving unit gaps between the neighboring integer points; now we will gradually fill in these gaps with rational and even more general numbers.

To begin with, we remind a couple of terms. Consider the unit segment of the number line between the integer numbers 0 and 1. The term *segment* here means that the end points 0 and 1 belong to this set, denoted by *brackets*, as $[0, 1]$. Eventually we extend this picture over any segment $[a, b]$, $a < b$. This segment is called *unit*, because its length is 1, $1 - 0 = 1$.

Figure 2.2: The unit segment $[0, 1]$ of the number line.

Now we want to populate this segment of the number line. The rational numbers represent ratios of the integers. Consider, for instance, the ratio $r = \frac{6}{2}$. Since 2 divides 6, we have nothing new, this rational number is the well familiar natural number $\frac{6}{2} = 3$. Thus, the integer numbers are particular instances of the rational numbers. But in general it is not the case.

Suppose you bought a pizza pie and paid $8. If you cut the pie into 8 slices, there is no problem, each slice costs $1. Now, if you cut the pie into 6 slices, every slice is clearly bigger than in the first division and must cost more. However, if you would pay $2 for slice, the total will be $6 \cdot 2 = \$12$, which is bigger than the initial $8. But there is *no* integer number between 1 and 2! To solve similar problems, people still in the ancient times had to introduce rational numbers. Similarly to the case $r = \frac{8}{6}$, for the most part, the rational numbers are not integers. Nevertheless, every rational number also has the corresponding point on the number line.

Let us say we have to divide the unity into two equal parts, obviously called *halves*. Each of these two equal parts is *one half* of the unity. The phrase 'one-half' can be compactly and conveniently written down as $\frac{1}{2}$. We can also consider "two halves" or $\frac{2}{2}$. However, two halves make the whole unity, thus, $\frac{2}{2} = 1$. Then we can use several unities, divide each of them in halves, and make $\frac{3}{2}$, $\frac{4}{2} = 2$, etc. Whence, the fractions have appeared quite naturally as symbols to represent the rational numbers.

Since we split the unity 1 into two equal halves, we divide the segment $[0, 1]$ into two halves, designate the middle point as representing the corresponding rational number, and mark this middle point by the fraction $\frac{1}{2}$ or by $1/2$:

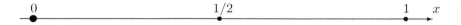

Figure 2.3: The rational number $1/2$ marks the middle point of the segment $[0, 1]$ on the number line.

In the same way, we can divide the unity into *three* equal parts, call each of these three equal parts by 'one-third' and denote it as the fraction $\frac{1}{3}$. We can take two out of these three equal parts, that is, 'two-thirds', and denote it as $\frac{2}{3}$, or all the three such equal parts, that is, 'three-thirds', and denote it as $\frac{3}{3} = 1$. To place the fractions with the denominator of 3 on the number line, we divide the unit segment $[0, 1]$ into *three* equal parts and designate these new points as representing the rational numbers (and the corresponding fractions) $1/3$ and $2/3$. The point 1 represents the total of all the three equal parts, thus we can write $3/3$.

Figure 2.4: Rational numbers $1/3$ and $2/3$ divide the segment $[0, 1]$ into three equal parts

But three "thirds" clearly make the whole unit segment, thus, $3/3 = 1$. Moreover, $0 = 0/3$, and we interpret this as if we take none of the three equal thirds. This is shown in Fig. 2.4. Further on, we can construct $\frac{4}{3}$, $\frac{5}{3}$, $\frac{6}{3}$, etc. To have *six-thirds*, we need two sets of three-thirds, thus we need two unities. Therefore, $\frac{6}{3} = 2$.

Let us take four such equal thirds of the unity – even if a pizza pie is cut only into three equal slices, we can easily imagine buying 4, or 5, or 77 slices – we just need many pies, each of them being cut into three equal parts. This fraction is written as $\frac{4}{3}$, and since $3/3 = 1$, it should be $4/3 = 1 + \frac{1}{3} > 1$, thus we do not have an appropriate space for it within the unit segment $[0, 1]$. Therefore, to show $4/3$ on the number line, we extend the unit segment by *one-third* to the right of the point 1 (Fig. 2.5):

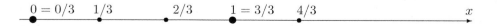

Figure 2.5: Rational numbers $1/3$, $2/3$, $3/3$ and $4/3$ on the number line.

Clearly, in the same way we can consider other fractions with the denominator of 3, starting with $0 = 0/3$; since $3/3 = 1$, then each three-thirds represent a unity, thus $3/3 = 1$, $6/3 = 1 + 1 = 2$, $9/3 = 1 + 1 + 1 = 3$, etc. In Fig. 2.6 these thirds are shown in succession.

$$0 = \frac{0}{3}, \frac{1}{3}, \frac{2}{3}, \quad 1 = \frac{3}{3}, \frac{4}{3}, \frac{5}{3}, \quad 2 = \frac{6}{3}, \frac{7}{3}, \frac{8}{3}, \quad 3 = \frac{9}{3}, \frac{10}{3}, \ldots$$

Now, if we extend the number line far enough to the right, we can place the fractions comprising as many thirds as we need:

Figure 2.6: Rational numbers $1/3$, $2/3$, $3/3$,..., $5 = 15/3$ on the number line.

In the same fashion we can consider fractions with the denominator of 4, $0 = \frac{0}{4}, \frac{1}{4}, \frac{2}{4}, \frac{3}{4}, \frac{4}{4} = 1, \frac{5}{4}, \ldots$ and plot them on the number line, see Fig. 2.7.

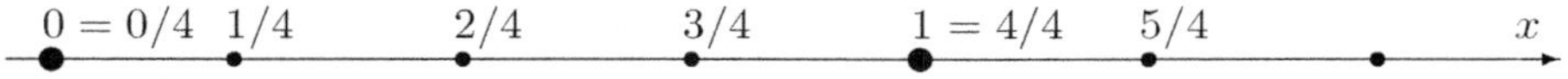

Figure 2.7: Rational numbers $0 = \frac{0}{4}, \frac{1}{4}, \frac{2}{4}, \frac{3}{4}, 1 = \frac{4}{4}, \frac{5}{4}$ on the number line.

Now on the same number line (or a copy of it) we plot both the fractions 0, $1/2$, 1 and the fractions 0, $1/4$, $2/4$, $3/4$, 1, $5/4$, see Fig. 2.8. It seems that both fractions

Figure 2.8: Rational numbers $0 = \frac{0}{4}, \frac{1}{4}, \frac{2}{4}, \frac{1}{2}, \frac{3}{4}, 1 = \frac{4}{4}, \frac{5}{4}$ on the number line.

$\frac{2}{4}$ and $\frac{1}{2}$ appear at the same point of the number line. It is not difficult to convince ourselves that this is not only our visual impression. Indeed, when we divide a unit segment into 4 equal parts and take 2 of them, we use exactly one-half of the four parts available or a half of the unit segment, thus $\frac{2}{4} = \frac{1}{2}$.

Exercise 2.2.1 *Write down fractions with denominators 5, then with 6, and with 7, whose numerators do not exceed denominators, and plot these fractions first separately on "different" number lines, that is, on different drawings, and then together on the same number line.*

Exercise 2.2.2 *What part, that is, what fraction of the area of each figure in Fig. 2.10 is shaded gray?*

Figure 2.9: The number line for exercise 2.2.1.

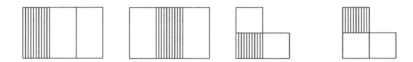

Figure 2.10: Exercise 2.2.2.

2.2.2   Properties of Fractions

Now we study some important properties of fractions. We saw (Fig. 2.3-2.8) that if denominators are increasing, there are more and more fractions with the same denominator. Observe also that there are more and more apparent coincidences, like $\frac{1}{2} = \frac{2}{4} = \frac{3}{6} = \frac{4}{8}$ or $\frac{1}{3} = \frac{2}{6}$, that is, two or more of the fractions attached to the same point of the number line. To explain this phenomenon, we remind the following definition.

Definition 2.2.1 *Two fractions, $\frac{a}{b}$ and $\frac{c}{d}$, are called equivalent if and only if*

$$a \cdot d = b \cdot c.$$

The equivalence of fractions is denoted by the equality sign, as

$$\frac{a}{b} = \frac{c}{d}.$$

For instance, the fractions $\frac{3}{7}$ and $\frac{15}{35}$ are equivalent, since $\frac{3}{7} = \frac{15}{35}$.

Now we assert, without a proof, the following fundamental property of fractions.

Claim. *Equivalent fractions represent the same rational number.*

For example, $\frac{1}{2} = \frac{2}{4}$ since $1 \cdot 4 = 2 \cdot 2$, $\frac{1}{2} = \frac{3}{6}$ for $1 \cdot 6 = 3 \cdot 2$, and $\frac{3}{7} = \frac{6}{14}$ since $3 \cdot 14 = 6 \cdot 7$. Thus, $\frac{1}{2} = \frac{2}{4} = \frac{3}{6}$, this series can be extended indefinitely, and all these fractions represent the same *rational number*, and are attached to the same point on the number line. We call such fractions *equivalent* and *not equal* to emphasize that these fractions are written by using different whole numbers.

Exercise 2.2.3 *Separate the following set of 15 fractions into subsets of equivalent fractions. For instance, the fractions $\frac{2}{3}, \frac{4}{6}, \frac{20}{30}$ are equivalent, that is, they belong to the* *same subset, but $\frac{2}{5}$ is not equivalent to them and belongs to another subset.*

$\frac{1}{2}$	$\frac{3}{4}$	$\frac{3}{2}$	$\frac{10}{20}$	$\frac{6}{3}$
$\frac{6}{4}$	$\frac{12}{8}$	$\frac{15}{10}$	$\frac{8}{12}$	$\frac{15}{20}$
$\frac{1}{5}$	$\frac{10}{5}$	$\frac{9}{6}$	$\frac{100}{50}$	$\frac{50}{100}$

Let us consider a fraction with the denominator of 1, say, $\frac{2}{1}$. This symbol means we want to split 2 into one whole piece, that is, leave as is, do not divide it at all; therefore, it must be $\frac{2}{1} = 2$. By the same token, $\frac{p}{1} = p$ for any integer p. Reading the latter equation from right to left, we see that any integer number can be written as a fraction, whence, every integer is a rational number and can be represented as a fraction in infinitely many ways. However, not every rational number is an integer: indeed, $\frac{5}{1} = 5$, but $\frac{1}{5}$ is not an integer number.

Look again at the equations $\frac{1}{2} = \frac{2}{4} = \frac{3}{6}$. In the third fraction, the numerator and the denominator have a common factor of 3: $3 = 3 \cdot 1$ and $6 = 3 \cdot 2$, while the numerator and the denominator of the first fraction are mutually prime (the "1" is not considered to be a common factor). This observation leads to the following definition.

Definition 2.2.2 *A fraction is called irreducible (in lowest terms) if its numerator and denominator have no common factor distinct from 1 (such whole numbers are called mutually prime); otherwise a fraction is called reducible.*

For example, the fractions $\frac{2}{4}$, $\frac{3}{6}$, and $\frac{40}{5}$ are reducible, since, for instance, $40 = 5 \cdot 8$ and $5 = 5 \cdot 1$ with the common factor of 5, while $\frac{1}{2}$ and $\frac{5}{7}$ are in lowest terms, irreducible.

Consider two equivalent fractions, say, $\frac{2}{3}$ and $\frac{8}{12}$ – they are equivalent for $2 \cdot 12 = 24 = 3 \cdot 8$. Of course, $8 = 2 \cdot 4$ and $12 = 3 \cdot 4$, thus, the fraction $\frac{8}{12}$ can be written as $\frac{2 \cdot 4}{3 \cdot 4}$. The number 4, which occurs both in the numerator and in the denominator of the fraction, is called the *common factor* of the numerator and denominator; we observe that to convert the fraction $\frac{8}{12}$ to an equivalent fraction $\frac{2}{3}$, we can *cross out* the common factor 4. This procedure of removing the common factor is called *cancelation*, we *cancel out* a common factor 4. Thus, we observe that the fraction $\frac{8}{12}$ can be *reduced* to the equivalent fraction in lowest terms $\frac{2}{3}$ by *canceling out* the common factor of 4.

Consider any other fraction, $\frac{a}{b}$, which is equivalent to $\frac{2}{3}$, thus, $\frac{2}{3} = \frac{a}{b}$. Hence, by Definition 2.2.1, $2 \cdot b = 3 \cdot a$. The left-hand side of the latter equation is an even number, thus the right-hand side is also even, that is, is divisible by 2. But 2 does not divide 3, therefore 2 must divide another factor on the right, a, that is, $a = 2 \cdot p$. Similarly, since $3 \cdot a$ is multiple of 3, the 3 must also be a factor of the left-hand side of that equation, $2 \cdot b$. Since 3 clearly is not a factor of 2, 3 must divide b, therefore, $b = 3 \cdot q$. Now we have $\frac{2}{3} = \frac{a}{b} = \frac{2 \cdot p}{3 \cdot q}$, and since the left-most and the right-most fractions are equal, we conclude that $2 \cdot 3 \cdot q = 3 \cdot 2 \cdot p$. Finally, dividing both sides of the latter equation by $6 = 2 \cdot 3$, we see that any fraction, equivalent to $\frac{2}{3}$, can be reduced to lowest terms by canceling a common factor of the numerator and denominator.

This fundamental property of equivalent fractions can be proven in general.

Theorem 2.2.1 *Any fraction can be reduced to the equivalent fraction in lowest terms by canceling out the GCF of its numerator and denominator.* $\square$

For example, consider a fraction $\frac{40}{50}$. The GCF(40,50)=10, hence, factoring the numerator and denominator of this fraction, we have $40 = 4 \cdot 10$ and $50 = 5 \cdot 10$. Thus, the common factor 10 can be canceled out (or just *crossed out*), giving us the equivalent fraction in lowest terms:

$$\frac{40}{50} = \frac{4 \cdot 10}{5 \cdot 10} = \frac{4 \cdot \cancel{10}}{5 \cdot \cancel{10}} = \frac{4}{5}.$$

It is also possible, after finding the common factors, to apply the fundamental property of fractions as follows:
$$\frac{40}{50} = \frac{40 \div 10}{50 \div 10} = \frac{4}{5}.$$

This is a general algorithm for *reducing a fraction to lowest terms*. Sometimes it is more convenient to cancel not the entire GCF of the numerator and the denominator, but proceed in smaller steps cancelling smaller common factors. Thus, in the previous example we can proceed, omitting some steps, as follows:

$$\frac{40}{50} = \frac{2 \cdot 20}{2 \cdot 25} = \frac{20}{25} = \frac{4 \cdot 5}{5 \cdot 5} = \frac{4}{5}.$$

Exercise 2.2.4 *Reduce the following fractions to lowest terms.*

$\frac{10}{12} =$	$\frac{30}{45} =$	$\frac{30}{20} =$	$\frac{100}{2000} =$	$\frac{6}{3} =$
$\frac{6}{4} =$	$\frac{12}{8} =$	$\frac{15}{105} =$	$\frac{84}{12} =$	$\frac{15}{20} =$
$\frac{100}{505} =$	$\frac{10}{5} =$	$\frac{9}{6} =$	$\frac{100}{50} =$	$\frac{50}{100} =$

Exercise 2.2.5 *Design and solve two more exercises similar to the previous one.*

There are also problems where it is convenient to replace a fraction, reduced or not, with an equivalent fraction having larger numerator and denominator. Reading the previous rule backward, we see that this can be achieved by multiplying both the numerator and denominator of a fraction by a non-zero integer (thus the resulting fraction certainly is not in lowest terms.) For example,

$$\frac{1}{2} = \frac{1 \cdot 7}{2 \cdot 7} = \frac{7}{14}$$

and $\frac{7}{14}$ is equivalent to $\frac{1}{2}$.

Exercise 2.2.6 *Find three equivalent fractions for each of the following ones.*

$\frac{1}{2} =$	$\frac{3}{4} =$	$\frac{3}{2} =$	$\frac{1}{20} =$	$\frac{6}{3} =$
$\frac{6}{5} =$	$\frac{50}{10} =$	$\frac{12}{8} =$	$\frac{15}{105} =$	$\frac{4}{12} =$

Exercise 2.2.7 *Design and solve two more exercises similar to the previous one.*

2.2.3   Like and Unlike Fractions

Definition 2.2.3 *Fractions with the same denominator are called like fractions. Otherwise, the fractions are called unlike fractions.*

For example, the fractions $\frac{1}{2}$ and $\frac{3}{2}$ are like fractions, while $\frac{1}{2}$ and $\frac{1}{3}$ are unlike fractions.

Exercise 2.2.8 *Separate the following set of fractions into subsets of like fractions.*

$$\frac{1}{2} \qquad \frac{3}{4} \qquad \frac{3}{2} \qquad \frac{10}{2} \qquad \frac{6}{3}$$

$$\frac{6}{4} \qquad \frac{12}{8} \qquad \frac{15}{2} \qquad \frac{8}{8} \qquad \frac{15}{20}$$

$$\frac{2}{4} \qquad \frac{12}{12} \qquad \frac{15}{30} \qquad \frac{1}{1} \qquad \frac{150}{30}$$

$$\frac{1}{5} \qquad \frac{10}{5} \qquad \frac{9}{6} \qquad \frac{100}{5} \qquad \frac{5}{100}$$

2.2.4 Arithmetic Operations with Fractions

When we add *three* identical items and *two* more items of the same kind, we get *five* items of that kind. In abstract terms we do the addition, $3 + 2 = 5$, where the integers 3 and 2 can stand for anything we want. For example, if we have to add *like fractions*, say $\frac{3}{7}$ and $\frac{2}{7}$, the identical items we want to add, are the equal *seventh* parts of the unity. Since $\frac{3}{7} = 3 \cdot \frac{1}{7}$ and $\frac{2}{7} = 2 \cdot \frac{1}{7}$, we have to add 3 such items and 2 more of the same items, thus,

$$\frac{3}{7} + \frac{2}{7} = (3 + 2) \cdot \frac{1}{7} = 5 \cdot \frac{1}{7} = \frac{5}{7}.$$

Theorem 2.2.2 *The sum or difference of* like *fractions is also a like fraction with the same denominator, whose numerator is the corresponding sum or difference of the numerators of the given fractions; in symbols,*

$$\frac{a}{b} + \frac{c}{b} = \frac{a+c}{b}. \tag{2.2.1}$$

$\square$

For example, $\frac{9}{6} + \frac{2}{6} - \frac{5}{6} + \frac{7}{6} = \frac{9+2-5+7}{6} = \frac{13}{6}$.

Every mathematical equation is a two-way street. Let us read equation (2.2.1) backward, from right to left,

$$\frac{a+c}{b} = \frac{a}{b} + \frac{c}{b}.$$

If we compare this with the distributive law (1.8.1) of the multiplication, we can say that the latter equation expresses, for division, the distributive law for fractions. For example, $\frac{20+7}{3} = \frac{20}{3} + \frac{7}{3}$, or in the same vein, $\frac{20-7}{3} = \frac{20}{3} - \frac{7}{3}$.

Example 2.2.1 *Compute $\frac{1}{5} - \frac{10}{5} - \frac{0}{5} + \frac{16}{5} - \frac{5}{5}$.*

Solution. Since the problem includes fractions, we look at their denominators and immediately observe that all the fractions given are like fractions with the denominator of 5. Moreover, there is a fraction with zero numerator, representing the number 0; hence the corresponding fraction is 0, it does not affect the result, and we can skip it. Thus, the solution is very simple, we work the non-zero numerators, $1 - 10 + 16 - 5 = -9 + 16 - 5 = 7 - 5 = 2$, and the result is $\frac{1}{5} - \frac{10}{5} - \frac{0}{5} + \frac{16}{5} - \frac{5}{5} = \frac{1-10+16-5}{5} = \frac{2}{5}$.

In the next section, when we study the mixed numbers, we will be able to do this problem in slightly different manner. $\square$

Exercise 2.2.9 *Compute the expressions and reduce the answers to lowest terms.*

$$\frac{10}{12} - \frac{30}{12} + \frac{30}{12} = \qquad\qquad\qquad \frac{12}{8} + \frac{8}{8} - \frac{15}{8} =$$

$$\frac{77}{12} - \frac{15}{12} - \frac{10}{12} - \frac{1}{12} + \frac{9}{12} = \qquad\qquad \frac{10}{2} - \frac{1}{2} + \frac{3}{2} =$$

$$\frac{6}{4} - \frac{1}{4} + \frac{15}{4} = \qquad\qquad\qquad\qquad \frac{15}{3} - \frac{6}{3} =$$

$$\frac{6}{3} + \frac{3}{3} - \frac{12}{3} + \frac{15}{3} = \qquad\qquad \frac{0}{3} + \frac{1}{3} + \frac{2}{3} - \frac{3}{3} + \frac{4}{3} =$$

Now we have to study how to add or subtract *unlike* fractions. We again reduce this problem to the previous one by changing the given unlike fractions to the equivalent *like* fractions. First of all, we consider an example.

Example 2.2.2 *Add the fractions $\frac{1}{9} + \frac{5}{6}$.*

Solution. The denominators of the fractions are 9 and 6, thus we have to deal with *unlike* fractions. We want to replace the fractions with *equivalent* but *like* ones, that is, we want to find two fractions whose denominators are multiples of 9 and 6, respectively. These numbers have *infinitely* many *common multiples*, for instance, 18, 36, 54, etc. But there is the *smallest* number among them, namely, 18. We choose this $LCM(9,6) = 18$ as the smallest or the *Least Common Denominator*, LCD, of the given fractions. Hence, we look for equivalent fractions with the denominator of 18 and notice that $18 = 9 \cdot 2$, thus

$$\frac{1}{9} = \frac{1 \cdot 2}{9 \cdot 2} = \frac{2}{18}.$$

The factor 2, which we multiply both the numerator and denominator by, is sometimes called an *additional factor* necessary to transform the fraction to an equivalent fraction with the denominator 18. Usually we do not write the middle step here and do it "by eyes". Similarly, $\frac{5}{6} = \frac{15}{18}$. The problem now becomes a familiar one about adding like fractions, and we easily finish it:

$$\frac{1}{9} + \frac{5}{6} = \frac{2}{18} + \frac{15}{18} = \frac{2+15}{18} = \frac{17}{18}.$$

$\square$

Sometimes after adding/subtracting we have to reduce the resulting fraction to lowest terms.

Example 2.2.3 *Compute $\frac{8}{9} - \frac{2}{3} + \frac{3}{5}$.*

Solution. In this example with unlike fractions, the $LCD(3,5,9) = 45$, thus we compute the equivalent fractions,

$$\frac{8}{9} = \frac{40}{45}, \frac{2}{3} = \frac{30}{45}, \frac{3}{5} = \frac{27}{45},$$

and their algebraic sum is

$$\frac{8}{9} - \frac{2}{3} + \frac{3}{5} = \frac{8 \cdot 5}{9 \cdot 5} - \frac{2 \cdot 15}{3 \cdot 15} + \frac{3 \cdot 9}{5 \cdot 9} = \frac{40}{45} - \frac{30}{45} + \frac{27}{45} = \frac{40 - 30 + 27}{45} = \frac{37}{45}.$$

$\square$

Exercise 2.2.10 *Compute and reduce the answers to lowest terms.*

$$\frac{6}{3} - \frac{6}{4} =$$
$$\frac{6}{3} + \frac{3}{4} - \frac{12}{3} + \frac{15}{5} =$$

$$\frac{12}{8} + \frac{8}{7} - \frac{15}{56} =$$
$$\frac{1}{5} - \frac{1}{12} + \frac{3}{2} =$$

$$\frac{6}{4} - \frac{3}{5} + \frac{5}{7} =$$
$$\frac{10}{13} - \frac{30}{12} + \frac{30}{11} =$$

Exercise 2.2.11 *Design and solve two more exercises similar to the previous one.*

Remark 2.2.1 *Sometimes, instead of computing the LCD, we use a* common *denominator, which is not the* lowest *one. It is not an error, however, it may lead to longer computations involving larger numbers, but the answer of course is to be the same. Let us again calculate the sum $\frac{1}{9} + \frac{5}{6}$, but instead of the $LCD(6,9) = 18$ we use the product of the denominators, $9 \cdot 6 = 54$, which is exactly 3 times the LCD. Then*

$$\frac{1}{9} + \frac{5}{6} = \frac{6}{54} + \frac{45}{54} = \frac{6+45}{54} = \frac{51}{54} \qquad (2.2.2)$$

and we have to reduce the latter fraction by canceling the common factor 3, $\frac{51}{54} = \frac{17}{18}$.

Remark 2.2.2 *If the numbers involved are small, then to add or subtract two fractions, we can avoid the explicit evaluation of the LCD and immediately perform three multiplications: multiply the denominators to find the common denominator, as in the previous remark, and cross-multiply the numerators and denominators. For instance, in the previous example,*

$$\frac{1}{9} + \frac{5}{6} = \frac{1 \cdot 6 + 5 \cdot 9}{9 \cdot 6} = \frac{6+45}{54}$$

and from this point we recognize the computations in (2.2.2).

Now we study how to multiply and divide fractions. Given two fractions, $\frac{a}{b}$ and $\frac{c}{d}$, their product and quotient are also fractions. To learn how to multiply fractions, we look back at the multiplication of integer numbers, say, $3 \cdot 4$. We know that the latter is an abbreviation of the sum $4 + 4 + 4$, thus, if we imagine that we have an infinite supply of the digits 4, we take any three of them. In the same fashion, any multiplication problem $a \cdot b$ can be interpreted as if we take a out of the many items of kind b.

In particular, if we have to multiply $\frac{1}{2} \cdot 6$, we have to take *a half* of 6, which is $6 \div 2 = 3$. Recalling now that any integer k can be written as a fraction $\frac{k}{1}$, we see that indeed,

$$\frac{1}{2} \cdot 6 = 3 = \frac{1 \cdot 6}{2 \cdot 1}.$$

Moreover, if we have to multiply $\frac{3}{2} \cdot 6$, we represent $\frac{3}{2}$ as

$$\frac{1}{2} + \frac{1}{2} + \frac{1}{2} = 3 \cdot \frac{1}{2},$$

and by the distributive rule,

$$\frac{3}{2} \cdot 6 = \frac{3}{2} \cdot \frac{6}{1} = \frac{3 \cdot 6}{2 \cdot 1} = \frac{18}{2} = 9.$$

Analyzing these examples, we *define* the product of any fractions as follows.

The product of fractions $\frac{a}{b}$ and $\frac{c}{d}$ is the fraction, whose numerator is the product of the numerators a and c, and whose denominator is the product of the denominators b and d, that is,

$$\frac{a}{b} \cdot \frac{c}{d} = \frac{a \cdot c}{b \cdot d}.$$

For example,

$$\frac{2}{3} \cdot \frac{6}{7} = \frac{2 \cdot 6}{3 \cdot 7} = \frac{2 \cdot (2 \cdot 3)}{3 \cdot 7} = \frac{2 \cdot 2}{1 \cdot 7} = \frac{4}{7},$$

where in the middle step we canceled out a 3.

While *multiplying* fractions, we do not have to write the product as one fraction, we can omit some intermediate steps and cancel out all common factors immediately. Thus, in the previous example, we do

$$\frac{2}{3} \cdot \frac{6}{7} = \frac{2 \cdot 6}{3 \cdot 7} = \frac{2 \cdot 2}{1 \cdot 7} = \frac{4}{7},$$

or even better,

$$\frac{2}{3} \cdot \frac{6}{7} = 2 \cdot \frac{2}{7} = \frac{4}{7}.$$

□

Exercise 2.2.12 *Multiply fractions. Reduce the answers if possible.*

$\frac{10}{3} \cdot \frac{1}{2} =$ $\qquad$ $\frac{6}{4} \cdot \frac{3}{4} \cdot \frac{15}{4} =$

$\frac{15}{4} \cdot \frac{6}{5} =$ $\qquad$ $\frac{12}{8} \cdot \frac{15}{20} =$

$\frac{1}{5} \cdot \frac{10}{5} \cdot \frac{0}{5} \cdot \frac{100}{5} \cdot \frac{5}{100} =$

Exercise 2.2.13 *Design and solve two more exercises similar to the previous one.*

To define the division of fractions, we can reason as follows. Let us try to find the quotient of two fractions, $\frac{a}{b} \div \frac{m}{n}$ as a fraction $\frac{p}{q}$, that is, set

$$\frac{a}{b} \div \frac{m}{n} = \frac{p}{q}.$$

Since the division is the inverse of multiplication, this is equivalent to the equation

$$\frac{a}{b} = \frac{m}{n} \cdot \frac{p}{q} = \frac{m \cdot p}{n \cdot q}.$$

Now we observe that if we set here $p = a \cdot n$ and $q = b \cdot m$, then the right-hand side becomes

$$\frac{m \cdot p}{n \cdot q} = \frac{m \cdot a \cdot n}{n \cdot b \cdot m} = \frac{a}{b}$$

after canceling out $m \cdot n$. Thus we have found that the quotient should be

$$\frac{a}{b} \div \frac{m}{n} = \frac{a \cdot n}{b \cdot m}.$$

Therefore, it makes sense to define the *division* of fractions as follows.

The quotient of the fractions $\frac{a}{b}$ and $\frac{c}{d}$ is the product of the same fraction $\frac{a}{b}$ by the fraction $\frac{d}{c}$, that is,

$$\frac{a}{b} \div \frac{c}{d} = \frac{a}{b} \cdot \frac{d}{c} = \frac{a \cdot d}{b \cdot c}.$$

For example,

$$\frac{2}{3} \div \frac{6}{7} = \frac{2 \cdot 7}{3 \cdot 6} = \frac{14}{18} = \frac{7}{9}.$$

It is convenient to rephrase this definition in terms of the next notion.

Definition 2.2.4 *The reciprocal of a number $a \neq 0$ is the number $\frac{1}{a}$. A reciprocal of zero is undefined.*

Thus, the reciprocal of the integer 3 is the fraction $\frac{1}{3}$, the reciprocal of the fraction $\frac{5}{7}$ is the fraction $1 \div \frac{5}{7} = \frac{7}{5}$, the reciprocal of the fraction $\frac{1}{8}$ is the integer $1 \div \frac{1}{8} = \frac{8}{1} = 8$.

Now we can say that to divide fractions $\frac{a}{b} \div \frac{c}{d}$, we have to multiply the dividend by the reciprocal of the divisor, that is,

$$\frac{a}{b} \div \frac{c}{d} = \frac{a}{b} \cdot \frac{d}{c} = \frac{a \cdot d}{b \cdot c}.$$

Exercise 2.2.14 *Divide fractions. Reduce the answers if possible.*

$$\frac{10}{2} \div \frac{1}{2} = \qquad\qquad \frac{6}{4} \div \frac{3}{4} = \qquad\qquad \frac{15}{3} \div \frac{6}{3} =$$

$$\frac{12}{8} \div \frac{15}{20} = \qquad\qquad \frac{1}{5} \div \frac{10}{5} = \qquad\qquad \frac{100}{5} \div \frac{5}{100} =$$

Exercise 2.2.15 *Compute and reduce the answers to lowest terms; make sure that the given fractions are in simplest form.*

$$\frac{10}{13} \div \frac{30}{13} + \frac{3}{11} = \qquad\qquad \frac{6}{3} + \frac{3}{4} \div \frac{2}{3} + \frac{15}{5} =$$

$$\frac{6}{4} \cdot \frac{3}{5} \div \frac{5}{7} = \qquad\qquad \frac{15}{3} \div \frac{16}{4} =$$

$$\frac{1}{2} + \frac{8}{7} \div \frac{3}{4} = \qquad\qquad \frac{1}{5} \cdot \frac{10}{15} \div \frac{0}{25} + \frac{100}{50} - \frac{5}{100} =$$

Exercise 2.2.16 *Design and solve two more exercises similar to the previous ones.*

Exercise 2.2.17 *Simplify*[3]

$$\frac{1/2 + 1/3 + 1/4 + 1/5}{1/2 + 1/3 - 1/4 - 1/5} + \frac{1/4 + 1/5 + 1/6 + 1/7}{1/4 + 1/5 - 1/6 - 1/7} - \frac{1024}{1357}.$$

Exercise 2.2.18 *Explain on what principle you determine the order of the operations in*

$$\frac{1}{2} + \frac{3}{4} \div \frac{5}{6} - \frac{7}{8} \times \frac{9}{10}$$

and express the value as a decimal fraction. Insert the brackets necessary to make the expression mean :

Add $\frac{3}{4}$ to $\frac{1}{2}$, divide the sum by $\frac{5}{6}$, from the quotient subtract $\frac{7}{8}$, and multiply this difference by $\frac{9}{10}$.

---

[3]This, the next exercise 2.2.18, and a few other problems are from the Great Britain Post Office Entrance Examination. Women And Girl Clerks. October 1897. The author is greatly indebted to Professor Alexandre Borovik for this information.

2.2.5 Mixed Numbers

It is convenient to distinguish two kinds of fractions.

Definition 2.2.5 *A fraction $\frac{a}{b}$ with positive numerator and denominator is called proper if $a < b$. Otherwise, that is if $a \geq b$, the fraction is called improper.*

For example, $\frac{2}{7}$ is a proper fraction, while $\frac{7}{2}$ and $\frac{2}{2} = 1$ are improper ones.

Exercise 2.2.19 *Among the following, which fractions are proper and which are improper?*

$$\frac{7}{8}; \quad \frac{8}{7}; \quad \frac{9}{3}; \quad \frac{4}{4}; \quad \frac{11}{13}; \quad \frac{18}{10}; \quad \frac{31}{3}; \quad \frac{3}{1}; \quad \frac{12}{11}; \quad \frac{43}{44}$$

Exercise 2.2.20 *Write three proper and three improper fractions.*

Definition 2.2.6 *A mixed number is the sum of an integer number, called the integer part of the mixed number and a proper fraction, called the fractional part of the mixed number. By a very old agreement, the mixed numbers are written without the "+" sign between the integer and the fractional parts.*

For example, $1\frac{3}{4}$ is the mixed number $1 + \frac{3}{4}$. In all the other cases, that is, if we have to *subtract, multiply,* or *divide* an integer and a fraction, we must *explicitly* show the symbol of the operation intended.

Every *improper fraction* can be written as a mixed number. For example, consider an improper fraction $\frac{19}{5}$. Dividing $19 \div 5$, we see that $19 = 3 \cdot 5 + 4$. From here, using the distributive law for division, we get the mixed number

$$\frac{19}{5} = \frac{3 \cdot 5 + 4}{5} = \frac{3 \cdot 5}{5} + \frac{4}{5} = 3 + \frac{4}{5} = 3\frac{4}{5},$$

where 3 is the integer part and $\frac{4}{5}$ the fractional part of the given improper fraction $\frac{19}{5}$ or, which is the same, of the mixed number $3\frac{4}{5}$.

Working backward, let us change the mixed number $3\frac{4}{5}$ to an equal improper fraction. Since we have to work here with the denominator of 5, we ask themselves, how many *fifths are in one unity?* The answer is clearly *five fifths*. Since we have three unities in the example, we have $3 \cdot 5 = 15$ fifths in the integer part. In addition to that, we have *four-fifths* in the fractional part, totaling to

$$3\frac{4}{5} = \frac{3 \cdot 5}{5} + \frac{4}{5} = \frac{3 \cdot 5 + 4}{5} = \frac{19}{5}.$$

We see that to change the mixed number $3\frac{4}{5}$ to an improper fraction, we must use the same denominator 5. To find the numerator, we have to multiply 3 by 5 and add 4, thus $3\frac{4}{5} = \frac{3 \cdot 5 + 4}{5} = \frac{19}{5}$. Now we state a general algorithm for converting a mixed number to an improper fraction, and vice versa, an improper fraction to the mixed number.

(1) *To change a positive improper fraction $\frac{a}{b}$, $a \geq b > 0$, to an equal mixed number, we have to:*

Divide a over b with a remainder: $a = Q \cdot b + R$, where Q is the quotient and $0 \leq R < b$ the remainder. Then we combine these numbers into a mixed number, as

$\frac{a}{b} = Q\frac{R}{b}$.

(2) *Vice versa, for a positive mixed number* $Q\frac{R}{b}$, *where* $Q \geq 1$ *is an integer part,
the equal improper fraction is* $Q\frac{R}{b} = \frac{Q \cdot b + R}{b}$.

These parameters in our first example were $a = 19$, $b = 5$, $Q = 3$, $R = 4$.

Example 2.2.4 *To change* $4\frac{3}{7}$ *to an improper fraction, we write*

$$4\frac{3}{7} = \frac{4 \cdot 7 + 3}{7} = \frac{28 + 3}{7} = \frac{31}{7}.$$

To change the improper fraction $\frac{111}{13}$ *to a mixed number, we divide* 13 *into* 111,
$111 = 8 \cdot 13 + 7$, *thus* $\frac{111}{13} = 8\frac{7}{13}$. $\square$

Exercise 2.2.21 *Change improper fractions to equal mixed numbers.*

$\frac{11}{2} =$ $\qquad$ $\frac{10}{2} =$ $\qquad$ $\frac{6}{4} =$ $\qquad$ $\frac{37}{14} =$ $\qquad$ $\frac{15}{4} =$

$\frac{15}{3} =$ $\qquad$ $\frac{16}{3} =$ $\qquad$ $\frac{123}{8} =$ $\qquad$ $\frac{8}{8} =$ $\qquad$ $\frac{159}{20} =$

Exercise 2.2.22 *Change mixed numbers to equal improper fractions.*

$3\frac{1}{2} =$ $\qquad$ $4\frac{1}{12} =$ $\qquad$ $5\frac{6}{11} =$ $\qquad$ $6\frac{3}{4} =$

$8\frac{1}{3} =$ $\qquad$ $9\frac{6}{13} =$ $\qquad$ $10\frac{2}{7} =$ $\qquad$ $1\frac{8}{13} =$

Exercise 2.2.23 *Design and solve two more exercises similar to the previous ones.*

Exercise 2.2.24 *What mixed number is equal to the* proper *fraction* $\frac{2}{3}$? *What is its
integer part?*

To perform four arithmetic operations with the mixed numbers, we *should* initially
convert them to improper fractions. Only *addition* can be done by adding separately
integer parts and separately fractional parts.

Example 2.2.5 *Compute* $3\frac{1}{2} + 4\frac{1}{12}$.

Solution. We have $3\frac{1}{2} = \frac{3 \cdot 2 + 1}{2} = \frac{7}{2}$ and $4\frac{1}{12} = \frac{4 \cdot 12 + 1}{12} = \frac{49}{12}$. The $LCD(2, 12) = 12$,
thus we change $\frac{7}{2} = \frac{42}{12}$ and

$$3\frac{1}{2} + 4\frac{1}{12} = \frac{42}{12} + \frac{49}{12} = \frac{42 + 49}{12} = \frac{91}{12} = 7\frac{7}{12}.$$

$\square$

Example 2.2.6 *Add (again) the mixed numbers* $3\frac{1}{2} + 4\frac{1}{12}$.

Solution. Now we proceed as follows:

$$3\frac{1}{2} + 4\frac{1}{12} = \left(3 + \frac{1}{2}\right) + \left(4 + \frac{1}{12}\right) = (3 + 4) + \left(\frac{1}{2} + \frac{1}{12}\right)$$

$$= 7 + \left(\frac{1}{2} + \frac{1}{12}\right) = 7 + \left(\frac{6}{12} + \frac{1}{12}\right) = 7 + \frac{7}{12} = 7\frac{7}{12},$$

with (Surely!) the same result, but in the case of *subtraction, multiplication* and
division this approach can immediately lead to *mistakes*. $\square$

Example 2.2.7 *Compute* $4\frac{1}{12} - 3\frac{1}{2}$.

Solution. Since the subtrahend is clearly less than the minuend, the difference must be positive. However, to subtract $\frac{1}{2}$ from $\frac{1}{12}$ and get a positive result, we must borrow from the integer part, that is why we begin by changing the mixed numbers to improper fractions. We have $4\frac{1}{12} = \frac{49}{12}, 3\frac{1}{2} = \frac{7}{2}$, whence

$$4\frac{1}{12} - 3\frac{1}{2} = \frac{49}{12} - \frac{7}{2} = \frac{49}{12} - \frac{42}{12} = \frac{7}{12}.$$

If we do this example *without* converting to improper fractions, we *must* write

$$4\frac{1}{12} - 3\frac{1}{2} = 4 + \frac{1}{12} - \left(3 + \frac{1}{2}\right) = 4 + \frac{1}{12} - 3 - \frac{1}{2},$$

and to subtract a larger fraction $\frac{1}{2}$ from a smaller one $\frac{1}{12}$. Thus, we have to *borrow* a unit from the integer part, and than do the same conversion. So that, it is usually simpler to immediately change the given mixed numbers to improper fractions.   □

Warning. Therefore, to perform arithmetic computations with mixed numbers, first of all, it is advisable to change the mixed numbers involved into improper fractions.

Example 2.2.8 *Compute* $4\frac{1}{12} \cdot 3\frac{1}{2}$.

Solution. We start by changing the mixed numbers to improper fractions. Otherwise, we have to use the distributive law, which is unwarranted complication in such a problem.

$$4\frac{1}{12} \cdot 3\frac{1}{2} = \frac{49}{12} \cdot \frac{7}{2} = \frac{343}{24} = 14\frac{7}{24}.$$

□

Example 2.2.9 *Compute* $4\frac{1}{12} \div 3\frac{1}{2}$.

Solution. Again, we first change to improper fractions:

$$4\frac{1}{12} \div 3\frac{1}{2} = \frac{49}{12} \div \frac{7}{2} = \frac{49}{12} \cdot \frac{2}{7} = \frac{49 \cdot 2}{12 \cdot 7} = \frac{7}{6} = 1\frac{1}{6}.$$

□

Warning. We mention a typical misunderstanding, often leading to unnecessary complications and errors: While *multiplying* and *dividing fractions*, there is *no need* to change them to like fractions.

Example 2.2.10 *Compute* $\frac{1}{5} \div \frac{1}{12} \div \frac{3}{2}$.

Solution. Since operations of the same level are done from left to right, we compute

$$\frac{1}{5} \div \frac{1}{12} \div \frac{3}{2} = \frac{1}{5} \cdot \frac{12}{1} \div \frac{3}{2} = \frac{1}{5} \cdot \frac{12}{1} \cdot \frac{2}{3} = \frac{1 \cdot 12 \cdot 2}{5 \cdot 1 \cdot 3} = \frac{4 \cdot 2}{5} = 1\frac{3}{5},$$

where in the second to the last step we canceled the fraction by 3. However,

$$\frac{1}{5} \div \left(\frac{1}{12} \div \frac{3}{2}\right) = \frac{1}{5} \div \left(\frac{1}{12} \cdot \frac{2}{3}\right) = \frac{1}{5} \div \frac{1}{18} = \frac{1}{5} \cdot \frac{18}{1} = \frac{18}{5} = 3\frac{3}{5}.$$

□

Exercise 2.2.25 *Compute.*

$$5\tfrac{6}{11} + 4\tfrac{3}{4} = \qquad\qquad 5\tfrac{6}{11} - 4\tfrac{3}{4} = \qquad\qquad 5\tfrac{6}{11} \cdot 4\tfrac{3}{4} =$$

$$5\tfrac{6}{11} \div \tfrac{3}{4} = \qquad\qquad 9\tfrac{15}{16} + \tfrac{1}{3} = \qquad\qquad 9\tfrac{15}{16} - \tfrac{1}{3} =$$

$$9\tfrac{15}{16} \cdot \tfrac{1}{3} = \qquad\qquad 9\tfrac{15}{16} \div \tfrac{1}{3} =$$

Exercise 2.2.26 *Design and solve two more exercises similar to the previous ones.*

2.2.6 Comparing Fractions

It is easy to compare two *like* fractions: $\tfrac{3}{2}$ is, obviously bigger than $\tfrac{1}{2}$, since the sum of three positive quantities, like three halves, is bigger than one such quantity, that is, one-half. Symbolically, $\tfrac{3}{2} > \tfrac{1}{2}$, and also $\tfrac{3}{5} < \tfrac{4}{5}$. Therefore:

Theorem 2.2.3 *Among several positive like fractions the one with the biggest numerator is the biggest* □

Now let us compare two *aliquot* fractions, these are fractions $\tfrac{1}{p}$ whose numerator is 1. If we want to compare, say, 1/2 and 1/3, then in the former we divide the unity into *two* equal parts, while in the latter the same unity is divided into *three* equal parts; it is clear that in the first case each part is bigger than in the second.

Figure 2.11: $1/3 < 1/2 < 2/3$.

As another illustration of the same property, we know that a quarter, which is $\tfrac{1}{4}$ of a dollar, is worthier than a dime, which is only $\tfrac{1}{10}$ of a dollar. The same is true if both numerators are equal, not necessarily the 1. Therefore:

Theorem 2.2.4 *Among several positive fractions with the same numerators the fraction with the biggest denominator is the smallest, and that with the smallest denominator is the biggest.* □

For example, $2 < 4$, however, $\tfrac{3}{2} > \tfrac{3}{4}$; $5 > 2$ while $\tfrac{3}{5} < \tfrac{3}{2}$.

The latter relationship is called the *inverse proportionality*:

With equal numerators, the bigger the denominator is, the smaller is the fraction.

If both numerators and denominators are not equal, the comparison is not so immediate. Sometimes no computation is necessary; indeed, $\tfrac{3}{4}$ is clearly smaller than $\tfrac{5}{3}$, since the first fraction is proper, that is, it is less than 1, while the second one is improper, it is bigger than 1. But in general, to compare two fractions we are to replace them with like fractions.

Example 2.2.11 *What fraction is bigger, $\tfrac{3}{4}$ or $\tfrac{5}{6}$?*

Solution. Since the $LCD(4,6) = 12$, we compute the equivalent fractions $\frac{3}{4} = \frac{9}{12}$, $\frac{5}{6} = \frac{10}{12}$, and since $9 < 10$, we have $\frac{9}{12} < \frac{10}{12}$, therefore, $\frac{3}{4} < \frac{5}{6}$.
$hfillqed$

Remark 2.2.3 *Another way to compare two* positive *fractions is to cross-multiply them. For example, if we want to check what fraction, $\frac{3}{4}$ or $\frac{5}{6}$ is larger, we can suppose for a second that $\frac{3}{4} > \frac{5}{6}$. Then, cross-multiplying the latter and dropping the equal denominators, we get $3 \cdot 6 > 4 \cdot 5$, or $18 > 20$, which is, clearly, false. Therefore, our assumption was wrong and the conclusion is $\frac{3}{4} < \frac{5}{6}$.*

However, if we have to compare three or more fractions, the first method may be better, since to compare three unlike positive fractions, in general, we must do three pair-wise comparisons of these fractions.

Remark 2.2.4 *The terms "increasing", "ascending", "from smaller to bigger" are synonyms, as well as "decreasing", "descending", "from larger to smaller".*

Example 2.2.12 *Arrange the fractions $\frac{3}{4}, \frac{1}{2}$, and $\frac{2}{3}$ in ascending order.*

Solution. Since the $LCD(2,3,4) = 12$, we compute the equivalent like fractions $\frac{3}{4} = \frac{9}{12}$, $\frac{1}{2} = \frac{6}{12}$, and $\frac{2}{3} = \frac{8}{12}$. Now we can arrange the numerators as

$$6 < 8 < 9, \text{ or } \frac{6}{12} < \frac{8}{12} < \frac{9}{12}.$$

Returning to the given fractions, we get finally, $\frac{1}{2} < \frac{2}{3} < \frac{3}{4}$. $\qquad\square$

Example 2.2.13 (1) *Compare the mixed numbers $3\frac{3}{4}$ and $4\frac{1}{2}$.*
(2) *Compare the mixed numbers $3\frac{3}{4}$ and $3\frac{1}{2}$.*

Solution. (1) Since the integer parts $3 < 4$, we obviously have $3\frac{3}{4} < 4\frac{1}{2}$, independently upon the magnitudes of the fractional parts $\frac{3}{4}$ and $\frac{1}{2}$.

(2) These mixed numbers have the same integer part, 3, hence we must compare the fractional parts, $\frac{3}{4}$ and $\frac{1}{2}$. Since $\frac{3}{4} > \frac{2}{4} = \frac{1}{2}$, we conclude that $3\frac{3}{4} > 3\frac{1}{2}$. $\qquad\square$

Exercise 2.2.27 (1) *Compare the mixed numbers $2\frac{3}{8}$ and $2\frac{1}{4}$.*
(2) *Arrange in increasing order:*

$$20\frac{2}{5}; \qquad 20\frac{4}{7}; \qquad 19; \qquad 3\frac{3}{5}; \qquad 3\frac{4}{9}; \qquad 3\frac{1}{2}$$

(3) *Arrange in descending order:*

$$6\frac{6}{11}; \qquad 6\frac{5}{9}; \qquad 6\frac{5}{8}; \qquad 6$$

(4) *Arrange in decreasing order:*

$$5\frac{2}{5}; \qquad 4\frac{3}{4}; \qquad 9\frac{5}{6}; \qquad 8\frac{1}{3}; \qquad 9; \qquad 19\frac{6}{7}; \qquad 10\frac{2}{7}; \qquad 5; \qquad 11\frac{1}{3}; \qquad 11\frac{5}{9}.$$

Exercise 2.2.28 *Archimedes derived the following boundaries for the number π,*

$$3\frac{10}{71} < \pi < 3\frac{1}{7}.$$

Prove that these boundaries are consistent, that is, the lower boundary $3\frac{10}{71}$ is indeed smaller than the upper one $3\frac{1}{7}$.

2.2.7 The Average

Given several quantities, it is often useful to compress the given information and represent (approximately!) the whole group by just one number. One of such representatives is the *mean* or the *arithmetic average*. The average of two quantities, a and b, is a half of their sum, $\frac{1}{2}(a+b)$. The average of three quantities, a, b, c, is one-third of their sum, $\frac{1}{3}(a+b+c)$, the average of four quantities, a, b, c, d, is one-fourth of their sum, $\frac{1}{4}(a+b+c+d)$, etc. In general, the average of n quantities, $a_1, a_2, \ldots, a_n$, is the $\left(\frac{1}{n}\right)^{th}$ part of their sum, and is often denoted by over-bar $\bar{a}$:

$$\bar{a} = Average(a_1; a_2; \ldots; a_n) = \frac{a_1 + a_2 + \cdots + a_n}{n}. \qquad (2.2.3)$$

In formulas like this we often do not know how many quantities are actually involved, we want to describe a general situation and give a definition, which can be applied to any number of quantities. That is why we denote the number of quantities by some *generic* parameter (we have chosen n, but this is immaterial) and write the generic formula as

$$\bar{a} = \frac{a_1 + a_2 + \cdots + a_n}{n},$$

where the symbol $\cdots$ (three dots) is the ellipsis.

Example 2.2.14 *Find the average of* $1\,344$ *and* 0.

Solution. There are just two numbers in the question, thus the sum in (2.2.3) for this problem consists of two addends, and

$$Average(1\,344; 0) = \frac{1}{2}(1\,344 + 0) = \frac{1\,344}{2} = 672.$$

$\square$

Example 2.2.15 *What is the average grade of a student who scored* $50, 75, 75, 80$ *and* 95 *at her five tests?*

Solution. To compute the average, we determine that the number of quantities (the tests) is $n = 5$, thus the sum contains five addends, and the average is

$$\frac{50 + 75 + 75 + 80 + 95}{5} = \frac{375}{5} = 75.$$

$\square$

Example 2.2.16 *A student scored* $50, 75, 75, 80$ *at four out of her five tests. What can be her average over five tests, if the grades are in range from* 0 *through* 100?

Solution. The worst-case scenario occurs if she scores only 0 at the fifth test; then the average will be $\frac{50+75+75+80+0}{5} = 56$. The best possible average results if she scores perfect 100, giving the average $\frac{50+75+75+80+100}{5} = 76$. Thus, the average can vary from 56 to 76 inclusive. $\square$

Exercise 2.2.29 *At three out of her five tests, the student scored* $50, 65$, *and* 79, *and got equal scores at two other tests. The average was* 70. *What are the missing grades?*

Exercise 2.2.30 *In this example, what is the average after 4 tests? After the first 3 or 2 tests? After the first test?*

Exercise 2.2.31 *Design and solve two more exercises similar to the previous one.*

The score like 50 in the example above, is called *outlier* because it lies well beyond the majority of scores. And even though the student's other scores are very good and steadily grow, the outlier will constantly pull her average down.

Example 2.2.17 *After the first four tests, the same student computed that her average is now $280 \div 4 = 70$ – Please check that out! What should her fifth score be to improve the average to 90?*

Solution. The average after the first four tests is $\frac{50+75+75+80}{4} = \frac{280}{4} = 70$, therefore, her computation is correct. If the average of five numbers is 90, then the sum of these five scores must be $90 \cdot 5 = 450$. But these 450 points include the total of the first four grades, which is 280, thus her fifth mark has to be $450 - 280 = 170$, which is hardly possible.   □

Exercise 2.2.32 *Find the averages; round off the fractional results to the nearest integer.*

$Average(870; 8) =$ $Average(1\,002\,344; 0) =$

$Average(1\,002;\ 345; 71) =$ $Average(709; 808; 2; 45) =$

$Average(128; 345; 9; 909) =$ $Average(2\,450; 67; 8) =$

$Average(3; 457; 128; 345; 9; 909) =$ $Average(2\,450; 67; 801) =$

$Average(870; 960; 45) =$ $Average(870; 960; 8; 456) =$

Exercise 2.2.33 *During the spring semester, Mike had 20 quizzes and got 3 grades of 90, 5 grades of 87, 10 grades of 75, one 99 and one 40. What was his average grade?*
  His friend Rosie had, in the same class, 3 grades of 90, 5 grades of 87, 10 grades of 75, one 99 and one 74. What was her average grade?

Exercise 2.2.34 *Three friends paid for lunch $1.40, $1.60, and 75 cents, respectively. What is the average cost of the lunch?*

Exercise 2.2.35 *Computing the average balance of her 5 accounts, the student calculated the correct sum of all the balances but then mistakenly divided the sum by 6 and got $555.40. What is the correct average balance?*

Exercise 2.2.36 *15 first-graders and 10 second-graders competed in throwing the ball. The first-graders scored on average 77 ft., while the second-graders scored on average 75 ft. What is the average score for all 25 students?*

Exercise 2.2.37 *Design and solve two more exercises similar to the previous one.*

2.2.8   The Mode and the Median

Let A be a set of elements, called also, depending upon the context, an *array*, a *population* or a *sample*. The same element $a \in A$ can appear in the array several times, and the number of the occurrences of a in A is called the *frequency* of a in A.

In addition to the mean, there are other numerical measures approximately representing an array in a compressed way. Two such quantities, commonly used in statistics, are the *mode* and the *median*.

Definition 2.2.7 *A mode of an array is an element, which occurs most often, that is, with the highest frequency among the elements of the array. If two elements occur with the same highest frequency, each of them is a mode and the array is called bimodal. If three or more elements appear with the same highest frequency, the array is said to have no mode.*

For example, the set $\{1, 2, 3, 5\}$ has no mode, the set $\{1, 2, 3, 5, 5\}$ has the mode of 5, the array $\{1, 2, 3, 5, 2, 3\}$ is bimodal, it has two modes, 2 and 3. It should be noted that the mode is always an element of the array, and similarly to the arithmetic mean of a set, the ordering of the elements of the array is irrelevant. However, the ordering is important for the sequel quantity.

Definition 2.2.8 *Consider an array of numbers, whose elements are ordered in increasing order (the opposite ordering leads to the same number). The median is a middle number of the array. Thus, if the array contains an odd number of elements, the median occupies the middle location within the array, and there are equally many elements of the array to the left and to the right of the median. If the array contains an even number of elements, then there are two middle elements, and the median is the average of these two scores.*

For example, the median of the set $\{1, 2, 3, 5\}$ is $\frac{1}{2}(2 + 3) = 2\frac{1}{2}$. To find the median of the set $\{1, 2, 3, 5, 2, 3\}$, we must first reorder it as $\{1, 2, 2, 3, 3, 5\}$, therefore, the median is $(2 + 3)/2 = 2\frac{1}{2}$. The array $\{1, 2, 3, 5, 2, 3, 6\}$ after re-arranging becomes $\{1, 2, 2, 3, 3, 5, 6\}$, thus the median is 3, since there are three numbers smaller than 3 and three numbers bigger than 3.

Exercise 2.2.38 *Find the means, modes and medians of the following arrays; round off the fractional results to the nearest integer.*

$\{870; 8\}$	$\{1\,002\,344; 0\}$
$\{1\,002;\ 345; 71\}$	$\{709; 808; 2; 45\}$
$\{128; 345; 9; 909\}$	$\{3; 457; 128; 345; 9; 909\}$
$\{2\,450; 67; 8\}$	$\{2\,450; 067; 801\}$
$\{870; 960; 45\}$	$\{870; 960; 8; 456\}$

Problem 2.2.1 *For the sets in Exercise 2.2.36, compare their means, modes, and medians. Is it possible to derive any conclusion with regard their relationship, that is, for example, that one of them is always bigger or smaller than another, or no such a relationship exists?*

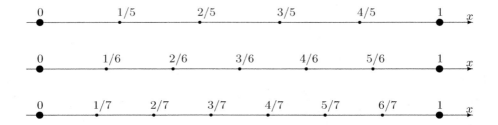

Figure 2.12: Number lines for exercise 2.2.1.

Answers 2.2

Exercise 2.2.1. $\frac{1}{5}, \frac{2}{5}, \frac{3}{5}, \frac{4}{5}; \frac{1}{6}, \frac{2}{6}, \frac{3}{6}, \frac{4}{6}, \frac{5}{6}; \frac{1}{7}, \frac{2}{7}, \frac{3}{7}, \frac{4}{7}, \frac{5}{7}, \frac{5}{7}.$

Exercise 2.2.2.

$$\frac{1}{2} = \frac{10}{20} = \frac{50}{100}; \qquad \frac{3}{4} = \frac{15}{20}; \qquad \frac{3}{2} = \frac{6}{4} = \frac{12}{8} = \frac{15}{10} = \frac{9}{6}; \qquad \frac{6}{3} = \frac{10}{5} = \frac{100}{50}; \qquad \frac{8}{12}; \qquad \frac{1}{5}.$$

Exercise 2.2.3.

$$\frac{10}{12} = \frac{5}{6}; \qquad \frac{30}{45} = \frac{2}{3}; \qquad \frac{30}{20} = \frac{3}{2} = 1\frac{1}{2}; \qquad \frac{100}{2000} = \frac{1}{20}; \qquad \frac{6}{3} = 2;$$

$$\frac{6}{4} = \frac{3}{2} = 1\frac{1}{2}; \qquad \frac{12}{8} = \frac{3}{2} = 1\frac{1}{2}; \qquad \frac{15}{105} = \frac{1}{7}; \qquad \frac{84}{12} = 7 \qquad \frac{15}{20} = \frac{3}{4};$$

$$\frac{100}{505} = \frac{20}{101}; \qquad \frac{10}{5} = 2 \qquad \frac{9}{6} = \frac{3}{2} = 1\frac{1}{2}; \qquad \frac{100}{50} = 2; \qquad \frac{50}{100} = \frac{1}{2}.$$

Exercise 2.2.5.

$$\begin{array}{lll}
\frac{1}{2} = \frac{2}{4} = \frac{10}{20} = \frac{11}{22}; & \frac{3}{4} = \frac{6}{8} = \frac{15}{20} = \frac{90}{120}; & \frac{3}{2} = \frac{6}{4} = \frac{12}{8} = \frac{300}{200}; \\
\frac{1}{20} = \frac{2}{40} = \frac{10}{200} = \frac{11}{220}; & \frac{6}{3} = \frac{2}{1} = \frac{12}{6} = \frac{400}{200}; & \frac{6}{5} = \frac{12}{10} = \frac{60}{50} = \frac{30}{25}; \\
\frac{50}{10} = \frac{5}{1} = \frac{10}{2} = \frac{100}{20}; & \frac{12}{8} = \frac{3}{2} = \frac{15}{10} = \frac{150}{100}; & \frac{15}{105} = \frac{1}{7} = \frac{10}{70} = \frac{2}{14}; \\
\frac{4}{12} = \frac{1}{3} = \frac{2}{6} = \frac{10}{30}; & \frac{8}{5} = \frac{1}{1} = \frac{10}{10} = \frac{100}{100}; & \frac{10}{50} = \frac{1}{5} = \frac{2}{10} = \frac{3}{15}; \\
\frac{10}{5} = \frac{2}{1} = \frac{4}{2} = \frac{100}{50}; & \frac{20}{4} = \frac{3}{44} = \frac{15}{44} = \frac{30}{40}; & \\
& \frac{9}{6} = \frac{3}{2} = \frac{15}{10} = \frac{30}{20} &
\end{array}$$

Exercise 2.2.7.

$$\{1/1\}; \{1/2, 3/2, 10/2, 15/2\}; \{6/3\}; \{2/4, 3/4, 6/4\};$$

$$\{1/5, 10/5, 100/5\}; \{9/6\}; \{8/8, 12/8\}; \{12/12\}; \{15/20\};$$

$$\{15/30, 150/30\}; \{5/100\}.$$

Exercise 2.2.8.

$$\begin{array}{ll}
\frac{10}{12} - \frac{30}{12} + \frac{30}{12} = \frac{10}{12} = \frac{5}{6} & \frac{12}{8} + \frac{8}{8} - \frac{15}{8} = \frac{5}{8} \\
\frac{77}{12} - \frac{15}{12} - \frac{10}{12} - \frac{1}{12} + \frac{9}{12} = \frac{60}{12} = 5 & \frac{10}{2} - \frac{1}{2} + \frac{3}{2} = \frac{12}{2} = 6 \\
\frac{6}{4} - \frac{1}{4} + \frac{15}{4} = \frac{20}{4} = 5 & \frac{15}{3} - \frac{6}{3} = \frac{9}{3} = 3 \\
\frac{6}{3} + \frac{3}{3} - \frac{12}{3} + \frac{15}{3} = \frac{12}{3} = 4 & \frac{0}{3} + \frac{1}{3} + \frac{2}{3} - \frac{3}{3} + \frac{4}{3} = \frac{4}{3}.
\end{array}$$

Exercise 2.2.9.

$$\begin{array}{ll}
\frac{6}{3} - \frac{6}{4} = \frac{24-18}{12} = \frac{1}{2}; & \frac{6}{3} + \frac{3}{4} - \frac{2}{12} = \frac{24+9-8}{12} = \frac{25}{12} = 2\frac{1}{12}; \\
\frac{84}{12} - \frac{15}{2} - \frac{10}{12} = \frac{84-90}{12} - 1 = \frac{-6}{12} - 1 = -\frac{1}{2} - 1 = -1\frac{1}{2}; & \frac{1}{5} - \frac{1}{12} = \frac{12-5}{60} = \frac{7}{60}; \\
\frac{6}{4} - \frac{3}{5} + \frac{2}{10} = \frac{30-12+8}{20} = \frac{26}{20} = 1\frac{3}{10}; & \frac{15}{3} - \frac{16}{4} = \frac{60-48}{12} = \frac{12}{12} = 1; \\
\frac{12}{8} + \frac{8}{7} - \frac{15}{56} = \frac{84+64-15}{56} = \frac{133}{56} = 2\frac{3}{8}; & \\
\frac{1}{5} - \frac{12}{10} - \frac{0}{25} + \frac{100}{50} - \frac{5}{100} = \frac{20-120-0+200-5}{100} = \frac{95}{100} = \frac{19}{20} &
\end{array}$$

Exercise 2.2.10. 1/3 for every figure.

Exercise 2.2.12.

$$\frac{\frac{10}{3} \cdot \frac{1}{2}}{\frac{10}{3} \cdot \frac{1}{2} = \frac{10}{6} = \frac{5}{3};} \qquad \frac{6}{4} \cdot \frac{3}{4} \cdot \frac{15}{4} = \frac{135}{32}; \qquad \frac{15}{4} \cdot \frac{6}{5} = \frac{9}{2};$$

$$\frac{12}{8} \cdot \frac{8}{8} \cdot \frac{15}{20} = \frac{9}{8}; \qquad \frac{1}{5} \cdot \frac{10}{5} \cdot \frac{0}{5} \cdot \frac{100}{5} \cdot \frac{5}{100} = 0.$$

Exercise 2.2.14.

$$\frac{10}{2} \div \frac{1}{2} = 10; \qquad \frac{6}{4} \div \frac{3}{4} = 2 \qquad \frac{15}{3} \div \frac{6}{3} = \frac{15}{6} = \frac{5}{2};$$

$$\frac{12}{8} \div \frac{15}{20} = 2 \qquad \frac{1}{5} \div \frac{10}{5} = \frac{1}{10}; \qquad \frac{100}{5} \div \frac{5}{100} = 400.$$

Exercise 2.2.15.

$$\frac{10}{13} \div \frac{30}{13} + \frac{3}{11} = \frac{20}{33}; \qquad \frac{6}{3} + \frac{3}{4} \div \frac{2}{3} + \frac{15}{5} = 6\frac{1}{8};$$

$$\frac{6}{4} \cdot \frac{3}{5} \div \frac{5}{7} = \frac{63}{50}; \qquad \frac{15}{3} \div \frac{16}{4} = \frac{5}{4};$$

$$\frac{1}{2} + \frac{7}{8} \div \frac{3}{4} = \frac{5}{3}; \qquad \frac{1}{5} \cdot \frac{10}{15} \div \frac{2}{25} + \frac{100}{50} - \frac{5}{3} = 2.$$

Exercise 2.2.17. 8

Exercise 2.2.18. 0.61254. $\left(\left(\frac{1}{2} + \frac{3}{4}\right) \div \frac{5}{8} - \frac{7}{8}\right) \times \frac{9}{10}$

Exercise 2.2.19. Proper fractions: $\frac{7}{8}, \frac{11}{13}, \frac{43}{44}$. Improper fractions: $\frac{8}{7}, \frac{9}{3}, \frac{4}{4}, \frac{18}{10}, \frac{31}{3}, \frac{3}{1}, \frac{12}{11}$.

Exercise 2.2.21.

$$\frac{11}{2} = 5\frac{1}{2}; \qquad \frac{10}{2} = 5 \qquad \frac{6}{4} = 1\frac{1}{2}; \qquad \frac{37}{14} = 2\frac{9}{14}; \qquad \frac{15}{4} = 3\frac{3}{4};$$

$$\frac{15}{3} = 5; \qquad \frac{16}{3} = 5\frac{1}{3}; \qquad \frac{123}{8} = 15\frac{3}{8}; \qquad \frac{8}{8} = 1 \qquad \frac{159}{20} = 7\frac{19}{20};$$

Exercise 2.2.22.

$$3\frac{1}{2} = \frac{7}{2}; \qquad 4\frac{1}{12} = \frac{49}{12}; \qquad 5\frac{6}{11} = \frac{61}{11}; \qquad 6\frac{3}{4} = \frac{27}{4};$$

$$8\frac{1}{3} = \frac{25}{3}; \qquad 9\frac{6}{13} = \frac{123}{13}; \qquad 10\frac{2}{7} = \frac{72}{7}; \qquad 1\frac{8}{13} = \frac{21}{13}.$$

Exercise 2.2.24. $\frac{2}{3} = 0\frac{2}{3}$, its integer part is 0.

Exercise 2.2.25.

$$5\frac{6}{11} + 4\frac{3}{4} = 10\frac{13}{44}; \qquad 5\frac{6}{11} - 4\frac{3}{4} = \frac{35}{44}; \qquad 5\frac{6}{11} \cdot 1\frac{3}{4} = 9\frac{13}{44}; \qquad 5\frac{6}{11} \div 1\frac{3}{4} = 3\frac{13}{77};$$

$$9\frac{15}{16} + \frac{1}{3} = 10\frac{13}{48}; \qquad 9\frac{15}{16} - \frac{1}{3} = 9\frac{29}{48} \qquad 9\frac{15}{16} \cdot \frac{1}{3} = 3\frac{5}{16}; \qquad 9\frac{15}{16} \div \frac{1}{3} = 29\frac{13}{48}.$$

Exercise 2.2.27. (1) $2\frac{"}{3}8 = \frac{19}{8} > \frac{18}{8} = \frac{9}{4}2\frac{1}{4}$.

(2) $3\frac{4}{9} < 3\frac{1}{2} < 3\frac{3}{5} < 19 < 20\frac{2}{5} < 20\frac{4}{7}$.

(3) $6\frac{5}{8} > 6\frac{5}{9} > 6\frac{6}{11} > 6$.

(4) $19\frac{6}{7} > 11\frac{5}{9} > 11\frac{1}{3} > 10\frac{2}{7} > 9\frac{5}{6} > 9 > 8\frac{1}{3} > 5\frac{2}{5} > 5 > 4\frac{3}{4}$.

Exercise 2.2.29. 78.

Exercise 2.2.31. The average after the first 4 tests was $(1/4)(50 + 75 + 85 + 80) = 290/4 = 72\frac{1}{2}$, after the first 3 tests the average was $(1/3)(50 + 75 + 85) = 210/3 = 70$, after the first 2 tests the average was $(1/2)(50 + 75) = 125/2 = 62\frac{1}{2}$, and after the first test the average was $(1/1)(50) = 50/1 = 50$.

Exercise 2.2.33.

$Average(870; 8) = 439;$ $Average(1\,002\,344; 0) = 501\,172;$

$Average(1\,002; 345; 71) = 473;$ $Average(709; 808; 2; 45) = 391;$

$Average(128; 345; 9; 909) = 87;$ $Average(2\,450; 67; 8) = 842;$

$Average(3; 457; 128; 345; 9; 909) = 309;$ $Average(2\,450; 67; 801) = 1\,106;$

$Average(870; 960; 45) = 625;$ $Average(870; 960; 8; 456) = 574.$

Exercise 2.2.34. Mike: $\frac{3 \cdot 90 + 5 \cdot 87 + 10 \cdot 75 + 1 \cdot 99 + 1 \cdot 40}{20} = 79\frac{7}{10};$

Rosie: $\frac{4 \cdot 90 + 5 \cdot 86 + 8 \cdot 70 + 1 \cdot 99 + 2 \cdot 74}{20} = 79\frac{17}{20}.$

Thus, Rosie performed slightly better than Mike.

Exercise 2.2.35. $\frac{1}{3}\left(1\frac{40}{100} + 1\frac{60}{100} + \frac{75}{100}\right) = 1\frac{25}{100}$; the average cost is \$1.25.

Exercise 2.2.36. \$555.40 · 6 = \$3 332.40; \$3 332.40 ÷ 5 = \$666.48.

Exercise 2.2.37. 76.2 ft.

Exercise 2.2.38. We give only the medians.

$Median(870; 8) = 439$; $\qquad$ $Median(1\,002\,344; 0) = 501\,172$;

$Median(1\,002; 345; 71) = 345$; $\qquad$ $Median(709; 808; 2; 45) = 377$;

$Median(128; 345; 9; 909) = 236\frac{1}{2}$; $\quad$ $Median(3; 457; 128; 345; 9; 909) = 236\frac{1}{2}$;

$Median(2\,450; 67; 8) = 67$; $\qquad$ $Median(2\,450; 67; 801) = 67$;

$Median(870; 960; 45) = 870$; $\qquad$ $Median(870; 960; 8; 456) = 663$.

2.3   Proportions

A *ratio* is relationship between two quantities expressed by fraction, when we look for how many times one quantity goes into another. Thus, instead of saying "A fraction two-thirds, $\frac{2}{3}$", we can say "A ratio of 2 to 3."

Consider four numbers, a, b, c, d, and make two ratios $\frac{a}{b}$ and $\frac{c}{d}$; of course, we assume that $b \neq 0$ and $d \neq 0$. It is said that these four numbers are *proportional* or are *in proportion*, if the two ratios above are equal:

$$\frac{a}{b} = \frac{c}{d}.$$

Sometimes we want to emphasize the validity and call it a *valid proportion*. Ratios and proportions can be written by making use of the symbol ÷, thus, $a \div b = c \div d$ has exactly the same meaning as $\frac{a}{b} = \frac{c}{d}$; in words, *a is to b as c is to d*.

Among the four terms of a proportion, a and d are called the *extreme terms* or just the *extremes*, and b and c are called the *middle terms*, or the *means*. For example, in a proportion $\frac{2}{5} = \frac{6}{15}$, the middle terms are 5 and 6, and the extremes are 2 and 15.

Example 2.3.1 *Why is the equation $\frac{2}{5} = \frac{6}{15}$ a (valid) proportion?*

Solution. The common factor of 6 and 15 is 3. If we reduce the second ratio to lowest terms by canceling out the 3, we get $\frac{6}{15} = \frac{2 \cdot 3}{5 \cdot 3} = \frac{2}{5}$, thus, both ratios are indeed equal to tone another, and we have proved that the given proportion is valid. □

If we look carefully at this problem, we notice that the product of the extreme terms and that of the mean terms are equal: $2 \cdot 15 = 6 \cdot 5$. It's not a coincidence, rather an instance of the following property of proportions:

Theorem 2.3.1 *The Fundamental Property of Proportions*. *In a (valid) proportion, the product of its extreme terms is equal to the product of the mean terms. In symbols, if*

$$\frac{a}{b} = \frac{c}{d}$$

then

$$a \cdot d = b \cdot c.$$

Moreover, the converse property *also holds good. Namely, if $b \neq 0$, $d \neq 0$ and*

$$a \cdot d = b \cdot c,$$

then the four quantities make a proportion, that is,

$$\frac{a}{b} = \frac{c}{d}.$$

□

Problem 2.3.1 *Prove that the two inequalities $b \neq 0$ and $d \neq 0$ together are equivalent to the inequality $b \cdot d \neq 0$.*

Exercise 2.3.1 *Determine whether the following proportions are valid, that is, whether the equations are true:*

$$\frac{3}{7} = \frac{4}{10} \qquad\qquad \frac{13}{5} = \frac{5}{2} \qquad\qquad \frac{1}{5} = \frac{4}{20}.$$

Exercise 2.3.2 *Replace each indeterminate, that is, symbols x, y, etc., in the following equations with a number, which makes the four numbers proportional. For example, given $\frac{1}{2} = \frac{x}{10}$, we can replace the x by 5 and get the proportion $\frac{1}{2} = \frac{5}{10}$, which is valid by the fundamental property of proportions, for $1 \cdot 10 = 2 \cdot 5 = 10$. But $x = 3$ is not good for this example, since $1 \cdot 10 \neq 2 \cdot 3$.*

$$\frac{1}{2} = \frac{x}{20} \qquad\qquad \frac{1}{y} = \frac{3}{9} \qquad\qquad \frac{5}{3} = \frac{20}{z}$$

$$\frac{3}{a} = \frac{4}{4} \qquad\qquad \frac{b}{100} = \frac{12}{48} \qquad\qquad \frac{c}{10} = \frac{1}{2}$$

$$\frac{p}{2} = \frac{10}{12} \qquad\qquad \frac{5}{q} = \frac{9}{5} \qquad\qquad \frac{r}{7} = \frac{2}{5}$$

Exercise 2.3.3 *Design and solve two more exercises similar to the previous one.*

Traditionally, in mathematics an unknown quantity is denoted by some character, the most popular and often used is, probably, x. The first proportion in Exercise 2.3.2, $\frac{1}{2} = \frac{x}{20}$, after cross-multiplication becomes $2x = 20$. Such statements are called *linear equations* (in unknown x); we study them in detail later on, in Chap. 2.6.

Consider the proportion $\frac{1}{2} = \frac{5}{10}$ and interchange the mean terms, thus getting $\frac{1}{5} = \frac{2}{10}$. This is also a proportion, since it comes down to the same equation $1 \cdot 10 = 2 \cdot 5$. Moreover, if we interchange the two extreme terms, we derive another proportion $\frac{10}{2} = \frac{5}{1}$, leading to the equivalent equation $10 \cdot 1 = 2 \cdot 5$. We can use the fundamental property of proportions to check that the following useful equations hold good in general, for any proportion.

Proposition 2.3.1 *Given a proportion $\frac{a}{b} = \frac{c}{d}$, we can derive the following proportions, which are also valid:*

$$\frac{b}{a} = \frac{d}{c}$$
$$\frac{a}{c} = \frac{b}{d}$$
$$\frac{d}{b} = \frac{c}{a}$$
$$\frac{a+b}{b} = \frac{c+d}{d}$$
$$\frac{a-b}{b} = \frac{c-d}{d}$$
$$\frac{a+b}{a-b} = \frac{c+d}{c-d}.$$

Exercise 2.3.4 *State these proportions in verbal form. For example, the first proportion can be stated as "For any proportion $\frac{b}{a} = \frac{d}{c}$, the reciprocals are also proportional."*

Consider a proportion where the means are equal,

$$\frac{a}{m} = \frac{m}{d}.$$

In this case the quantity m is called *the mean proportional between a and d*. By the fundamental property, $m^2 = a \cdot d$, or $m = \sqrt{a \cdot d}$. For example, $2 \div 4 = 4 \div 8$, therefore, 4 is the mean proportional between 2 and 8; indeed, $2 \cdot 8 = 4^2$. On the other hand, 6 is not the mean proportional between 5 and 7, since $6^2 = 36$, while $5 \cdot 7 = 35 \neq 36$. The mean proportional between 5 and 7 is $\sqrt{35}$, which is not a rational number. If a problem allows negative numbers, then there would be two means, $\sqrt{35}$ and $-\sqrt{35}$.

Exercise 2.3.5 *Compute the (positive) mean proportionals between the following pairs of numbers, 3 and 0, 3 and 12, 3 and 3.*

Example 2.3.2 *The dog Drim weighs 20 pounds, and the cat Crim weighs 4 pounds. Their owner wants to divide 12 pounds of beef jerky proportionally to their weights. How much of jerky will get each of them?*

Solution. Suppose Drim will get d pounds and Crim c pounds. Then d is to c as 20 to 4, or as a proportion, $\frac{d}{c} = \frac{20}{4}$. Reducing the fraction on the right, we have $\frac{d}{c} = 5$, or $d = 5c$. Since $d + c = 12$, we insert here $5c$ instead of d and get $5c + c = 12$, thus, $6c = 12$, hence $c = 2$, and finally $d = 5c = 5 \cdot 2 = 10$. Drim will get 10 pounds and Crim 2 pounds of jerky. $\qquad\square$

Exercise 2.3.6 *From the proportions in Proposition 2.3.1, derive as many equivalent proportions as you can. For example, the proportion $\frac{a+b}{b} = \frac{c+d}{d}$ implies the following one: $\frac{b}{a+b} = \frac{d}{c+d}$. Verify this by making use of the fundamental property of proportions.*

Exercise 2.3.7 *My friend pays $500 a year taxes on property worth $10 000, while his neighbor pays $700. What is the neighbor's property worth if both are in the same tax brackets?*

Exercise 2.3.8 *On a map, Sky-Rise county is represented by a rectangle 9 in. long and 6 in. wide. If the actual length of the county is 150 mi., find its width.*

Exercise 2.3.9 *A supermarket has sugar in packs of two sizes, 2 lb. at $1.50 per pack, and 5 lb. at $3.50 per pack. Which is the better buy? How the manager should price the bigger pack, so that both will have the same unit price?*

Exercise 2.3.10 *Your new car uses 2 gal. of gas to travel 70 mi. on highway. How many gal. of gas do you need to travel 320 mi. in the same conditions?*

Exercise 2.3.11 *You need 70 chocolates to feed your two dogs for 5 days. How many chocolates do you need to feed the same dogs for 10 days? For 6 days? One such a dog for a week?*

Exercise 2.3.12 *Three friends, Alpha, Beta, and Gamma, of ages 9, 9, and 10 years, respectively, have to split 84 hours of community service proportionally to their ages. How many hours must work each of them?*

Exercise 2.3.13 *Three crocodiles eat 5 fishermen in 2 days. Assuming that all people have the same weight and volume, how many days is it necessary for 5 crocodiles with the same appetite to eat 7 fisherwomen?.*

Exercise 2.3.14 *A $9\frac{1}{3}$-gallon drum is $\frac{2}{5}$ empty. How much of the drum, in gallons, is filled and how much is empty?*

Exercise 2.3.15 *A machinist can make 4 details in 48 minutes. How many details can she make during an 8-hour work day?*

Exercise 2.3.16 *Design and solve two more exercises similar to the previous ones.*

Answers 2.3

Exercise 2.3.1. $\frac{3}{7} = \frac{4}{10}$ – No, since $3 \cdot 10 \neq 7 \cdot 4$; $\frac{13}{5} = \frac{5}{2}$ – No, since $13 \cdot 2 \neq 5 \cdot 5$; $\frac{1}{5} = \frac{4}{20}$ – Yes, since $1 \cdot 20 == 5 \cdot 4$.
Exercise 2.3.2. $x = 10, y = 3, z = 12, a = 3, b = 25, c = 5, p = 5/3, q = 25/9, r = 14/5$.
Exercise 2.3.4. 0; 6; 3.
Exercise 2.3.7. Denote the unknown cost by x and set the proportion $500 \div 10\,000 = 700 \div x$. From this proportion, $x = \$14\,000$.
Exercise 2.3.8. Denoting the unknown width by w, we set the proportion $9 \div 150 = 6 \div w$, thus, $w = 100$ mi. The proportion can be also set as $9 \div 6 = 150 \div w$, surely, leading to the same answer.
Exercise 2.3.10. $320/35 = 9\frac{1}{7}$ gal.
Exercise 2.3.11. $\frac{70}{2 \cdot 5} = 7$ chocolates per dog per day, thus the answers are 140; 84; 49 chocolates, respectively.
Exercise 2.3.12. 27, 27, and 30, respectively.
Exercise 2.3.13. $\frac{42}{25} = 1\frac{17}{25}$ days.
Exercise 2.3.14. The drum contains $5\frac{3}{5}$ (gallons) and is $3\frac{11}{15}$ (gallons) empty.
Exercise 2.3.15. 40 details.

2.4 Decimals and Percents

2.4.1 Decimals. Basic Properties

Since we use the *place-value number system* with the base of 10, the *powers of ten,* that is, the numbers $10 = 10^1$, $10^2 = 10 \cdot 10 = 100$, $10^3 = 1,000$, $10^4 = 10,000, 10^5 = 100,000$, $10^6 = 1,000,000$, ..., etc., are singled out, they play a special role in computations. We remind that positive powers of ten are called, in increasing order,

$$10 = 10^1 - ten$$

$$100 = 10^2 - hundred$$

$$1\,000 = 10^3 - thousand$$

$$10\,000 = 10^4 - ten\ thousand$$

$$100\,000 = 10^5 - hundred\ thousand$$

$$1\,000\,000 = 10^6 - million$$

etc. In the opposite direction,

$$10^{-1} = \frac{1}{10} \text{ - one-tenth}$$

$$10^{-2} = \frac{1}{100} \text{ - one-hundredth}$$

$$10^{-3} = \frac{1}{1000} \text{ - one-thousandth, etc.}$$

Definition 2.4.1 *Decimals are mixed numbers, maybe, with zero integer part, such that the numerator and denominator of the fraction part are positive integer numbers, and moreover, the denominator is a* positive integer power of ten.

For example, $3\frac{12}{100}$ is a decimal. However, this writing may be cumbersome. Due to the omnipresence of the decimals, a special, shortened notation for the decimals has been designed many years back. Namely, the integer part is written as a whole number, but only the *numerator* of the fractional part is written explicitly. The integer part and the fractional part are separated by a *decimal dot*[4] '.', like 1.5. To avoid confusion, the dot must be clearly written at the lower level of a line of the text. This is important, since the 'middle' dot signifies the *multiplication*, namely, $3 \cdot 4 = 3 \cdot 4 = 12$, while 3.4 is the decimal *Three and four-tenths*.

Since we do not see denominators of the decimals explicitly, how to distinguish, say, $\frac{13}{100}$ from $\frac{13}{1000}$? This is possible, since every place in the fractional part of decimals represents some unique power of ten. The first place to the right of the decimal dot is reserved for the *tenths*, thus, $0.3 = \frac{3}{10}$ and is read "three-tenths". The sequel, second place to the right is reserved for the *hundredths*, thus, $0.03 = \frac{3}{100}$ and is read "three-hundredths", etc. For instance, 0.003 means $\frac{3}{1000}$ and is read "three-thousandths". The decimal $0.1203 = \frac{1203}{10000}$ is read "one thousand, two hundred, three ten-thousandths".

Let us have more practice. $\frac{3}{100} = 0.03$ – since the fraction is read "three-hundredths", so that the 3 must be in the place for hundredths. $\frac{2}{10} = 0.2$, since this is "two-tenths"; $\frac{345}{100} = 3\frac{45}{100} = 3.45$, since this is an improper fraction, $\frac{3456}{100} = 34\frac{56}{100} = 34.56$, while $-\frac{13}{10000} = -0.0013$.

Exercise 2.4.1 (1) *In a number* 102.980765432, *what digit is in the place of hundreds? Tens? Unities? Thousands? Tenths? Hundredths? Thousandths? Ten-thousandths? Hundred-thousandths? Millionths, etc.?*

(2) *In this number, at what place the digit* 0 *is? The same question about the digits* $1, 2, \ldots, 9$.

(3) *How many times bigger is the left-most* 2 *than the right-most* 2 *in the number* 102.980765432?

Example 2.4.1 *Change the fractions* $\frac{17}{100}$ *and* $\frac{217}{100}$ *to the equal decimals.*

Solution. The fraction $\frac{17}{100}$ can be written as

$$\frac{17}{100} = \frac{10+7}{100} = \frac{10}{100} + \frac{7}{100} = \frac{1}{10} + \frac{7}{100},$$

---

[4]In some countries the comma ',' is used instead of the decimal dot '.'.

hence, the digit of the tenths is 1 and the digit of the hundredths is 7. Moreover, the fraction is proper, therefore, its whole part is 0 and we write

$$\frac{17}{100} = 0.17,$$

or even .17, since this 0 is *insignificant* and is not compulsory.

The second fraction, $\frac{217}{100}$ is improper. We convert it to a mixed number as $\frac{217}{100} = 2\frac{17}{100}$, and using the previous example, write the answer as

$$\frac{217}{100} = 2.17.$$

In the same fashion, $\frac{1304}{100} = 13.04$, and $\frac{1304}{1000000} = 0.001304$ - since the latter denominator has six zeros, we have to add two zeros between the decimal dot and a four-digit numerator. Here are a few more examples how to change fractions to decimals:

$$\frac{3}{10} = 0.3, \quad \frac{3}{100} = 0.03, \quad \frac{345}{100} = 3.45, \quad \frac{345}{1000} = 0.345, \quad -\frac{13}{10000} = -0.0013.$$

$\square$

Remark 2.4.1 *In examples like the last one, the zero to the left of the decimal point is optional, we can write 0.3 = .3 and 0.03 = .03. Nevertheless, we recommend to preserve initially this 0 and write 0.1.*

But of course, .3 and .03 are two different numbers, the zero in .03 is significant.

An integer number can also be written as a decimal, for instance, $7 = \frac{7}{1} = 7.0$.

Example 2.4.2 *Change the following fractions to decimals.*

$$\frac{13}{100}, \quad \frac{13}{1000}, \quad \frac{130}{100}, \quad \frac{103}{100}, \quad \frac{103}{10}, \quad \frac{13}{1000}, \quad \frac{13}{10000}$$

Solution. The fraction $\frac{13}{100}$ means "thirteen-hundredths", that is, "ten-hundredths" and "three-hundredths". Since "ten-hundredths" $\frac{10}{100} = \frac{1}{10}$ and means "one-tenth", we must place a 1 in the place of tenths and a 3 in the place of hundredths. Therefore, $\frac{13}{100} = 0.13$. However, the fraction $\frac{13}{1000}$ is "thirteen-thousandths", hence $\frac{13}{1000} = 0.013$.

In the numerator of $\frac{130}{100}$, the zero is significant, $\frac{130}{100} = 1\frac{30}{100} = 1.30 = 1.3$, but $\frac{103}{100} = 1\frac{3}{100} = 1.03$ and $\frac{103}{10} = 10\frac{3}{10} = 10.3$. Moreover, $\frac{13}{1000} = 0.013$ and $\frac{13}{10000} = 0.0013$.
$\square$

Exercise 2.4.2 *Write down three different numbers (1) between 1.9 and 2.05; (2) between $\frac{3}{2}$ and $\frac{7}{4}$.*

Exercise 2.4.3 *Design and solve two more exercises similar to the previous one.*

Exercise 2.4.4 *Change the sequel fractions to decimals.*

$\frac{1}{10} =$	$\frac{30}{10} =$	$\frac{1}{1000} =$	$\frac{12}{10000} =$
$\frac{50}{10} =$	$\frac{20}{10} =$	$\frac{20}{100} =$	$\frac{12}{1000} =$
$\frac{23}{10} =$	$\frac{11}{10000} =$	$\frac{101010101}{10000} =$	$\frac{3}{1} =$

Changing a decimal to a fraction is even simpler: just read the decimal and write it down as a fraction whose denominator is a power of ten; reduce if necessary. For example, 0.205 is read *Two hundred and five thousandths*, therefore,

$$0.205 = \frac{205}{1000} = \frac{41 \cdot 5}{200 \cdot 5} = \frac{41}{200},$$

and 1.02, that is, "one and two-hundredths" is

$$1.02 = 1 + \frac{2}{100} = 1 + \frac{1}{50} = 1\frac{1}{50}.$$

Exercise 2.4.5 *Change decimals to fractions. Simplify if possible.*

1.1 =	30.10 =	10.098 =	1.2109 =
10.98 =	10.09 =	100.008 =	1000.0001 =
3.1 =	1110000.12 =	10000.045 =	−12.098 =

Exercise 2.4.6 *Design and solve two more exercises similar to the previous ones.*

2.4.2   Comparing Decimals

Decimals are compared exactly as the integers, starting from the left-most digits carrying the biggest value. For example, 0.0206 > 0.01999 since in both numbers the left-most *significant digits* represent hundredths, and 2 > 1; all the other digits are irrelevant for the conclusion. We remind that the right-most zeros in the *fractional part* of a decimal are *insignificant*, and we can write them (or not) as a matter of convenience. Thus, 2.23 = 2.230 = 2.23000.

As another example, 1.9999 < 20.0000, since the first number does not show the digit of tens at all, meaning that this digit is 0. However, 1.9999 > 1.9998, since the only difference is at the fourth place after the decimal dot ("ten-thousandths"), and here 9 > 8.

Exercise 2.4.7 *Replace the "?" with an appropriate inequality symbol* $<, >, \leq, \geq$.

$$1.04 \; ? \; 1.004 \qquad\qquad 0.234 \; ? \; 0.229 \qquad\qquad 0.10203 \; ? \; 1.0$$

2.4.3   Arithmetic Operations with Decimals

When we do arithmetic with the decimals, all the rules of operating with signed numbers remain the same as in the case of integer numbers. However, we have a new concern – where to place the decimal dot in the result.

The addition and subtraction of decimals are simple – we line both decimals up, so that the decimal dots are in the same column; this way the dot in the result will *automatically* occur in the same column. Let us consider an example.

Example 2.4.3 *Add* 18.597 + 321.84.

Solution. We line both addends up, so that the decimal dots are in the same column and bring down the dot in this column as it should appear in the sum.

$$18.597$$
$$- \; \underline{+321.84} \; -$$

After that, the addition works exactly as in the case of the whole numbers, starting at the right-most column. The right-most significant digit, 7, of the first addend stands for the thousandths, while there is no thousandths in the second addend, the corresponding digit is 0; thus, we start by adding $7 + 0 = 7$,

$$18.597$$
$$\underline{+321.840}$$
$$.7$$

Now we have to add the digits of hundredths, $9+4 = 13$. Thus, the digit of hundredths in the sum is 3, and 1 must be carried on to the left, to the column of tenths,

$$\mathbf{1}$$
$$18.597$$
$$\underline{+321.840}$$
$$.37$$

For the digit of tenths we get $1 + 5 + 8 = 14$, thus we record 4 in the tenths column and carry-on 1 to the left,

$$\mathbf{11}$$
$$18.597$$
$$\underline{+321.840}$$
$$.437$$

We end the job by adding the integer parts,

$$\mathbf{1\,11}$$
$$18.597$$
$$\underline{+321.840}$$
$$340.437$$

Whence, $18.597 + 321.84 = 340.437$ □

Example 2.4.4 *Subtract* $12.097 - 21.12$.

Solution. We have to take away a bigger number from a smaller one, hence exactly as with the integer numbers, the difference must be negative, and we proceed as in Chapter 1.7. To work with positive numbers, that is, with the absolute values, we switch the order to get a positive result and then apply the $-$ sign to the difference. Therefore, we subtract $21.12 - 12.097$, keeping in mind that in the end we must change the sign of this result. We do $21.120 - 12.097$ and to subtract 7 from 0, we borrow 1 from 2 and get $10 - 7 = 3$ in the place of the tenths. Continue in the same way, we calculate $21.12 - 12.097 = 9.023$, but being careful to change sign; we finally have $12.097 - 21.12 = -9.023$. □

Exercise 2.4.8 *Compute.*

$1.04 + 0.004 =$	$0.0234 + 0.229 =$	$0.10203 + 1.0 =$
$1.04 - 0.004 =$	$0.0234 - 0.00229 =$	$0.10203 - 0.012 =$

$1.04 - 0.004 + (0.0234 + 0.229 - 0.10203 + 1.0) =$ $\qquad$ $21.8 - 0 =$ $\qquad$ $0 - 34.6 =$

Exercise 2.4.9 *Design and solve two more exercises similar to the previous one.*

To learn how to multiply the decimals, as always, we first consider examples.

Example 2.4.5 *Multiply* $0.1 \cdot 0.01$.

Solution. We change these decimals to fractions and multiply the latter;

$$0.1 \cdot 0.01 = \frac{1}{10} \cdot \frac{1}{100} = \frac{1 \cdot 1}{10 \cdot 100} = \frac{1}{1000} = 0.001.$$

It is useful to compare this example with the product $10 \cdot 100 = 1\,000$, that is, with an obvious result, *ten times a hundred is a thousand*. However, when we multiply the reciprocals, we get *one-tenth times one-hundredth is one-thousandth*.   □

Example 2.4.6 *Multiply* $2.9 \cdot 0.02$.

Solution. We change these decimals to fractions as well and multiply the latter;

$$2.9 \cdot 0.02 = \frac{29}{10} \cdot \frac{2}{100} = \frac{29 \cdot 2}{10 \cdot 100} = \frac{58}{1000} = 0.058.$$

□

In these two examples, we first changed the decimals to fractions to show the procedure. What is essential here is the denominator, which is the product of two powers of 10. Therefore, it contains as many zeros as the total of the numbers of zeros in the decimals multiplied. But these numbers of zeros are exactly the numbers of the decimal places in the decimal factors involved, that is, the numbers of the significant digits to the right of the decimal dot. Whence, we have derived the rule for multiplying the decimals.

Theorem 2.4.1 *To multiply decimals, we first neglect the decimal dots and multiply these numbers as the integers. Then, to locate the decimal dot in the product, we add the numbers of decimal places in all the factors – the sum gives the number of decimal places in the product.*   □

Corollary 2.4.1 *The product of a decimal and an integer contains exactly as many decimal places as the decimal.*

Problem 2.4.1 *Consider a special case of the previous corollary, when the integer ends with a few zeros.*

In Example 2.4.6, we first multiply $29 \cdot 2 = 58$. Second, the factor 2.9 has one decimal place and the factor 0.02 has two decimal places, therefore, the product $2.9 \cdot 0.02$ has $1 + 2 = 3$ decimal places, that is, $2.9 \cdot 0.02 = 0.058$, as we computed before. Let us have more practice.

Example 2.4.7 *Multiply* $1.001 \cdot (-0.301) \cdot 3.11$.

Solution. There is one negative factor, therefore the product is negative. Having said that, we "forget" about signs and multiply the absolute values. Thus, $1.001 \cdot 0.301 = 0.302\,301$, and $0.302\,301 \cdot 3.11 = 0.93704611$, but it is not the answer, the answer is -0.93704611.   □

Remark 2.4.2 *To multiply decimals, we do not have to line them up in any way. It is convenient to write the longer number as the first factor.*

Exercise 2.4.10 *Compute.*

$$1.04 \cdot 0.004 = \qquad 0.0234 \cdot 0.229 = \qquad 0.10203 \cdot 1.03 =$$

$$1.04 \cdot 1.054 = \qquad 0.0234 \cdot 0.209 = \qquad 0.1203 \cdot 1.009 =$$

$$1.04 - 0.004 \cdot (0.02 + 0.2 \cdot 0.102 + 1.0) = \qquad 1.04 - 0 \cdot (0.02 + 1.0) =$$

Exercise 2.4.11 *Design and solve two more exercises similar to the previous one.*

We take up the division of decimals now. Remind that any move of the decimal dot in a given decimal changes the value of the decimal – if the dot shifts one step to the *right*, the decimal becomes ten times *larger*. For example, if the dot in 0.1, which is *one-tenth*, has moved one step to the right, the number becomes 1.0, that is, the integer *one*. In the same way, if the decimal dot moves k steps to the right, the decimal becomes 10^k times bigger. Indeed, 341 is hundred times more than 3.41.

In the opposite direction, when we shift the decimal dot k steps to the *left*, the decimal number becomes 10^k times *smaller*. For instance, given a decimal 100.1, that is, *one hundred and one-tenth*, if we move the dot one step to the *left*, the number becomes 10.01, that is, just *ten and one-hundredth*.

Considering these and similar examples, we convince ourselves in the validity of the following rule for multiplying or dividing decimals *by a power of ten*.

Theorem 2.4.2 (1) *To multiply a decimal by a power of ten, 10^k, where k is a natural number, it is sufficient to shift the decimal dot k steps to the right.*

(2) *To divide a decimal by a power of ten, 10^k, where k is a natural number, it is sufficient to shift the decimal dot k steps to the left.* □

Thus, $1.023 \cdot 10^3 = 1\,023$ getting an integer, but $1.023 \div 10^3 = 0.001023$.

Exercise 2.4.12 *Compute.*

$$1.04 \cdot 10 = \qquad 0.0234 \cdot 10^2 = \qquad 0.10203 \cdot 10^3 = \qquad 1.4 \cdot 10^5 =$$

$$0.0234 \cdot 10^2 = \qquad 0.1203 \cdot 10^9 = \qquad 1.04 \div 10 = \qquad 0.0234 \div 10^2 =$$

$$0.10203 \div 10^3 = \qquad 1.4 \div 10^5 = \qquad 0.0234 \div 10^2 = \qquad 0.1203 \div 10^9 =$$

Exercise 2.4.13 *Design and solve two more exercises similar to the previous one.*

Next we study how to divide a decimal over any positive integer number. The algorithm is very similar to one for dividing integer numbers in Section 1.11. The only new element is, where to place the decimal dot in the quotient. However, division is the inverse of multiplication, and we have just learnt in Corollary 2.4.1, that if we multiply a decimal by an integer, then the product has exactly as many decimal points as the decimal. So that, when we divide a decimal over an integer number, we immediately set the dot in the future quotient in the same column as in the dividend. Let us demonstrate the algorithm by the example.

Example 2.4.8 *Divide* 1.203 *by* 14.

Solution. We write exactly as in the long-division algorithm, compare with Example 1.9.3 above,

$$14 \;\overline{)\,1.203}$$

and first of all, set the decimal dot in the quotient in the same column as in the dividend:

$$14 \;\overline{)\,\overset{.}{1.203}}$$

Since 14 goes into 1 zero times, the integer part of the quotient is 0, and we can write

$$14 \;\overline{)\,\overset{0.}{1.203}}$$

in agreement with our common sense, since $1.203 \div 14$ is a proper fraction. Next, we try to use two digits of the dividend and divide 14 into 12, thus getting another 0 in the quotient.

$$14 \;\overline{)\,\overset{0.0}{1.203}}$$

Now as in Example 1.9.3, we divide 14 into 120, thus, the left-most non-zero digit of the quotient is 8, which must be recorded above the 0 in the dividend; 0 in 120 is the digit of *hundredths* in the dividend, hence 8 is also the digit of *hundredths* in the quotient, and it follows two zeros to the left of 8:

$$14 \;\overline{)\,\overset{0.08}{1.203}}$$

According to the algorithm, we multiply $14 \cdot 8 = 112$, put this product beneath 120 and subtract it from the latter number:

$$
\begin{array}{r}
\overset{0.08}{14\;\overline{)\,1.203}} \\
-\,112 \\
\hline
8
\end{array}
$$

Next we bring down the right-most digit 3 of the dividend:

$$
\begin{array}{r}
\overset{0.08}{14\;\overline{)\,1.203}} \\
-\,112 \\
\hline
83
\end{array}
$$

Now we divide 14 into 83 and by trial find the next digit, 5, of the quotient:

$$
\begin{array}{r}
\overset{0.08\,5}{14\;\overline{)\,1.203}} \\
-\,112 \\
\hline
83
\end{array}
$$

The crucial question is how long should we continue this process? There are two possible outcomes: either after finitely many steps the remainder is zero, therefore the division is finished. Otherwise, the division can last endlessly. Therefore, the quotient must be rounded off, and the problem should provide us with the information as to what decimal position the result must be rounded off.

Suppose, in this problem we want the answer to be precise up to the hundredths, that is, we want to have two correct digits in the result. To assure this, we need one more digit of the quotient, the digit of the thousandths, and we have to make the last loop in this example: $14 \cdot 5 = 70$ and $83 - 70 = 13$ gives the remainder 13:

$$\begin{array}{r} 0.08\,5 \\ 14\ \overline{)\ 1.203} \\ -\,1\,12 \\ \hline 83 \\ -70 \\ \hline 13 \end{array}$$

We did this extra division to compute the third digit of the quotient – since this digit is 5, we must increase the previous digit, and the quotient, *rounded up to the hundredths*, is 0.09.

Sometimes we can avoid the extra division, if after computing the digit of hundredths 8, we look at the remainder, which is (by chance!) also $8 > 5$, which tells us that the digits of hundredths in the answer must be $8 + 1 = 9$, hence the answer is 0.09.   □

Example 2.4.9 *Divide* $1.203 \div 1\,203$ *and round off to the nearest tenth.*

Solution. If we notice that both the dividend and the divisor have the same significant digits, we can proceed as follows:

$$\frac{1.203}{1\,203} = \frac{1\,203}{1\,203 \cdot 1\,000} = \frac{1}{1\,000} = 0.001,$$

which after the required rounding to the tenths is $\approx 0.0 = 0$. This example illustrates how, while rounding, we loose precision and the significant digits – they are "run away" from the screen. Had we rounded to the thousandths, the answer would be $0.001 \neq 0$. □

Exercise 2.4.14 *Compute. If necessary, round off all the answers to three decimal places after the decimal dot.*

$$1.04 \div 52 = \qquad 1.04 \div 520 = \qquad 1.04 \div 5\,200 =$$
$$0.0234 \div 234 \approx \qquad 2.34 \div 234 = \qquad 0.0234 \div 2\,340 =$$

Exercise 2.4.15 *Design and solve two more exercises similar to the previous one.*

Now we can easily divide a decimal over any decimal by reducing the problem to the previous case.

Example 2.4.10 *Divide* 1.203 *over* 1.4.

Solution. The denominator here has only one decimal place. Thus, keeping in mind the fundamental property of fractions, we multiply both the numerator and denominator by $10 = 10^1$. Now the problem reads

$$1.203 \div 1.4 = \frac{1.203}{1.4} = \frac{1.203 \cdot 10}{1.4 \cdot 10} = \frac{12.03}{14},$$

and we have to divide a decimal over an integer. In other problems, if the denominator contains k decimal places, we would multiply both numerator and denominator by 10^k. To finish the problem, we now proceed as in the previous examples,

$$14\ \overline{)\ 12.03}$$

and first of all, set the decimal dot in the quotient in the same column as in the dividend, as follows:

$$14 \ )\overline{12.03}$$

We again divide 14 into 120, thus, the left-most significant digit of the quotient is 8, and it must be recorded above the 0 in the dividend. Since 0 is the digit of the *tenths* in the dividend, 8 is also the digit of the *tenths* in the quotient, and the integer part of the quotient is 0:

$$14 \ )\overline{12.03}^{\,0.8}$$

According to the long-division algorithm, we multiply $14 \cdot 8 = 112$, put this product beneath 120 and subtract it from the latter number:

$$
\begin{array}{r}
0.8 \\
14 \ )\overline{12.03} \\
-\ 112 \\
\hline
8
\end{array}
$$

Next we bring down the 3,

$$
\begin{array}{r}
0.8 \\
14 \ )\overline{12.03} \\
-\ 112 \\
\hline
83
\end{array}
$$

and divide 14 into 83. By trial we find the next digit, 5, of the quotient,

$$
\begin{array}{r}
0.8\,5 \\
14 \ )\overline{12.03} \\
-\ 112 \\
\hline
83
\end{array}
$$

If we want the answer to be precise up to the hundredths, we must know whether to preserve this 5 or to increase it to 6. Thus, we compute one more digit of the quotient as $14 \cdot 5 = 70$, $83 - 70 = 13$:

$$
\begin{array}{r}
0.8\,5 \\
14 \ )\overline{12.03} \\
-\ 112 \\
\hline
83 \\
-70 \\
\hline
13
\end{array}
$$

At this step we exhausted all digits of the dividend, therefore, we just attach 0 to the 13 and divide 14 into 130; since $130 = 14 \cdot 9 + 4$, the next digit of the quotient is 9:

$$
\begin{array}{r}
0.8\,59 \\
14 \ )\overline{12.03} \\
-\ 112 \\
\hline
83 \\
-70 \\
\hline
130 \\
-126 \\
\hline
4
\end{array}
$$

Thus, we must increase the 5, and the answer, *rounded up to the hundredths*, is 0.86. It is worth noting that the divisor in this example, 1.4, is ten times smaller than 14 in the previous example, and the rounded quotient, $0.86 \approx 0.9$, is approximately 10 times larger than 0.09 in Example 2.4.7.   □

Example 2.4.11 *Divide* $28,342 \div 0.28342$.

Solution. We write

$$28,342 \div 0.28342 = 2\ 834\ 200 \div 28\ 342 = 100$$

and

$$1.631 \div 0.05 = 163.1 \div 5 = 32.62$$

$\square$

Remark 2.4.3 *If we have to round off in many-step problems, we must keep a couple of extra digits at every intermediate step; for example, if the final result must have the right digit of tenths, all the intermediate steps of rounding must be up to the hundredths.*

Exercise 2.4.16 *Compute. If necessary, round off all the intermediate answers to three decimal places, and the final answers to two places.*

$1.04 \div 52 =$	$1.04 \div 5.2 =$	$1.04 \div 0.52 =$
$0.0234 \div 234 =$	$0.0234 \div 23.4 =$	$0.0234 \div 2.34 =$
$0.0234 \div 0.117 =$	$0.103 \div 0.00103 =$	$0.103 \div 10.3 =$
$0.103 \div 1.03 =$	$0.103 \div 0.0103 =$	$1.4 \div 10.5 =$
$1.4 \div 1.05 =$	$1.4 \div 0.105 =$	$1.4 \div 0.00105 =$
$0.0234 \div 1.2 =$	$0.0234 \div 0.12 =$	$0.0234 \div 0.00012 =$
$0.1203 \div 10.9 =$	$0.1203 \div 1.09 =$	$0.1203 \div 0.0109 =$

$$1.04 - 0.00004 \div (10.4 + 0.26 \div 0.13 + 1.0) =$$

Exercise 2.4.17 *Design and solve two more exercises similar to the previous one.*

2.4.4   Percents

Percents are the decimals with the denominator $100 = 10^2$, thus, one percent is *one-hundredth* part of the whole thing; percents are denoted by the symbol %. Vice versa, since $1\% = \frac{1}{100}$ of the total amount, then the latter, the whole quantity is *always* 100%. Percents are convenient in many book-keeping and similar every-day tasks[5]. If you made $200 by moonlighting, then one percent of this amount is $\frac{1}{100}$-th part of the amount, that is,

$$\frac{1}{100} \cdot 200 = \$2.$$

In computations we mostly use *decimal equivalents* of the percents. It is useful to remember a few basic percentage values as the decimals:

$$1\% = \frac{1}{100} = 0.01 \text{ of the amount given}$$

$$5\% = \frac{5}{100} = 0.05 = \frac{1}{20} \text{ of the amount given}$$

---

[5]A rarely used unit, one-thousandth of the entire quantity or one-tenth of one percent, is called *one promille* and is denoted as $1°/_{oo}$.

$$10\% = \frac{10}{100} = 0.1 = \frac{1}{10} \text{ of the amount given}$$

$$20\% = \frac{20}{100} = 0.2 = \frac{1}{5} \text{ of the amount given}$$

$$25\% = \frac{25}{100} = 0.25 = \frac{1}{4} \text{ of the amount given}$$

$$50\% = \frac{50}{100} = 0.5 = \frac{1}{2} \text{ of the amount given}$$

$$75\% = \frac{75}{100} = 0.75 = \frac{3}{4} \text{ of the amount given}$$

$$100\% = \frac{100}{100} = 1.0 = 1, \text{ that is, the whole amount}$$

$$200\% = \frac{200}{100} = 2, \text{ that is, twice the whole amount}$$

On the other hand,

$$0.2 = 0.2 \cdot 100\% = 20\%$$

$$0.3 = 0.3 \cdot 100\% = 30\%$$

$$0.4 = 0.4 \cdot 100\% = 40\%.$$

It is clear from the definition and these examples that to change a percentage value to its decimal equivalent, one has to divide the percentage value over 100. Since $100 = 10^2$, to convert a percentage value to its decimal equivalent, it is enough to shift a decimal dot *two places to the left*. Thus, the decimal equivalent of, say, 16% is $16/100 = 0.16$. In the opposite direction, to convert a decimal to the equivalent percentage point, it is enough to multiply the decimal by 100, or to move the dot *two places to the right*. For example, 3.05 is equivalent to $100 \cdot 3.05 = 305\%$.

Example 2.4.12 *Eugene's annual salary was $65 000. He got a 6% raise. what is his current salary?*

Solution. The solution is straightforward. First we find the 6% of $65 000. To do that, we must multiply this amount by the decimal equivalent of 6%, that is, by $6\% \cdot 0.01 = 0.06$, and get $0.06 \cdot 65\,000 = \$3\,900$. This is Eugene's raise. His new salary is $65\,000 + 3\,900 = \$68\,900$.

Slightly more sophisticated but shorter solution is to notice that now Eugene makes $100\% + 6\% = 106\% = 1,06$ of his previous salary, which can be momentarily computed without any calculator, and find the new salary as $1.06 \cdot 65\,000 = \$68\,900$. □

In this example we solve one of the basic problems of arithmetic – *Find a part (or a percent) of a quantity*. As we saw in the example, this problem can be always solved by *multiplication* of the given quantity by the *decimal* measure of the required part. If the part is expressed as a *percent*, we must convert it into the decimal.

Example 2.4.12 relates three quantities, two given and one unknown - Eugene's old salary, the given raise, and his new, yet unknown salary. However, every percentage problem involves the fourth quantity, which is always numerically known - 100%. If instead of percents we use the decimals, then instead of 100% we must use 1. These four quantities can be arranged in a proportion. If we denote the initial quantity (the base) as B, the percentage of change as P, and the value of the change as C, then the proportion is

$$\frac{B}{100} = \frac{C}{P}. \tag{2.4.1}$$

Thus, in the preceding example, which we initially solved without a proportion, we have $B = 65\,000$, $P = 6\%$, and the proportion (2.4.1) is

$$\frac{65\,000}{100} = \frac{C}{6},$$

resulting in the same raise $C = \$3900$.

Any term of proportion (2.4.1) can be unknown, except for the 100%. Let us consider examples.

Example 2.4.13 *Eugene's annual salary was $65 000. After a raise, his salary is $70 000. What was the raise?*

Solution. We again have $B = 65\,000$, while P is unknown. If we denote the new salary as $S = \$70\,000$, then the proportion is

$$\frac{B}{100} = \frac{S}{P},$$

or

$$\frac{65\,000}{100} = \frac{70\,000}{P},$$

therefore, $P \approx 107.69\%$. Of course, this number is not the raise, the latter is $107.69 - 100 = 7.69\%$. It is also possible to begin by finding the monetary value of the raise, which is again a mental exercise, since $70\,000 - 65\,000 = 5\,000$, and arrange the information in a proportion as follows,

$$\frac{65\,000}{100} = \frac{5\,000}{x},$$

hence we get $x \approx 7.69\%$.   □

Example 2.4.14 *After a 5%−raise, Eugene's annual salary became $67, 500. What was his initial salary?*

Solution. Now the proportion becomes

$$\frac{B}{100} = \frac{67\,500}{105},$$

therefore, the initial salary was $64\,285.71.   □

Remark 2.4.4 *Proportion (2.4.1) is universal in the sense that it can be used to solve any percent-related problem.*

It should be also noted that any derived proportion is as good as (2.4.1). for example, we can flip it and write as

$$\frac{100}{B} = \frac{P}{C},$$

or we can switch the columns and use the proportion

$$\frac{C}{P} = \frac{B}{100}.$$

What proportion to use is just the matter of convenience, they all give the same result.

Exercise 2.4.18 *Convert decimals and fractions to percents, and percents to decimals and to fractions.*

$$1.04 = \qquad 12 = \qquad 1041.2 = \qquad 0.0234 =$$

$$10.2 = \qquad 0.3402 = \qquad 0.10203\% = \qquad 10.3\% =$$

$$2030.3\% = \qquad 0.00105\% = \qquad 1.05\% = \qquad 1.4\% =$$

$$\frac{1}{4} = \qquad \frac{11}{400} = \qquad \frac{13}{4} = \qquad \frac{21}{50} = \qquad \frac{11}{25} = \qquad \frac{17}{20} =$$

Exercise 2.4.19 *Sasha earns 9% commission of the sales she makes. What was the gross amount of her sales when her commission was $405?*

Exercise 2.4.20 *Sasha invested $1 000, part at 4% and the other part at 2% annual rate. After the first year, the interest he received was $32. how much did he invest at each rate?*

Exercise 2.4.21 *Design and solve two more exercises similar to the previous ones.*

Answers 2.4

Exercise 2.4.1. (1) The digit of hundreds is 1, the digit of tens is 0, the digit of unities is 2, that of tenths is 9, of hundredths is 8, of thousandths is 0, of ten-thousandths is 7, of hundred-thousandths is 6, of millionths is 5.
(2) 0 occurs at the tens and thousandths, 1 occupies the place of the hundreds, ... , 9 occupies the place of the tenths.
(3) The left 2 is 10^9 times bigger than the right-most 2.
Exercise 2.4.2. The problems have infinitely many solutions, for example,
(1) $1.9 < 1.92 < 2 < 2.049 < 2.05$; and (2) $1.5 < 1.5001 < 1.50011 < 1.7 < 1.75$.
Exercise 2.4.4.

$$\frac{1}{10} = 0.1; \qquad \frac{30}{10} = 3; \qquad \frac{1}{1000} = 0.001; \qquad \frac{12}{10000} = 0.0012;$$
$$\frac{50}{10} = 5; \qquad \frac{22}{10} = 2.2; \qquad \frac{20}{100} = 0.2; \qquad \frac{12}{1000} = 0.012;$$
$$\frac{203}{10} = 20.3; \qquad \frac{11}{10000} = 0.0011; \qquad \frac{101010101}{10000} = 10101.0101; \qquad \frac{3}{1} = 3.$$

Exercise 2.4.5.

$$1.1 = \tfrac{11}{10} = 1\tfrac{1}{10}; \qquad\qquad\qquad 30.10 = \tfrac{301}{10} = 30\tfrac{1}{10};$$
$$10.098 = \tfrac{10\,098}{1\,000} = 10\tfrac{49}{500}; \qquad\qquad 1.2109 = \tfrac{12109}{10\,000} = 1\tfrac{2109}{10\,000};$$
$$10.98 = \tfrac{1098}{100} = 10\tfrac{49}{50}; \qquad\qquad 10.09 = \tfrac{1009}{100} = 10\tfrac{9}{100};$$
$$100.008 = \tfrac{100\,008}{1\,000} = 100\tfrac{1}{125}; \qquad\qquad 1000.0001 = \tfrac{10\,000\,001}{10\,000} = 1\,000\tfrac{1}{10\,000};$$
$$3.1 = \tfrac{31}{10} = 3\tfrac{1}{10}; \qquad\qquad 1110000.12 = \tfrac{111\,000\,012}{12} = 1\,110\,000\tfrac{3}{25};$$
$$10000.045 = \tfrac{10\,000\,045}{1\,000} = 10\,000\tfrac{9}{200}; \qquad -12.098 = -\tfrac{12\,098}{1\,000} = -\tfrac{6\,049}{500} = -12\tfrac{49}{500}.$$

Exercise 2.4.7. $1.04 > 1.004; 0.234 > 0.229; 0.10203 < 1.0.$
Exercise 2.4.8.

$$1.04 + 0.004 = 1.044; \quad 0.0234 + 0.229 = 0.2524; \qquad 0.10203 + 1.0 = 1.10203;$$
$$1.04 - 0.004 = 1.036; \quad 0.0234 - 0.00229 = 0.02111; \quad 0.10203 - 0.012 = 0.9003;$$
$$1.04 - 0.004 + (0.0234 + 0.229 - 0.10203 + 1.0) = 2.18637; 21.8; -34.6.$$

Exercise 2.4.10.

$$1.04 \cdot 0.004 = 0.00416; \qquad 0.0234 \cdot 0.229 = 0.0053586;$$
$$0.10203 \cdot 1.03 = 0.1050909; \quad 1.04 \cdot 1.054 = 1.09616;$$
$$0.0234 \cdot 0.209 = 0.0048906; \quad 0.1203 \cdot 1.009 = 0.1213827;$$

$$1.04 - 0.004 \cdot (0.02 + 0.2 \cdot 0.102 + 1.0) = 1.0358384; \qquad 1.04$$

Exercise 2.4.13.

$1.04 \cdot 10 = 10.4;$	$0.0234 \cdot 10^2 = 2.34;$
$0.10203 \cdot 10^3 = 102.03;$	$1.4 \cdot 10^5 = 140\,000;$
$0.234 \cdot 10^2 = 23.4;$	$0.1203 \cdot 10^9 = 120\,300\,000;$
$1.04 \div 10 = 0.104;$	$0.0234 \div 10^2 = 0.000234;$
$0.10203 \div 10^3 = 0.00010203;$	$1.4 \div 10^5 = 0.000014;$
$2.34 \div 10^2 = 0.0234;$	$0.1203 \div 10^9 = 0.0000000001203$

Exercise 2.4.15.

$1.04 \div 52 = 0.02;$	$1.04 \div 520 = 0.002;$	$1.04 \div 5\,200 = 0.0002;$
$0.0234 \div 234 = 0.0001;$	$2.34 \div 234 = 0.01;$	$0.0234 \div 2\,340 = 0.00001$

Exercise 2.4.17.

$1.04 \div 52 = 0.02;$	$1.04 \div 5.2 = 0.2;$
$1.04 \div 0.52 = 2;$	$0.0234 \div 234 = 0.0001 \approx 0.0;$
$0.0234 \div 23.4 = 0.001;$	$0.0234 \div 2.34 = 0.01;$
$0.0234 \div 0.117 = 0.2;$	$0.103 \div 0.00103 = 100;$
$0.103 \div 10.3 = 0.01;$	$0.103 \div 1.03 = 0.1;$
$0.103 \div 0.0103 = 10;$	$1.4 \div 10.5 \approx 0.133;$
$1.4 \div 1.05 \approx 1.333;$	$1.4 \div 0.105 \approx 13.333;$
$1.4 \div 0.00105 \approx 1333.333;$	$0.0234 \div 1.2 \approx 0.020;$
$0.0234 \div 0.12 \approx 0.195;$	$0.0234 \div 0.00012 \approx 195.0;$
$0.1203 \div 10.9 \approx 0.011;$	$0.1203 \div 1.09 \approx 0.110;$
$0.1203 \div 0.0109 \approx 11.037;$	

$$1.04 - 0.00004 \div (10.4 + 0.26 \div 0.13 + 1.0) \approx 1.040.$$

Exercise 2.4.18.

$1.04 = 104\%;$	$12 = 1\,200\%;$
$1041.2 = 104\,120\%;$	$0.0234 = 2.34\%;$
$10.2 = 1\,020\%;$	$0.3402 = 34.02\%;$
$0.10203\% = 0.0010203 = \frac{10203}{10000000};$	$10.3\% = 0.103 = \frac{103}{1000};$
$2030.3\% = 20.3 = \frac{203}{10};$	$0.00105\% = 0.0000105 = \frac{21}{2000000};$
$1.05\% = 0.0105 = \frac{21}{2000};$	$1.4\% = 0.014 = \frac{7}{500};$
$\frac{1}{4} = 0.25 = 25\%;$	$\frac{11}{400} = 0.00275 = 0.275\%;$
$\frac{13}{4} = 3.25 = 325\%;$	$\frac{21}{50} = 0.42 = 42\%;$
$\frac{11}{25} = 0.44 = 44\%;$	$\frac{17}{20} = 0.85 = 85\%.$

Exercise 2.4.19. \$4\,500.
Exercise 2.4.20. \$600 at 4% and \$00 at 2%.

2.5 Like Terms

2.5.1 Algebraic Expressions

Until now, we have dealt with expressions containing only numbers. In *Algebra* we deal with expressions involving various *indeterminate* symbols, usually Latin, Greek, etc. characters, whose numerical values are either unknown or irrelevant and can be replaced by certain non-numerical symbol. Such *formulas* are called *algebraic expressions*, and in many problems we must evaluate a numerical value of the expression, given the values of indeterminates or parameters, which are in the expression.

Example 2.5.1 *Evaluate the expression* $(3a^2 - b^2) \div (a^2 + b^2 - 2)$, *if* $a = 2$ *and* $b = 3$.

Solution. We straightforwardly substitute the given numbers instead of the corresponding symbols, so that

$$\frac{3a^2 - b^2}{a^2 + b^2 - 2} = \frac{3 \cdot 2^2 - 3^2}{2^2 + 3^2 - 2} = \frac{3 \cdot 4 - 9}{4 + 9 - 2} = \frac{3}{11}.$$

□

Example 2.5.2 *Evaluate the expression* $(a^2 - b^2) \div (a^2 + b^2 - 2)$, *if* $a = b = 1$.

Solution. We proceed in the same way, but now

$$\frac{3a^2 - b^2}{a^2 + b^2 - 2} = \frac{3 \cdot 1^2 - 1^2}{1^2 + 1^2 - 2} = \frac{3 - 1}{1 + 1 - 2} = \frac{2}{0}.$$

Therefore, we arrived at a fraction with zero denominator, and if $a = b = 1$, then the given expression is undefined.   □

Example 2.5.3 *Evaluate the expression* $(a^2 - b^2) \div (a^2 + b^2 - 2)$ *if* $b = 0$.

Solution. No numerical value for a is given, hence the answer will contain this variable as an undefined parameter. We have

$$\frac{3a^2 - b^2}{a^2 + b^2 - 2} = \frac{3 \cdot a^2 - 0^2}{a^2 + 0^2 - 2} = \frac{3a^2}{a^2 - 2}.$$

□

Exercise 2.5.1 *Evaluate the formulas* **(1)** $\frac{4ab}{b-a}$ **(2)** $\frac{2bc}{a^2-b}$ *if* $a = 3$ *and* $b = -1$.

2.5.2   Transposition

If we have a correct statement like $2 = 1 + 1$, and add the same quantity, say 3, to both sides of this equation, we obviously again have a true statement, $2 + 3 = 1 + 1 + 3$, or $5 = 5$. Since subtraction is just the addition of the opposite quantity, we can both add and subtract the same quantity to both sides of an equation without changing its *sense* – the latter means that a true statement remains true and false remains false. This is a crucial property of equations, being known at least since Euclidean time. Let's state it again:

If $a = b$, then for any x, $a + x = b + x$ and $a - x = b - x$.

Since x can be both positive and negative, we do not have to write the second equation here, but it is convenient to have it here explicitly.

This property allows one to *bring over* any term of an equation from one side of the equation to the other side. Indeed, if

$$a + b = c,$$

then by adding $-b$ to both sides of the latter we get $a + b + (-b) = c + (-b)$, and since $a + b + (-b) = a + (b + (-b)) = a + 0 = a$, the equation becomes

$$a = c - b.$$

The property $b + (-b) = b - b$ allows us instead of adding $-b$ to subtract b with the same effect. Either way, we see that the quantity b disappears on the left-hand side of the equation and emerges at the opposite side with the opposite ("-") sign. This procedure is called *transposition*, we *transpose* b from one side to another by *simultaneously changing its sign*. This is a useful shortcut – instead of adding/subtracting a quantity to/from both sides of the equation, we just move this quantity from one side to the other. Just *do not forget to change the sign of the number* transposed.

For example, $3 + 15 = 18$ is definitely true. Transposing 15 to another side, we have $3 = 18 - 15$, which is evidently also true, as well as $15 = 18 - 3$ and $3 + 15 - 18 = 0$. The same true for inequalities of any sense: $3 + 1 \neq 5$, hence $3 \neq 5 - 1$. Or in other words, $3 + 1 < 5$ is a true inequality, thus $3 < 5 - 1$ also is true – the *transposition* can be applied both to equations and to inequalities.

We can transpose not only numbers but also literal expressions. Say, given an equation $a + 2b = -c$, we can add c, which is the additive inverse of $-c$, to both sides of the equation and get $a + 2b + c = -c + c$. Since $-c + c = c - c = 0$ for every c, we have an equivalent equation $a + 2b + c = 0$. Therefore we again observe that the term $-c$ appears on the *opposite side* with the *opposite sign*; for short, we *have transposed* $-c$ to another side of the equation by changing its sign. Whence, the transposition applies to expressions containing indeterminates as well.

Depending upon a problem, we can move different terms of an equation or of an inequality in different directions. For example, the inequality $90p < 456q + 12r$ can be rewritten as $0 < -90p + 456q + 12r$, and as $90p - 456q < 12r$, and as $90p - 456q - 12r < 0$, and as $90p - 12r < 456q$, and in many other ways.

Exercise 2.5.2 (1) *Rewrite the following expressions so that all the indeterminates are on the left side and all numbers on the right side.*

$12 = 908 + 78 - a$	$79 \geq 45 - b - 33$
$37 + 45 - c = -9$	$2 < d + 8$
$67 - f \leq 80 - 6$	$80 - g < 8 + 12$
$2d > k + 78 - h$	$8 \geq l - 33$
$7 \leq 12n - 9m$	$67p < 81q$
$20r \leq 8s - 5t$	$6x < 8y + 3z$

(2) *Rewrite the preceding expressions so that the right-hand side is* 0.

The transposition is useful in solving equations with unknowns. We discuss them in more detail later on; here we only look at a few simple examples. The expressions like $x - 3 = 7$ are called *linear equations in the unknown* x. x is called the *unknown*, because at the moment this is just a symbol, and the problem is to find all the numbers, which after plugging them in instead of x make the equation *true* numerical statement. Thus, in this example, if we choose $x = 2$, then the equation becomes $2 - 3 = 7$, that is, $-1 = 7$, which is false. However, if we choose $x = 10$, then the equation becomes $10 - 3 = 7$, that is, $7 = 7$, which is true. The number 10 is called the *root* or the *solution* of this equation.

When we have already known that $x = 2$ (or any other specific number), x is not unknown anymore, it is a *known quantity* now. Of course, an equation can have several, even infinitely many roots, however, in this example we write "the root" for this equation has the unique root.

We found a root $x = 10$ of the equation by a guess. However, there are infinitely many numbers, and we physically cannot try all of them by the substitution instead of the unknown. Therefore, we need some regular methods for solving mathematical equations. Transposition gives us a convenient method for solving certain equations. Indeed, in the example above, let us transpose the term -3 to the right-hand side of the equation, where it must appear with the " $+$ " sign. So that, we get $x = 7 + 3$, or $x = 10$. Hence, we found the *unique* solution $x = 10$ of the equation without guessing, by simple algebra (transposition).

Exercise 2.5.3 *Solve the following equations for the unknowns presented.*

$90 = g + 70$	$8 = k - 31$
$1 + n = -9$	$7 = 1 - b$
$2 + c = 8 - c$	$x + 6 = 8 + x$
$\|x\| = 3$	$\|x\| = -3.$

Exercise 2.5.4 *Design and solve two more exercises similar to the previous one.*

2.5.3   Combining Like Terms

In this chapter we have started studying *algebra*. We work with expressions containing various *variables*, called also *indeterminates* or *unknowns*.

In arithmetic, if we have a few numbers connected by plus or minus sings, we can compute this expression. In algebra such expressions can sometimes be simplified. The sums or differences of various *terms*, with no regard to the $+$ or $-$ signs, are called *algebraic sums*. However, the terms under consideration have a special structure. We allow only *terms* consisting of two factors, a numerical factor and a variable one. The numerical factor is called the (numerical) *coefficient* of the term. Whence, the products **102**d, $-g$, **7**h, **709**abc $-$**45**k, **331**lx, **3**x^2 $-$**3**n^3, $\frac{1}{2}x^2$ and $-$**9**m^8, with the coefficients (**shown here in bold**) $102, -1, 7, 709, -45, 331, 3, -3, \frac{1}{2}$ and -9 respectively, can be terms of some algebraic expressions.

Given a term of an algebraic expression, the product of indeterminates in this term is called the *variable part* of the term, because replacing the indeterminates with various numbers, we can compute different numerical values of the term. In the examples above, the variable parts are d, g, h, abc k, x, x^2 n^3, x^2 and m^8, respectively. We reiterate that at this stage only indeterminates, that is, single characters, independently upon the font, alphabet, etc., can be factors of variable parts.

Exercise 2.5.5 *Identify the coefficients and variable parts of the following terms.*

$102dg$	$709f$	$357g^4h^6$
$67ab$	$-450cdj^7$	$-56yz$

Exercise 2.5.6 *Design and solve two more exercises similar to the previous one.*

We often have to operate with several terms having the *same variable part* but different coefficients. If there are three students in a classroom, two more students come in, and we are asked how many students are in the classroom now, then everyone, without any hesitation claims that now there are $3 + 2 = 5$ students, since any individual characteristics of the students are immaterial and we are interested only in the property of being a student. In such computations we deal only with the numbers, 3 and 2, that is, with the numerical coefficients.

The terms with the same variable parts are called *like terms*. For example, if we denote a student by an indeterminate s, then in the example above we have two like terms, $3s$ and $2s$, and we found $3s + 2s = 5s$.

This procedure is called *combining like terms*.

Example 2.5.4 *The terms $3xy$, $-3xy$, xy, $-xy$, $13xy$, $\frac{3}{4}xy$ are like terms since these six terms have the same variable part xy, while $3xyz$, x^2 and $3x$ are not like terms. We can simplify $5xyz - 2xyz = 3xyz$, $2xyz - 5xyz = -3xyz$, and $7f - 7f = (7-7)f = 0f = 0$, however, $2xy - 2x$ cannot be simplified, since $2xy$ and $2x$ are NOT like terms. For the most part, we do not write down these small steps explicitly. We can cancel out the like terms with the opposite signs, as follows:*

$$3ab + 2a^2b - 4ab - 5 - 2a^2b = 3ab + \cancel{2a^2b} - 4ab - 5 - \cancel{2a^2b} =$$

$$= 3ab - 4ab - 5 = -ab - 5.$$

□

Exercise 2.5.7 *Separate the following six terms in groups of like terms.*

$$102dg, \quad 709dgf, \quad -357dg, \quad ad, \quad -dg, \quad d^2g$$

Exercise 2.5.8 *Simplify by combining like terms.*

$x - 2y + 8x + 7y =$ $7s + s - s^2 + 8s - 5s - 3s^2 + 4s^3 =$

$-a - 3a^7 + a =$ $2a^2 - a^2 - a^2 =$

$2ab - 8ab + b - 8a =$ $3c + 6d - 8cd + 3d =$

Exercise 2.5.9 *Design and solve two more exercises similar to the previous ones.*

Answers 2.5

Exercise 2.5.1. (1) 3; (2) $-c/5$.
Exercise 2.5.2.

(1)	$a = 974$;	$b \geq -67$;	$c = 91; -d < 6$;	
	$-f \leq 7$;	$-g < -60$;	$2d + h - k > 78$	$-l \geq -41$;
	$9m - 12n \leq -7$;	$67p - 81q < 0$;	$20r + 5t - 8s \leq 0$;	$6x - 8y - 3z < 0$.

(2)	$a - 974 = 0$;	$b + 67 \geq 0$;;	$c - 91 = 0$;	$-d - 6 < 0$;
	$-f - 7 \leq 0$;	$60 - g < 0$;	$2d + h - k - 78 > 0$;	$41 - l \geq 0$;
	$9m - 12n + 7 \leq 0$;	$67p - 81q < 0$;	$20r + 5t - 8s \leq 0$;	$6x - 8y - 3z < 0$.

Exercise 2.5.3.

$g = 20; k = 39; n = -10; b = -6; c = 3;$ No solution; $x = \pm 3;$ No solution .

Exercise 2.5.5.

The coefficient is 102, the variable part is dg
The coefficient is 709, the variable part is f
The coefficient is 357, the variable part is $g^4 h^6$
The coefficient is 67, the variable part is ab
The coefficient is -450, the variable part is cdj^7
The coefficient is -56, the variable part is yz.

Exercise 2.5.7. There is only one group of like terms, $102dg, -357dg,$ and $-dg$.
Exercise 2.5.8.

$x - 2y + 8x + 7y = 9x + 5y; \quad 7s + s - s^2 + 8s - 5s - 3s^2 + 4s^3 = 4s^3 - 4s^2 + 11s;$
$-a - 3a^7 + a = -3a^7; \quad\quad\quad\quad 2a^2 - a^2 - a^2 = 0;$
$2ab - 8ab + b - 8a = -8a + b - 6ab; \quad 3c + 6d - 8cd + 3d = 3c + 9d - 8cd.$

2.6   Linear Equations and Inequalities

2.6.1   Linear Equations

We have already briefly discussed linear equations, now we can study them thoroughly. These equations and corresponding linear inequalities appear in endless applications.

There are many simple problems, where we can appeal to our *common sense* and compute the answer immediately, without any algebra. For instance, if a pizza pie costs \$16, and we want only a half of the pie, we have to pay $\$16 \div 2 = \$8$. However, there are many more problems, where we cannot see the answer immediately, but we can easily compose a certain *relation* between the given pieces of information. Consider an example.

Example 2.6.1 *A pizza pie costs* \$16, *a slice of pizza and a bottle of water each cost* \$2. *How many slices of pizza can we buy at most if we have* \$11, *and we also want to buy a bottle of water and still save* \$1 *for the next morning cup of coffee?*

Surely, we can proceed without any algebra. Indeed, we immediately set aside $1 + 2 = \$3$ for water and coffee, leaving us with $11 - 3 = \$8$. At this point we have enough skills to realize that since $8 = 2 \cdot 4$, we can buy 4 slices of pizza.   □

However, in more advanced problems it is often advantageous to use *algebraic* approach[6].

To solve the previous problem again, this time *algebraically,* let us denote the number of slices, we can buy, as s (for *slice*). The power and beauty of algebraic approach is that we do not know the number of slices yet, but we can *denote* it by any convenient symbol and manipulate this symbol as if it were a number, leading to the solution of the problem. Since each slice costs \$2, then for 2 slices we must pay $2 \cdot 2 = \$4$, for 3 slices we must pay $3 \cdot 2 = \$6$, for 4 slices we must pay $4 \cdot 2 = \$8$, etc.

---

[6]Try, for instance, to solve for x, without using any algebraic tools, the equation $171x - 342 = 1025$.

It is clear now that for s slices we must pay $s \cdot 2 = 2s$ dollars, independently upon the value of s.

Next, to account for drinks, we must add $2 + 1 = \$3$ to these $2s$ dollars, amounting to $2s + 3$ dollars. If we want to spend all the money, we have to set the equation

$$2s + 3 = 11.$$

This equation is called a *linear equation in one unknown*, more specifically, in the unknown s. The meaning of the adjective *linear* will be explained later on We start by discussing a couple of general issues regarding the linear equations.

First of all, a remark about writing is in order. Of course, $2s$ here means $2 \cdot s$, but the formula $2s$ is unambiguous. However, if we have to multiply numbers, say $2 \cdot 4$, we cannot skip a symbol for multiplication; $2 \cdot 4$ is also good, but 24 means a two-digit number, consisting of two tens and four unities, far from $2 \cdot 4 = 8$.

Let us further explore the equation $2s + 3 = 11$. Replace the symbol s in the equation with the number 4; this procedure is called *substitution*, we *substitute*, or *insert*, or *plug in* 4 instead of s. The equation becomes $2 \cdot 4 + 3 = 11$, which is evidently true. However, if we set $s = 3$ in the equation, we get $2 \cdot 3 + 3 = 11$, which is definitely false, since $2 \cdot 3 + 3 = 6 + 3 = 9 \neq 11$.

We observed that some numbers made an equation a *true* numerical statement, while others made is *false*. The former are called the *solutions* or *roots* of the equation. Thus, we see that 4 is a root of the equation $2s + 3 = 11$, while 3 is not a root.

This example shows that we can, if the equation is simple enough, verify whether any given number is a root of the equation by replacing the unknown in all of its occurrences in the equation by the number and comparing the numerical values of the left-hand and the right-hand sides – if these values are equal, the number is a root, otherwise the number is not a root.

Exercise 2.6.1 *Verify whether each of the numbers* $3, 5, -6, -3, 6, -1$ *satisfy (is a root of) any of the following equations,* **(1)** $3x - 5 = 2x$ **(2)** $31(y - 15) = 8y$ **(3)** $3(k - 15) + 40 = 2(4 - k) - 8$.

For example, inserting 3 into the left-hand side of the first equation, we get $3 \cdot 3 - 5 = 9 - 5 = 4$, *while the right-hand side gives us* $2 \cdot 3 = 6$. *Since* $4 \neq 6$, *we conclude that 3 is not a root of this equation.*

Exercise 2.6.2 *Design and solve two more exercises similar to the previous one.*

An equation does not have to have a solution. For example, the equation $x^2 = -1$ *has no real solutions*, since the square of any real number, positive or negative, is a positive number, maybe 0. After these remarks, it is natural to state the following.

To solve an equation means to find all its roots or to prove that the equation has no root at all.

Let us solve a *literal* linear equation

$$a \cdot x + b = c \tag{2.6.1}$$

in unknown x. It is called *literal* because the coefficients are characters rather than numbers. In our initial problems, the *coefficient* of the unknown a and the free terms b and c are given numbers. For instance, the equation $2x = 8$, is a linear equation (2.6.1) with $a = 2$, $b = 0$, and $c = 8$. The equation $2y+3 = 11$ also is a linear equation, now in the unknown y, and $2s + 3 = 4s - 11$ is a linear equation as well, this time in s. The latter is not exactly of kind (2.6.1), but can be reduced to this form. What is important here, is that the unknown x, or y, or s..., in all its occurrences is of first degree, that is, its exponent must everywhere be 1. The equation $2x - 3 = 5 + 6x$ also is a linear equation. The equation $x^2 = 8$ is *not a linear equation*, because the exponent of x is not 1. Nor $2^x = 1$ is a linear equation. It is also immaterial what symbol denotes the unknown, thus, $2x + 3 = 11$ and $2y + 3 = 11$ are linear equations with the same *root* 4.

Now we are ready to develop a general procedure for solving linear equations. Start with a simple example 2.6.1, that is,

$$2s + 3 = 11. \tag{2.6.2}$$

Our goal is to solve the equation, that is, to compute a number a, which makes the equation a true numerical statement. This conclusion is often written as

$$s = a. \tag{2.6.3}$$

If the unknown in the equation were x, or y,..., we would write $x = a$, or $y = a$, etc. To eliminate this dependance upon the symbol of the unknown, it is convenient to introduce *the solution set* $\{a\}$, which shows only the *roots* and does not mention the symbol of the unknown.

We have computed already $a = 4$, now our goal is to develop a general algebraic procedure for solving linear equations like (2.6.1). Equation (2.6.3) tells us that we have to isolate the *unknown*. Thus, we must remove the 3 from the left-hand side, and the transposition was developed exactly for this. So that, we transpose 3 in equation (2.6.2) from left to the right side and deduce a simpler equation with the same root $2s = 11 - 3$, or $2s = 8$.

The latter equation contains $2s$ instead of s that we want. The operation between the coefficient 2 and x is multiplication, and we remember that the inverse of multiplication is division. Therefore, we *divide* now both sides of the latter equation by 2 and get

$$\frac{2s}{2} = \frac{8}{2}.$$

Reducing the fractions, we get $s = 4$, the solution we found before without any algebra. But the *algebraic approach* works in incomparably more complicated problems, where simple "common sense" does not work. Moreover, this algebraic approach can be easily realized on computers. Using the algebraic approach, we gradually, step by step, simplify an equation.

The important lesson here is that, while solving equations, we often use *inverse operations*. At the second to the last step, the equation was $2s = 8$, and we applied division, that is the inverse of multiplication. And the transposition also is the inverse of either addition or subtraction.

Solving our equation above, we arrive at the conclusion $s = 4$. This is a part of mathematical jargon. We do not claim here that the letter s is equal to the number 4. We claim that this number being substituted for the unknown s, makes the initial equation true, that is, 4 is a root of the equation $2s + 3 = 11$. Actually we can write "the root", because our calculations inevitably lead to the number 4, this linear equation has *only* one root, the solution of this equation is *unique*. If we apply the same transformations to the equation $2z + 3 = 11$, where the unknown is denoted by z, we will arrive at the same answer $z = 4$. The solution set of any of these equations is $\{4\}$. It should be remarked that the solution set is a *set*, thus in the latter notation one must use *curly braces*.

Example 2.6.2 *Solve equation (2.6.1).*

Solution. Applying the procedure developed while solving the examples above, first we get the equation $ax = c - b$. Next, we are tempted to divide over a, but this is impossible if $a = 0$. Whence, we have to consider two cases. If $a \neq 0$, we can divide, and the solution is unique, $x = \frac{c-b}{a}$. If $a = 0$, the equation becomes $0 \cdot x = c - b$, or $0 = c - b$ independently on x. Therefore, if $c = b$, the equation is the identity $0 = 0$ independently upon x, thus, any real number is a solution. In the opposite direction, if $c \neq b$, the equation is the contradiction, again independently upon x. □

To solve linear equations, in addition to the transposition, we often are to use another algebraic property. First, let us consider an example.

Example 2.6.3 *Solve linear equation $2 + 3x = 4 - x$.*

Solution. Since the unknown x appears in the equation twice, we first transpose $-x$ from right to the left, getting $2 + 3x + x = 4$ or combining like terms $3x$ and x, to $2 + 4x = 4$. To *isolate* the x-term, we transpose the 2 from left to the right and get the equation $4x = 4 - 2$ or $4x = 2$. We remember that we want to compute x, but so far we have found $4x$. It is clear now that to "un-do" the multiplication, $4 \cdot x$ on the left, we should use its *inverse* operation, that is, division, but we must divide by 4 *both sides of the equation.* Thus we write $4x \div 4 = 2 \div 4$. For calculations it is, maybe, more convenient to write the latter by making use of the fractions, as

$$\frac{4x}{4} = \frac{2}{4}.$$

As in the previous example, we see why this division is useful: we cancel out the 4 on the left and derive an equation $x = \frac{2}{4}$, or after reducing the fraction in the right-hand side, $x = \frac{1}{2}$. Whence, we have found that there is only one number, namely the fraction $\frac{1}{2}$, which *satisfies the equation*. In other words, the *root* of the equation $2 + 3x = 4 - x$ is $\frac{1}{2}$. In other words, the solution set of this equation is a one-element set $\{\frac{1}{2}\}$. □

This procedure is justified by the following property, which we state here without a proof.

Theorem 2.6.1 *If we multiply or divide both sides of an equation by the same non-zero quantity, the resulting equation is equivalent to the initial one, that is, both equations have the same solution set; in particular, either both have a solution, or both have no solution.* □

Example 2.6.4 *Solve equation $2 + 3x = 4 + 3x$.*

Solution. After the transposition, we get $3x - 3x = 4 - 2$ or $0 = 2$. This equation does not contain the unknown at all and represents a false, contradictory statement. There is no way to satisfy this equation, the statement $0 = 2$ is false for *any* number x. Therefore, the equation has no solution, its solution set is the *empty set*, denoted by special symbol $\emptyset$. ☐

Example 2.6.5 *Solve equation* $1 + 2x = 4 + 2x - 3$.

Solution. Now, after the transposition we get $2x - 2x = 4 - 3 - 1$ or $0 = 0$. Similarly to the previous example, there is no unknown here, but the numerical statement $0 = 0$ is true. Therefore, any numerical value of x makes the original equation true, and the solution set of this equation contains all real numbers; the set of real numbers is denoted by **R**. If in the problem we consider *complex numbers*, then the solution set is the set of complex numbers **C**. ☐

Example 2.6.6 *Find three consecutive integers, such that their sum is 90.*

Solution. Let the middle number be x, then the previous number is $x - 1$ and the next, third number is $x + 1$. Their sum is $x - 1 + x + x + 1 = 3x$, and the condition of the problem reads $3x = 90$. From this equation, $x = 90/3 = 30$, and the numbers are $30 - 1 = 29$, 30, $30 + 1 = 31$.

   In some problems it is more convenient to start with the first number and set this number to be, say, k, thus two other numbers are $k + 1$ and $k + 2$, and the equation is $(k) + (k + 1) + (k + 2) = 90$, or $3k + 3 = 90$. Therefore, $3k = 90 - 3 = 87$ and $k = 29$, leading, surely, to the same answer, $k + 1 = 30$ and $k + 2 = 31$, or $\{29, 30, 31\}$. ☐

Example 2.6.7 *Find three consecutive odd integer numbers, such that the sum of the first two of them is 13 more than the third number.*

Solution. Let the first number be n, then the second number is $n + 2$, and the third one is $n + 4$, because the step (the difference) between consecutive odd, or consecutive even integer numbers is 2. The equation is $n + n + 2 = n + 4 + 13$, or $2n + 2 = n + 17$. Transposing the terms and combining like terms, we get $n = 15$, therefore, $n + 2 = 17$ and $n + 4 = 19$; the answer is $\{15, 17, 19\}$. ☐

Example 2.6.8 *Find three consecutive odd integer numbers, such that the sum of the first two of them is 14 more than the third number.*

Solution. Again, let the first number be n, then the second number is $n + 2$, and the third one is $n + 4$. The equation is $n + n + 2 = n + 4 + 14$, or $2n + 2 = n + 18$. Solving this equation, we get $n = 16$. We must be alert and stop here, for 16 *is not an odd* number. Therefore, the problem has no solution. This could be seen from the beginning. Indeed, the sum of an odd and an even number if odd, thus the sum of an odd third number and 14 is odd. On the other hand, the sum of two odd numbers is even, therefore, the left-hand side of this equation cannot be equal to the right-hand side – the equation has no solution. ☐

Exercise 2.6.3 *Solve linear equations.*

$x - 2 = 5$ $5x - 7 = 5x - 8$

$-a - 3 = a + a$ $2a - 2 = 2$

$2b - 8b = b$ $3c - 8c = 15$

$x - 2 = x + 5$ $2x - 2 = 2x + 5 - 3$

$3x - 8 + 4x = 5$ $3x - 7 + 2x = -7 + 5x$

$5x - 7 = 5x - 7$ $7s + s - 2 + 8s = 18 - 5s - 3s + 4s$

$|x| = 7$ $|x| = -2$

$|x| + x = 0$ $|x| - 2x = 1$

Exercise 2.6.4 *A phone call from the International Space Station (ISS) to Houston, TX, costs \$15 for the first 3 min., \$3 for every minute after that, and \$20 space surcharge independently upon the time used.*
   (1) What is the cost of 14-min. call?
   (2) How long was the call If it cost \$335?

Exercise 2.6.5 *What is the number if twice the 'sum of the number and 6 is 9 less than 5 times the number.*

Exercise 2.6.6 *At 2 P.M. John leaves his place and goes north at 4 mph. At the same time from the same point Kate goes south at 3 mph. At what time the distance between them will be 14 miles?*

2.6.2   Interval Notation

To represent some sets of numbers on the number line, it is convenient to use so-called *interval notation*. In section 2.2.1 we considered the number line and its subsets, segments and intervals. We will use the symbol $x \in X$, meaning that x is an *element* of the set X. For instance, since 3 is a natural number, we write $3 \in \mathbb{N}$. Since 0 was *designated* as whole number but not natural, $0 \notin \mathbb{N}$, however, $0 \in \mathbb{W}$. The entire set of real numbers represented by the number line is denoted by the symbol $\mathbb{R}$.

Exercise 2.6.7 *Let $\mathbb{N}$ be the set of natural numbers and $\mathbb{W}$ the set of whole numbers. Replace the ellipsis ... with an appropriate symbol $\in$ or $\notin$ to make the expression true. Explain why or why not an expression is "true".*

$0 \ldots \mathbb{N}$	$6 \ldots \mathbb{N}$	$\frac{2}{3} \ldots \mathbb{N}$	$5 \ldots \mathbb{W}$	$1.5 \ldots \mathbb{N}$
$55 \ldots \mathbb{N}$	$-50 \ldots \mathbb{N}$	$100 \ldots \mathbb{W}$	$10.5 \ldots \mathbb{N}$	$-5 \ldots \mathbb{W}$

The set of all those real numbers, which are *bigger* than a number a and *smaller* than a number b, is called an *open (real) interval* with the end-points a and b and is denoted by (a, b); hence the end-points a and b *are not included* in an open interval. Thus, the decimal $2.3 \in (2, 4)$ and the integer $3 \in (2, 4)$, but $2 \notin (2, 4)$, $4 \notin (2, 4)$, and $1.99 \notin (2, 4)$. *Closed intervals*, containing the end-points a and b, are called *segments* and are denoted by *brackets* $[a, b]$. For instance, $2 \in [2, 4]$ and $4 \in [2, 4]$; all the other inclusions from the previous example remain the same. We can consider *semi-open* (or

Figure 2.13: $0 \in [0, 1)$, $1 \notin [0, 1)$, $\frac{2}{3} \in [0, 1)$.

semi-closed) intervals containing only one of its two end-point; thus $2 \notin (2, 4]$ while $4 \in (2, 4]$.

Of course, we suppose in these definitions that $a \leq b$, otherwise the interval is *empty*; the interval $(1, 1)$ is empty, but $[1, 1]$ contains only one number 1. There is a special symbol $\emptyset$ to signify the empty set, thus, $(1, 1) = \emptyset$, $(1, 1] = \emptyset$, and $[1, 1) = \emptyset$, but $[1, 1] \neq \emptyset$, it contains one element 1.

One or both of the end-points can be *infinite*. For example, $(-\infty, 4)$ stands for the set of all the real numbers *smaller than* 4; this set can be written as $\{x : x < 4\}$. Similarly, $[4, \infty)$ is the set of all real numbers greater than or equal to 4. Since ∞ is just a symbol and not a specific number, any interval on its 'infinite' end is always open and denoted by a parenthesis (or).

Exercise 2.6.8 *Among the following sets of real numbers, which are empty?*

$(0, 9]$	$[7, 6)$	$(0, 1)$	$[5.5, 5.6]$	$(1.4, 1, 4)$
$(0, 0)$	$(-100, 100)$	$(100, 100]$	$[100, 100)$	$[-10, -10]$

Warning. Keep in mind that $0 \notin (0, 9]$, for the elements of the interval $(0, 9]$ are only the strictly positive numbers which are smaller than or equal to 9, but 0 is not a positive number.

Unlike the empty sets $(0, 0)$, $[100, 100)$ and $(100, 100]$, the segment $[-10, -10]$ is not empty, it contains the number -10.

Exercise 2.6.9 *Let $\mathbb{N}$ be the set of natural numbers and $\mathbb{W}$ of whole numbers. Replace the dots ... with an appropriate symbol $\in$ or $\notin$ to make the statements true. For example, $0 \notin (0, 9]$, but $5 \in [5, 5.6]$.*

0 ... $(0, 9]$	6 ... $(1, 6)$	$\frac{2}{3}$ ... $(0, 1)$
5 ... $[5, 5.6]$	1.5 ... $(1.4, 1, 6)$	6 ... $(0, 60)$
-5 ... $(-10, -5]$	-50 ... $(-100, 100)$	10.5 ... $(10.5, 11]$
1 ... $(-\infty, 4)$	-1 ... $(-\infty, -3]$	16.2 ... $[0, \infty)$
-543 ... $(-\infty, \infty)$	-234 ... $[-234, 0)$	6 ... $(6, 60)$
0 ... $[0, 1)$	100 ... $(-100, 100)$	1 ... $[0, 1)$

2.6.3   Linear Inequalities In One Unknown

We considered numerical inequalities in Section 1.3. Similarly to an equation, an inequality can contain an unknown, and we have to find the solutions, that is, those numbers that make the inequality true. Consider, for instance, the inequality $x^2 > 0$. We can immediately realize that if $x = 0$, the inequality becomes $0^2 > 0$ or $0 > 0$, which is false. However, if $x = a \neq 0$, any non-zero positive or negative number, then the square $a^2 > 0$ is strictly positive, thus the inequality becomes true. Therefore, the solution set of this problem consists of all real numbers except for the zero. Quite similarly, all real numbers, now without any exception, satisfy the inequality $x^2 \geq 0$, while the inequality $x^2 < 0$ has no solution at all, its solution set is the empty set.

Whence the situation with inequalities is more complicated than with equations – as we have just observed the solution set of an inequality can be empty, or can contain finitely many numbers, or can be infinite. Here we study *linear* inequalities, containing only first powers of the unknown, for example, $x > 9$ or $3 - 7y \leq 5y + 5$. To solve them, we can use the same machinery that we used for solving *linear equations*, that is, the transposition and combining like terms. However, first of all we are to give an important definition, which was used in the case of equations *implicitly*, and have to learn how to multiply or divide inequalities by a number.

Definition 2.6.1 *Two inequalities (or equations) are called equivalent if they have the same solution set.*

For example, the equations $2x = x + 4$ and $x = 4$ are equivalent, the solution set in both cases is $\{4\}$. The inequalities $x^2 < 0$ and $x^4 < -1$ are equivalent, since both have the empty solution set. The inequalities $x^2 > 0$ and $x^2 \geq 0$ are not equivalent, for the number $x = 0$ satisfies the second inequality but does not satisfy the first one.

Exercise 2.6.10 *Are there equivalent equations among those in Exercise 2.6.3?*

To learn how to multiply or divide the inequalities, let us consider a simple example, say, the inequality $2 > 1$, which is surely *true*. If we multiply *both sides* of the inequality by a *positive* number, for instance, by $+3$, we get $3 \cdot 2 > 3 \cdot 1$, or $6 > 3$, which is again true. However, if we multiply *both sides* of the inequality by a *negative* number -3, we get $(-3) \cdot 2 > (-3) \cdot 1$, or $-6 > -3$, which is *false*. If the original inequality were *false*, then after multiplying by a negative number we would get a true statement. Analyzing such examples, we arrive at the following statement.

Theorem 2.6.2 (1) *If we multiply or divide both sides of an inequality by a (strictly) positive number or an expression, we derive an equivalent inequality, meaning that a true inequality remains a true inequality, and a false inequality remains false.*

(2) *On the contrary, if we multiply or divide both sides of an inequality by a (strictly) negative number or an expression, the resulting inequality has the opposite sense, that is, a true inequality becomes a false inequality, and a false inequality becomes true. Therefore, simultaneously with multiplying or dividing an inequality by a negative number, to get an equivalent inequality, we must change the sign of the inequality for the opposite.* □

For instance, if we have to multiply the true inequality $2 > 1$ by -3, we must flip the inequality symbol and the correct result is $-6 < -3$, which is also true.

Exercise 2.6.11 *Multiply and divide the following inequalities by* (1) *5;* (2) *-5; change the sense of the inequality if necessary.*

$x - 2 > 8x + 5$	$7s + s - 2 + 8s < 18 - 5s - 3s + 4s$
$-a - 3 \geq a + a$	$2a - 2 \leq 2$
$2b - 8b \leq -b$	$3c - 8c \geq 15$
$x - 2 < x + 5$	$2x - 2 > 2x + 5 - 3$

Exercise 2.6.12 *Design and solve two more exercises similar to the previous one.*

Now we show on several examples, how to solve linear inequalities.

Example 2.6.9 *Solve for x the inequality*

$$2x > 4 - x. \tag{2.6.4}$$

Solution. The inequality contains two x−terms. To combine them, we bring the term $-x$ from the right-hand side to the left by changing its sign, and get an equivalent inequality $2x + x > 4$, or $3x > 4$. Now we have to divide by the positive coefficient of x, thus the inequality preserves its sense, and the answer is $x > \frac{4}{3}$ or $\frac{4}{3} < x < \infty$. In interval notation, the solution set is $(\frac{4}{3}, \infty)$. The left boundary of the interval, that is, the number $\frac{4}{3}$ does not satisfy the given inequality, it does not belong to the solution set, that is why the left boundary of the interval is denoted by a parenthesis. □

It is useful to visualize the answer by making use of the number line, see Fig. 2.14.

Figure 2.14: The interval $(\frac{4}{3}, \infty)$ in Example 2.6.9.

Example 2.6.10 *Solve the inequality*

$$2x > 4 + 4x. \tag{2.6.5}$$

Solution. To combine the two x−terms, we again bring the term $4x$ from the right-hand side to the left by changing its sign, and get an equivalent inequality $2x - 4x > 4$, or $-2x > 4$. However, here we have to divide by the *negative* coefficient of x, thus the inequality must be reverted, and the answer is
$x < \frac{4}{-2} = -2$, or $-\infty < x < -2$, which in interval notation is $(-\infty, -2)$, see Fig. 2.15.
To avoid division over a negative number, we can from the beginning transpose the $2x$−term from left to the right and simultaneously transpose the constant term 4 to the left, getting an equivalent inequality $-4 > 4x - 2x$, or $-4 > 2x$, leading after dividing by 2, to the equivalent answer $-2 > x$. Reading the latter from right to the left, we get $x < -2$. □

Figure 2.15: The interval $-\infty < x < -2$ in example 2.6.10.

Analyzing these two examples, we see that solving linear inequalities is no more difficult than that of linear equations. Transposing the terms of the inequality (or equation) and combining like terms, any linear inequality in one unknown can be transformed to one of the following simplest inequalities.

$$(1) \qquad ax > b$$

$$(2) \qquad ax \geq b$$

$$(3) \qquad ax < b$$

$$(4) \qquad ax \leq b$$

where, of course, ax stands for the multiplication, $ax = a \cdot x$, and the coefficients a and b are real numbers. When solving linear equations, after dividing both sides of the equation through by a (presuming that $a \neq 0$), we derive the solution of the equation as $x = b/a$. In the problems with inequalities we must distinguish the two cases, whether the a is positive or a is negative. If $a > 0$, we divide both sides of the inequality over a and find the solutions in the cases (1) - (4) as $x > \frac{b}{a}$, $x \geq \frac{b}{a}$, $x < \frac{b}{a}$, $x \leq \frac{b}{a}$, respectively. If $a < 0$, we also divide both sides of the inequality over a, however we have to revert the inequality sign; the solutions in the cases (1) - (4) are now $x < \frac{b}{a}$, $x \leq \frac{b}{a}$, $x > \frac{b}{a}$, $x \geq \frac{b}{a}$, respectively.

Problem 2.6.1 *Solve the inequalities (1) - (4) above in the special case $a = 0$.*

For example, in case (1) we have $0 \cdot x > b$, that is, $0 > b$. Thus, if $b \geq 0$, the inequality $0 > b$ has no solution since we require zero to be bigger than itself or than a positive number. However, if $b < 0$, we require zero to be larger than a negative number, which is always true – therefore in this case any real number satisfies the inequality $0 \cdot x > b$.

The other three cases (2) - (4) are left as exercises for the reader.

Exercise 2.6.13 *Solve the following inequalities; give the answers in interval notation; graph the solution sets on the number line.*

$x - 2 > 8x + 5$	$7s + s - 2 + 8s < 18 - 5s - 3s + 4s$
$-a - 3 \geq a + a$	$2a - 2 \leq 2$
$2b - 8b \leq b$	$3c - 8c \geq 15$
$x - 2 < x + 5$	$2x - 2 > 2x + 5 - 3$
$|x| > 0$	$|x| \geq 0$
$|x| < 0$	$|x| < 1$
$|x| \geq 1$	$|x + 1| > 2$
$-6 \leq x + 2 < 9$	$5 > 2x - 3 \geq -4$

Exercise 2.6.14 *Design and solve two more exercises similar to the previous one.*

2.6.4 Operations with Powers. Negative Exponents

Consider two powers with the same base $b > 0$, say, b^2 and b^3. Since $b^2 = b \cdot b$ and $b^3 = b \cdot b \cdot b$, then while multiplying $b^2 \cdot b^3$, we have

$$b^2 \cdot b^3 = (b \cdot b) \cdot (b \cdot b \cdot b) = b \cdot b \cdot b \cdot b \cdot b = b^5.$$

It is evident from this example, that for any positive integer exponents k and l,

$$b^k \cdot b^l = b^{k+l}.$$

Using some calculus, one can prove that this rule holds good for any real, not only natural, exponents k and l.

Theorem 2.6.3 *To multiply powers with the same base, we must raise the base to the sum of the exponents.* □

For example, $b^{12} \cdot b^{13} = b^{25}$.

Let us now divide b^3 over b^2. We have

$$\frac{b^3}{b^2} = \frac{b \cdot b \cdot b}{b \cdot b},$$

and we can cancel exactly two factors of b, since there are only two such factors in the denominator; thus,

$$\frac{b^3}{b^2} = \frac{b \cdot b \cdot b}{b \cdot b} = b = b^{3-2}.$$

Generalizing this example, we arrive at the next *rule*.

Theorem 2.6.4 *To divide powers with the same base, we must subtract the exponents:*

$$\frac{b^k}{b^l} = b^{k-l}.$$

□

What happens if $l > k$? Again, we start by considering an example. Let us divide $b^3 \div b^5$; we have

$$\frac{b^3}{b^5} = \frac{b \cdot b \cdot b}{b \cdot b \cdot b \cdot b \cdot b},$$

and after canceling out $b^3 = b \cdot b \cdot b$, we have

$$\frac{b^3}{b^5} = \frac{1}{b \cdot b} = \frac{1}{b^2},$$

while by the previous rule it should be $\frac{b^3}{b^5} = b^{3-5} = b^{-2}$. Comparing the two expressions, the latter and $\frac{1}{b^2}$, we see that it makes sense to *define*[7] the powers with negative exponents as follows.

Definition 2.6.2 *For any base $b > 0$ and for any exponent $k \geq 0$,*

$$b^{-k} = \frac{1}{b^k}.$$

For instance, $2^{-3} = \frac{1}{2^3} = \frac{1}{8}$ and

$$\frac{1}{2^{-3}} = 1 \div \frac{1}{2^3} = 2^3 = 8.$$

If the exponent is an integer, we can consider powers with a negative base, for example, $(-3)^{-2} = \frac{1}{(-3)^2} = \frac{1}{9}$. However, in general, in the case of negative exponents, we

---

[7]Because we cannot prove it in the "Primer".

consider only powers with positive bases.

Keeping this definition in mind, we see that the following division rule is valid for any real exponents k and l:

To divide powers with the same base, we must subtract the exponents.

Example 2.6.11 *Compute* -10^2, $(-10)^2$, $(-10)^{-4}$, -10^{-4}, $(-10)^{-3}$, -10^{-3}.

Solution. $-10^2 = -10 \cdot 10 = -100$ – here the base is positive 10 and the whole power must be negated. However, $(-10)^2 = (-10) \cdot (-10) = 100$, since the parentheses indicate that the base of the power is the *negative* number -10. In the same fashion, $(-10)^{-4} = \frac{1}{(-10)^4} = \frac{1}{10\,000}$, $-10^{-4} = -\frac{1}{10\,000}$, $(-10)^{-3} = \frac{1}{(-10)^3} = -\frac{1}{1\,000}$, and also $-10^{-3} = -\frac{1}{1\,000}$. $\square$

Remark 2.6.1 *Use these examples to analyze the relationship between positive and/or negative bases, on the one hand, and the parity of the exponents, on the other hand.*

Exercise 2.6.15 *Compute the powers.*

$10^2 \div 10 =$	$10^2 \div 10^0 =$	$10^{12} \div 10^{-6} =$
$(-10)^2 \div 10^3 =$	$-10^2 \div 10^{-2} =$	$10^2 \div (-10)^{-4} =$
$10^{-3} \div 10^9 =$	$10^{-1} \div 10^{-5} =$	$10^6 \div 10^{-4} =$
$10^2 \div 10^{-5} =$		

2.6.5   Scientific Notation

The so-called *scientific notation* is no more and no less scientific than any other notations we have used before or we will use later, it is just a convenient way to write very big or very small numbers, or decimals with too many digits to the right of the decimal dot. For example, the mass of Earth is

$$\approx 59\,722\,000\,000\,000\,000\,000\,000\,000\,kg,$$

while the rest mass of electron is

$$\approx 0.000\,000\,000\,000\,000\,000\,000\,000\,000\,001 kg,$$

and both these numbers are extremely inconvenient to use in computations. However, in scientific notation these numbers are easy to handle:

$$59\,722\,000\,000\,000\,000\,000\,000\,000 \approx 59\,722 \cdot 10^{24}$$

and

$$0.000\,000\,000\,000\,000\,000\,000\,000\,000\,001 \approx 1 \cdot 10^{-30}.$$

The name "scientific" is used, because these representations of numbers are often used in sciences. When a calculator is used, you often see on its screen the answer shown in scientific notation.

Definition 2.6.3 *A positive number A is said to be written in scientific notation if it is represented as the product*

$$A = a \times 10^k,$$

where the exponent k is an integer number, positive, negative or zero, and the factor a satisfies $1 \leq a < 10$.

Example 2.6.12 *The decimal 230.004 can be written in many different ways, for example, as*

$$230.004 = 23.0004 \times 10 = 2.30004 \times 10^2 = 0.230004 \times 10^3 = 2300.04 \times 10^{-1}, \ldots$$

but only $230.004 = 2.30004 \times 10^2$ gives its scientific notation. As another example, we consider the number 0.000305, which representation in scientific notation is

$$0.000305 = 3.05 \times 10^{-4}.$$ □

Example 2.6.13 *As another example, we compute*

$$43.18 \div 10^{-4} \times 10^5 = 43.18 \div 0.0001 \times 100\,000$$

$$= 0.004318 \times 100\,000 = 431.8.$$

□

Exercise 2.6.16 *Compute and write the answer in scientific notation.*

$10^2 \times 0.010203 \div 10 =$	$10^2 \div 10 =$
$12.098 \div 10^{-6} =$	$-10.123 \div 10^3 =$
$10^2 \div 100 =$	$31.09 \times 10^2 \div (-10)^{-4} =$
$54.098 \times 10^{-3} \div 10^9 =$	$54.098 \times 10^{-3} \times 10^{-9} =$

Exercise 2.6.17 *Design and solve two more exercises similar to the previous one.*

Answers 2.6

Exercise 2.6.1. There is only one match: 5 satisfies the first equation $3x - 5 = 2x$.
Exercise 2.6.3. $x = 7$; No solution; $a = -1$; $a = 2$;
$b = 0$; $c = -3$; No solution; No solution;
$x = 13/7$; Infinitely many solutions; Infinitely many solutions; $s = 1$
Exercise 2.6.4. (1) \$68; (2) 103 min.
Exercise 2.6.5. The number is 7.
Exercise 2.6.6. At 4 P.M.
Exercise 2.6.7.

$$0 \notin \mathbb{N}; \quad 6 \in \mathbb{N}; \quad \tfrac{2}{3} \notin \mathbb{N}; 5 \in \mathbb{W}; \quad 1.5 \notin \mathbb{N};$$
$$55 \in \mathbb{N}; \quad -50 \notin \mathbb{N}; \quad 100 \in \mathbb{W}; \quad 10.5 \notin \mathbb{N}; \quad -5 \notin \mathbb{W}.$$

Exercise 2.6.8. $(7,6) = \emptyset$; $(100,100] = \emptyset$; $(-10,-10) = \emptyset$.
Exercise 2.6.9.

$$0 \notin (0,9]; \qquad 6 \notin (1,6); \qquad \tfrac{2}{3} \in (0,1); \qquad 5 \in [5,5.6];$$
$$1.5 \in (1.4,1,6); \qquad 6 \in (0,60); \qquad -5 \in (-10,-5] \qquad -50 \in (-100,100)$$
$$10.5 \notin (10.5,11] \qquad 1 \in (-\infty,4) \qquad -1 \notin (-\infty,-3] \qquad 16.2 \in (0,\infty);$$
$$-543 \in (-\infty,\infty); \qquad -234 \in [-234,0); \quad 6 \notin (6,60); \qquad 0 \in [0,1;\,)$$
$$100 \notin (-100,100); \quad 1 \notin [0,1).$$

Exercise 2.6.10. All the equations with no solution are equivalent to one another. Another family of mutually equivalent equations consists of the identities – equations whose solution set consists of all real numbers.

Exercise 2.6.11. $5x - 10 > 40x + 25$ but $-5x + 10 < -40x - 25$.

Exercise 2.6.13.

$x < -1$ or $x \in (-\infty, -1)$; $s < 1$ or $s \in (-\infty, 1)$;

$a \leq -1$ or $a \in (-\infty, -1]$; $a \leq 2$ or $a \in (-\infty, 2]$;

$b \geq 0$ or $b \in [0, \infty)$; $c \leq -3$ or $c \in (-\infty, -3]$;

$(-\infty, \infty)$, i.e., all real numbers; $\emptyset$, i.e., no solution;

$x \in [-8, 7)$; $[-1/2, 4)$.

Exercise 2.6.15.

$10^2 \div 10 = 10$ $10^2 \div 10^0 = 10^2 = 100$

$10^{12} \div 10^{-6} = 10^{18}$ $(-10)^2 \div 10^3 = 10^{-1} = 0.1$

$-10^2 \div 10^{-2} = -10^4 = -10\,000$ $10^2 \div (-10)^{-4} = 10^6 = 1\,000\,000$

$10^{-3} \div 10^9 = 10^{-12}$ $10^{-1} \div 10^{-5} = 10\,000$

$10^6 \div 10^{-4} = 10^{10}$ $10^2 \div 10^{-5} = 10\,000\,000$

Exercise 2.6.16.

$10^2 \times 0.010203 \div 10 = 1.0203 \times 10^{-1}$; $10^2 \div 10 = 1.0 \times 10$;

$12.098 \div 10^{-6} = 1.2098 \times 10^7$; $-10.123 \div 10^3 = -1.0123 \times 10^{-2}$;

$10^2 \div 100 = 1 = 1.0 \times 10^0$; $31.09 \times 10^2 \div (-10)^{-4} = 3.109 \times 10^7$;

$54.098 \times 10^{-3} \div 10^9 = 5.4098 \times 10^{-11}$; $54.098 \times 10^{-3} \times 10^{-9} = 5.4098 \times 10^{-11}$.

2.7 Arithmetic Operations With Mixed Units

Problems often contain different units of the same quantity, for example, time is measured in both hours and minutes, angles are given in degrees and radians, etc. In such cases we must be careful to change the data into one unit; the choice is usually based on the convenience and simplicity of computations. Let us practice.

Example 2.7.1 *A prepaid SIM card is good for 2 hrs and 30 min. You spoke with your friend for 37 min. 19 sec. How much time is left on the card?*

Solution. We have to subtract 37 min. 19 sec. from 2 hrs 30 min. A universal approach is to convert everything into seconds. Of course, we can use hours or minutes, but this would involve fractions, which is less convenient. So that, 2 hrs and 30 min. is $2 \cdot 60 + 30 = 150$ minutes. in turn, this is $150 \cdot 60 = 9\,000$ seconds. On the other hand, 37 min. and 19 sec, is $37 \cdot 60 + 19 = 2239$ seconds. Now the subtraction is simple, $9000 - 2239 = 6761$ seconds. It is natural now to change the answer into bigger units. Thus, first we divide by 60 with remainder, $6761 = 112\frac{41}{60}$, or 112 min. and 41 sec. In turn, 112 min is 1 hr and 52 min., therefore, the time left is 1 hr. 52 min. and 41 sec. □

Example 2.7.2 *The carpenter cut 2 ft 4 in piece from a 2 yd board. what is the length of the piece left?*

Solution. to avoid fractions, we again move to inches. The basic relations are 1 yd = 3 ft and 1 ft = 12 in, hence 1 yd = 3 · 12 = 36 in. Thus, the initial board is 2 · 36 = 72 inches, and the first piece is 2 · 12 + 4 = 28 inches. Now, the remaining piece is 72 − 28 = 44 inches or, if we prefer, since 44 ÷ 12 = $3\frac{8}{12}$, 3 ft and 8 in.   □

Example 2.7.3 *A standard A4 sheet of paper has measurements* 210mm · 297mm. *A student has chosen the size of printing area as* $7\frac{1}{2}in \cdot 9\frac{2}{3}in$. *What part of the total paper area is occupied by the text?*

Solution. Let us choose the units to use. Suppose we want to use decimal units, then we are to change inches to millimeters. Since 1 inch = 2.54 cm = 25.4 mm, we have

$$7\frac{1}{2} \cdot 25.4 = 190\frac{1}{2} \text{ mm}$$

and

$$9\frac{2}{3} \cdot 25.4 = 245\frac{8}{15} \text{ mm}.$$

The area of a rectangle is the product of its sides, thus, the printing area is

$$190.5 \cdot 245\frac{8}{15} = 46774.1 \text{ sq. mm.}$$

Since the total paper area is 210 · 297 = 62370 sq. mm, the printing area occupies 46774.1 ÷ 62370 = 0.7499 ≈ 0.75 = 75%.   □

Problem 2.7.1 *A car moving with speed of 65 mph, has to travel 100 km. A cyclist with the speed of 32 km per hour, has to travel 18 miles. Who finish the race faster?*

Chapter 3

Radicals and Irrational Numbers

We started the "Primer" with natural numbers and gradually expanded this number set to positive and negative integers and to rational numbers. However in many problems, for example, if we want to solve an equation $x^2 = 2$, we must expand the number world even further and introduce *irrational numbers*, considered in this chapter.

We study here some basic algebraic properties of radicals, and review also a few results, which are important in calculus.

3.1 Square Roots and Beyond

In Section 1.9 we studied the squaring, that is, the operation $a \mapsto a^2$ that puts into correspondence to every number a its square a^2. Now we are to construct the inverse operation to a^2; this operation is denoted by the symbol $\sqrt{\ }$, called *square root* or square *radical*. Let us consider the infinite sequence of all whole numbers,

$$0, 1, 2, 3, 4, 5, 6, 7, 8, 9, 10, 11, 12, 13, \ldots$$

Some of them, like $0 = 0^2, 1 = 1^2, 4 = 2^2, 9 = 3^2, 16 = 4^2, 25 = 5^2, \ldots$ are squares of integer numbers and called the *perfect squares*; for example, $9, 25, 36, 49, 100, 225$ are perfect squares, while 7 and 101 are not. Since every integer can be squared, the sequence of perfect squares is *infinite* together with the integers themselves.

Exercise 3.1.1 *Separate the sequence* $0, 1, 2, 3, \ldots, 99, 100, 101$ *of the first 102 whole numbers into two subsequences, the sequence of perfect squares and that of non-squares. How many terms are in each of these sets?*

Problem 3.1.1 *Here is a more difficult question: What sequence do you think is longer, the sequence of integers or the sequence of perfect squares?*

Definition 3.1.1 *Consider two positive numbers a and b, such that b is the square of a, that is*

$$b = a^2. \tag{3.1.1}$$

The positive number a is called the (principal) square root of b and is denoted by

$$a = \sqrt{b}. \tag{3.1.2}$$

The symbol $\sqrt{b}$ is also called the square radical of b and the quantity b the radicand of this radical.

Example 3.1.1 *For instance, $5 = \sqrt{25}$ since $5^2 = 25$, and $8 = \sqrt{64}$ since $8^2 = 64$. Next, $\left(\frac{1}{2}\right)^2 = \frac{1}{4}$, therefore, $\sqrt{\frac{1}{4}} = \frac{1}{2}$; $\left(\frac{2}{3}\right)^2 = \frac{4}{9}$, therefore, $\sqrt{\frac{4}{9}} = \frac{2}{3}$. We also have $0 = \sqrt{0}$ since $0^2 = 0$, and $\sqrt{1} = 1$.* □

A few smallest *perfect squares* are listed in the following exercise.

Exercise 3.1.2 *Compute.*

$\sqrt{0} =$	$\sqrt{1} =$	$\sqrt{4} =$	$\sqrt{9} =$
$\sqrt{16} =$	$\sqrt{25} =$	$\sqrt{36} =$	$\sqrt{49} =$
$\sqrt{64} =$	$\sqrt{81} =$	$\sqrt{100} =$	$\sqrt{121} =$
$\sqrt{144} =$	$\sqrt{169} =$	$\sqrt{196} =$	$\sqrt{225} =$

By definition 3.1.1, the equation $a^2 = b$ for $a \geq 0$ implies that $\sqrt{b} = a$ and vice versa, thus we can combine these equations together and write $\sqrt{a^2} = a$. Moreover, if we square both sides of the former equation and eliminate a, then we have $\left(\sqrt{b}\right)^2 = b$. We know that the square of any real number b is positive or zero, $b^2 \geq 0$, that is why in the definition we require the radicand b to be non-negative, $b \geq 0$.

Later on you will learn that square roots of negative numbers also exist, but those are not real numbers. These are quantities of new nature. When many centuries back people discovered some problems leading to the square roots of negative numbers, it was difficult to even *imagine* what are these new numbers. Eventually, these new quantities, like $\sqrt{-1}$, were called *imaginary* or *complex numbers*.

In all these examples the radicands were perfect squares, and we see that $\sqrt{0} = 0 < \sqrt{1} = 1 < \sqrt{4} = 2 < \sqrt{9} = 3 < \cdots$. Thus we can presume[1] that if $0 \leq a < b$, then $\sqrt{a} < \sqrt{b}$. Now, what about $\sqrt{2}$? By the preceding observation, since $1 < 2 < 4$, the number $\sqrt{2}$ must be between $\sqrt{1} = 1$ and $\sqrt{4} = 2$. However, there is no integer number between 1 and 2, therefore, together with Pythagoras, we must make a huge intellectual leap forward and assume that the number $\sqrt{2}$, which represents the side of a square of area 2, cannot be an integer.

But do these "numbers", whatever they are, exist? Yes, they exist in specific mathematical sense. It turns out that numbers like $\sqrt{2}$, $\sqrt{3}$, $\sqrt{5}$ and other radicals, where the radicand is not a perfect square, are *infinite, non-periodical, non-truncating* decimals, they are called *irrational* numbers. As an example, we prove now that $\sqrt{2}$ cannot be a fraction, thus it is an irrational number. For that we need the following observation.

Let us look again at the squares of several natural numbers, $1^2 = 1$, $2^2 = 4$, $3^2 = 9$, $4^2 = 16$, $5^2 = 25, \ldots$, etc. One immediately observes that the square of an odd number is also odd, while the square of an even number is also even. Of course the observation of several examples, even from much bigger sample *cannot* prove a

---

[1]This is correct, but a proof requires more advanced mathematics.

statement about infinitely many numbers. However, this observation is true and can be proved.

Problem 3.1.2 *Prove that every even integer n can be written as $n = 2k$, where k is another integer, and that every odd integer m can be represented as $m = 2l + 1$, where l is also an integer.*

Problem 3.1.3 *Use the representations $2k$ for even numbers and $2k+1$ for odd numbers to prove that the square of an even number is even and the square of an odd number is odd. Moreover, the converse is also true, that is, if a perfect square a^2 is even, then a is even and if a perfect square a^2 is odd, then a is also odd.*

Theorem 3.1.1 *There exists no rational number $\frac{a}{b}$, such that $\sqrt{2} = \frac{a}{b}$.*

Proof. We give this proof as an example of one of the oldest and most beautiful proofs in mathematics. The proof is by *contradiction*. This means that we assume the opposite, that is, that $\sqrt{2}$ can be written as a fraction, say $\sqrt{2} = \frac{a}{b}$, where a and b are positive integer numbers, and show that this assumption leads to contradiction. First of all, we reduce the fraction $\frac{a}{b}$ to the lowest terms. That is, we cancel out all the common factors, if there are any, in the fraction $\frac{a}{b}$, and write the reduced fraction is $\frac{p}{q}$.

So that we assume that $\sqrt{2} = \frac{p}{q}$, where p and q are mutually prime positive integers. Clearing the denominator, we write the latter as $q\sqrt{2} = p$. Now we square both sides of this equation and since $\left(\sqrt{2}\right)^2 = 2$, we get $2q^2 = p^2$. The left-hand side of the latter equation contains a factor of 2, thus it definitely is an even number. Hence the right-hand side, p^2, also is an even number. But we have proved in Problem 3.1.2 that in this case the p itself is an even number. Since any even number can be written as $p = 2r$, we have $p^2 = (2r)^2 = 4r^2$. Combining this with the equation $2q^2 = p^2$, we derive the equation $2q^2 = 4r^2$. Canceling out the 2 on both sides, we get $q^2 = 2r^2$. Now we observe that q^2 is even, and by the same reasoning we conclude that q itself is even, thus $q = 2s$. Therefore, we derived the two equations, $p = 2r$ and $q = 2s$, telling us that the numbers p and q have a common factor 2. But this is a contradiction, because we started our proof by assuming that the numbers p and q are mutually prime. This contradiction proves that $\sqrt{2}$ cannot be represented by a fraction with integer terms. □

Problem 3.1.4 *Prove that $\sqrt{3}$ and $\sqrt{5}$ are not rational numbers.*

Problem 3.1.5 *Apply this method to $\sqrt{4}$ and $\sqrt{9}$ and explain what you discover.*

If we try to compute $\sqrt{2}$ by making use of a calculator, we will get something like $\sqrt{2} = 1.41421$ – nothing infinite here. There is no mystery and no error, the decimal 1.41421 is not the precise value of $\sqrt{2}$, this is only an approximation; we can write $\sqrt{2} \approx 1.41421$. Using computers, one can find as many digits of $\sqrt{2}$ as is necessary, but nobody can compute all infinitely many digits of this or any other irrational number. In Section 3.4 we will learn how to compute a few digits of $\sqrt{2}$ or the square root of any other positive integer number.

Exercise 3.1.3 *Use a calculator to find $\sqrt{14}$, $\sqrt{\frac{1}{625}}$, $\sqrt{\frac{9}{1234567891011121314}}$ and try to determine whether you see the precise result or an approximation.*

We have to perform the arithmetic operations with irrational numbers. In general, the sum, difference, product, and ratio of two irrational numbers is again irrational, even though the proof is not elementary. In mathematical parlance, "in general" means that there may be some exceptions; for example, $\sqrt{2} + (2 - \sqrt{2}) = \sqrt{2} + 2 - \sqrt{2} = 2$, which is an integer number. All rational and irrational numbers together make the set of *real numbers*. Every point of the number line represents a real number, either rational or irrational. And vice versa, exactly as we have done with the integers, for any real number we can find the corresponding point on the number line.

3.1.1   Properties of Square Roots

Let us study some properties of the square roots. We know that $\sqrt{9} = \sqrt{3^2} = 3$. However, together with $9 = 3^2$, we also have $9 = (-3)^2$. We *must remember* that $\sqrt{9} = 3$ only, because by the definition, the symbol $\sqrt{a}$ can be only positive (or zero); if a is a positive real number, then the radical $\sqrt{a}$ is *never negative*. It is *wrong* to write $\sqrt{4} = -2$, but we can write $-\sqrt{4} = -2$, $\sqrt{(-169)^2} = \sqrt{(169)^2} = 169$, but $\sqrt{(-169)^2} \neq -169$.

Example 3.1.2 $\sqrt{|-9|} = 3$, $-\sqrt{9} = -3$, $|-\sqrt{9}| = 3$.   □

Exercise 3.1.4 *Compute or write "not a real number"; for the time being, until we learn complex numbers, "undefined" is also acceptable.*

$-\sqrt{0} =$ $\sqrt{-1} =$ $-\sqrt{4} =$ $\sqrt{|9|} =$

$\sqrt{|-16|} =$ $-\sqrt{|-25|} =$ $|\sqrt{|-36|}| =$ $\sqrt{-49} =$

$|-\sqrt{64}| =$ $\sqrt{81} =$ $\sqrt{100 - 36} =$ $\sqrt{121 - 122} =$

$\sqrt{144^2} =$ $\sqrt{(-169)^2} =$ $-\sqrt{(-196)^2} =$ $\sqrt{225} =$

Consider now the true equation $\sqrt{36} = 6$. Since $36 = 4 \cdot 9$ and $6 = 2 \cdot 3$, we have $\sqrt{4} \cdot \sqrt{9} = 2 \cdot 3 = 6$ as before, leading us to a guess that $\sqrt{a \cdot b} = \sqrt{a} \cdot \sqrt{b}$; this property is valid for any nonnegative a and b:

$$\sqrt{a \cdot b} = \sqrt{a} \cdot \sqrt{b} \text{ for any } a \geq 0,\ b \geq 0.$$

The left-hand side of the latter makes sense also if simultaneously $a < 0$ and $b < 0$, but then the right-hand side of the equation is not a real number at all. In this case, the equation must be changed as $\sqrt{a \cdot b} = \sqrt{|a|} \cdot \sqrt{|b|}$, where $|x|$ stands for the absolute value of a number x. A similar property connects the square roots and fractions:

$$\sqrt{\frac{a}{b}} = \frac{\sqrt{a}}{\sqrt{b}} \text{ for any } a \geq 0,\ b > 0,$$

and

$$\sqrt{\frac{a}{b}} = \frac{\sqrt{|a|}}{\sqrt{|b|}} \text{ for any } a \leq 0,\ b < 0.$$

Warning. We reiterate that if $a < 0$ or we do not know the sign of a, we must write

$$\sqrt{a^2} = |a|.$$

For example, $\sqrt{(-4)^2} = |-4| = 4$, but $\sqrt{-4^2} = \sqrt{-16}$ is not a real number.

In certain problems it is useful to apply these equations from right to left, that is, as

$$\sqrt{a} \cdot \sqrt{b} = \sqrt{a \cdot b},$$

and

$$\frac{\sqrt{a}}{\sqrt{b}} = \sqrt{\frac{a}{b}}$$

for appropriate a and b. We will employ the latter two equations more than once in the sequel.

We can say that the radicals *distribute* with respect to the multiplication and division of *positive* numbers. However, please be aware that there is no simple connection between radicals and addition or subtraction. In particular, this "distributive" property of square roots is NOT VALID for addition or subtraction. Indeed, let us compute

$$\sqrt{9 + 16} = \sqrt{25} = 5,$$

while $\sqrt{9} = 3$, $\sqrt{16} = 4$, thus

$$\sqrt{9} + \sqrt{16} = 3 + 4 = 7 \neq 5 = \sqrt{9 + 16}.$$

The two properties connecting the radicals with multiplication and division, allow us to simplify many radicals. Consider, for example, $\sqrt{12}$. Since $12 = 4 \cdot 3$, we can write $\sqrt{12} = \sqrt{4 \cdot 3} = \sqrt{4} \cdot \sqrt{3}$. The 3 is not a perfect square, so that $\sqrt{3}$ cannot be simplified, but $\sqrt{4} = 2$ and finally we get $\sqrt{12} = 2 \cdot \sqrt{3} = 2\sqrt{3}$.

In the same way,

$$\sqrt{\frac{27}{25}} = \frac{\sqrt{27}}{\sqrt{25}} = \frac{\sqrt{9 \cdot 3}}{5} = \frac{3 \cdot \sqrt{3}}{5}.$$

We have said that $2 \cdot \sqrt{3}$ is simpler than $\sqrt{12}$. The term *simplify* may have many different meanings. In particular, a radical without fractions in the radicand is said to be in *simplest radical form* if all those factors of the radicand, which are perfect squares, moved out of the radical as in the example above, that is, simplified to $\sqrt{a^2} = a$. Certainly, in some problems we may prefer to write $\sqrt{25}$ instead of 5, but in most cases 5 is definitely simpler than $\sqrt{25}$; that is why we call this *simplification*.

Exercise 3.1.5 *Simplify.*

$$\sqrt{2^2} = \qquad \sqrt{(-17)^2} = \qquad \sqrt{234^2} = \qquad \sqrt{-2^2}$$

$$\left(\sqrt{3}\right)^2 = \qquad \sqrt{(-2)^2} = \qquad \left(\sqrt{453}\right)^2 = \qquad \left(\sqrt{234}\right)^2 =$$

$$\sqrt{8} = \qquad -\sqrt{8} = \qquad \sqrt{98} = \qquad \sqrt{|-32|} =$$

$$|-\sqrt{128}| = \qquad \sqrt{18} = \qquad \sqrt{1000} = \qquad -\sqrt{75} =$$

$$\sqrt{675} = \qquad \sqrt{\tfrac{1}{9}} = \qquad \sqrt{\tfrac{4}{4}} = \qquad \sqrt{\tfrac{9}{4}} =$$

$$\sqrt{\tfrac{100}{144}} = \qquad \sqrt{\tfrac{36}{81}} = \qquad \sqrt{\tfrac{625}{1}} = \qquad \sqrt{\tfrac{1}{625}} =$$

Example 3.1.3 *Compute* $-2 + (-4) \cdot \sqrt{3^2 - 10 \div 2}.$

Solution. Clearly, before adding we must multiply, but the product involves a radical, and the latter is to be calculated first. In the radicand, we start by computing the power, $3^2 = 9$, then we divide, $10 \div 2 = 5$, and finally we subtract these two intermediate results, $3^2 - 10 \div 2 = 9 - 5 = 4$. Thus, the radical computes to $\sqrt{3^2 - 10 \div 2} = \sqrt{9 - 5} = \sqrt{4} = 2$, and now, before adding, we must multiply $(-4) \cdot \sqrt{3^2 - 10 \div 2} = -4 \cdot 2 = -8$. To finish the job, we add $-2 + (-4) \cdot \sqrt{3^2 - 10 \div 2} = -2 + (-8) = -10$.   □

In the following examples we show how to deal with radicals having the same radicand but, maybe, different coefficients – we treat them exactly as like terms.

Example 3.1.4 *Simplify the expression* $\sqrt{75} + \sqrt{80} - \sqrt{27} + \sqrt{36} - 11$.

Solution. The first obvious step is to compute $\sqrt{36} = 6$. The three other radicands are not perfect squares, therefore, we try to factor the radicands. We have $\sqrt{75} = \sqrt{25 \cdot 3} = 5\sqrt{3}$, $\sqrt{80} = \sqrt{16 \cdot 5} = 4\sqrt{5}$, and $\sqrt{27} = \sqrt{9 \cdot 3} = 3\sqrt{3}$, hence the whole expression reads now

$$5\sqrt{3} + 4\sqrt{5} - 3\sqrt{3} + 6 - 11 = 5\sqrt{3} + 4\sqrt{5} - 3\sqrt{3} - 5.$$

We treat the radicals $5\sqrt{3}$ and $3\sqrt{3}$ as like terms, it is the same as $5x - 3x = 2x$. Whence

$$5\sqrt{3} - 3\sqrt{3} = (5 - 3)\sqrt{3} = 2\sqrt{3},$$

and the expression becomes

$$5\sqrt{3} + 2\sqrt{5} - 3\sqrt{3} - 5 = 5\sqrt{3} - 3\sqrt{3} + 2\sqrt{5} - 5 = 2\sqrt{3} + 2\sqrt{5} - 5.$$

Since $3 \neq 5$, $\sqrt{3} \neq \sqrt{5}$ and the radicals $\sqrt{3}$ and $\sqrt{5}$ cannot be considered as like terms, the answer is

$$\sqrt{75} + \sqrt{80} - \sqrt{27} + \sqrt{36} - 11 = 2\sqrt{3} + 2\sqrt{5} - 5.$$

□

Example 3.1.5 *Simplify the expression* $2\sqrt{9} - 3\sqrt{18} + 4\sqrt{72} + 9$.

Solution. We have $2\sqrt{9} - 3\sqrt{18} + 4\sqrt{72} + 9$

$$= 2 \cdot 3 - 3\sqrt{9 \cdot 2} + 4\sqrt{2 \cdot 36} + 9$$

$$= 6 - 3 \cdot 3\sqrt{2} + 4 \cdot 6\sqrt{2} + 9$$

$$= 6 + 9 - 9\sqrt{2} + 24\sqrt{2} = 15 + 15\sqrt{2}.$$

□

Exercise 3.1.6 *Simplify.*

$$\sqrt{8} - \sqrt{8} = \qquad\qquad\qquad \sqrt{8} + \sqrt{8} =$$

$$\sqrt{8} - 2\sqrt{2} = \qquad\qquad\qquad \sqrt{8} - 3\sqrt{2} =$$

$$\sqrt{8} - \sqrt{32} = \qquad\qquad\qquad \sqrt{98} - \sqrt{|-32|} =$$

$$|-\sqrt{128}| + \sqrt{18} = \qquad\qquad \sqrt{1000} - \sqrt{75} + \sqrt{675} =$$

Example 3.1.6 *Simplify* $(2\sqrt{27} - \sqrt{3})(\sqrt{18} - \sqrt{2})$.

Solution. First we reduce the radicals to simplest radical form, $2\sqrt{27} = 2 \cdot 3\sqrt{3} = 6\sqrt{3}$ and $\sqrt{18} = 3\sqrt{2}$. After that we apply the distributive law and multiply radicals as $\sqrt{3} \cdot \sqrt{2} = \sqrt{6}$, etc.,

$$(2\sqrt{27} - \sqrt{3})(\sqrt{18} - \sqrt{2}) = (6\sqrt{3} - \sqrt{3})(3\sqrt{2} - \sqrt{2}) = (5\sqrt{3})(2\sqrt{2}) = 10\sqrt{6}.$$

$\square$

Example 3.1.7 *Simplify* $(2\sqrt{27} - \sqrt{2})(\sqrt{18} + 2\sqrt{3})$.

Solution. As in the previous example, we have $2\sqrt{27} = 6\sqrt{3}$ and $\sqrt{18} = 3\sqrt{2}$, thus

$$(2\sqrt{27} - \sqrt{2})(\sqrt{18} + 2\sqrt{3}) = (6\sqrt{3} - \sqrt{2})(3\sqrt{2} + 2\sqrt{3}).$$

Initially, there is no like terms here, hence we use the distributive rule,

$$(6\sqrt{3} - \sqrt{2})(3\sqrt{2} + 2\sqrt{3}) = 6 \cdot 3\sqrt{3 \cdot 2} + 6 \cdot 2\sqrt{3 \cdot 3} - 3\sqrt{2 \cdot 2} - 2\sqrt{2 \cdot 3}$$

$$= 18\sqrt{6} + 12\sqrt{9} - 3\sqrt{4} - 2\sqrt{6} = 18\sqrt{6} + 12 \cdot 3 - 3 \cdot 2 - 2\sqrt{6}$$

$$= 18\sqrt{6} + 36 - 6 - 2\sqrt{6} = 18\sqrt{6} + 30 - 2\sqrt{6}.$$

Now we get the like terms, $18\sqrt{6} - 2\sqrt{6} = 16\sqrt{6}$, and finally,

$$(2\sqrt{27} - \sqrt{2})(\sqrt{18} + 2\sqrt{3}) = 16\sqrt{6} + 30.$$

$\square$

Example 3.1.8 *Simplify* $(2\sqrt{27} - \sqrt{2})(\sqrt{18} + \sqrt{5})$.

Solution. As in the previous examples, we do $2\sqrt{27} = 6\sqrt{3}$ and $\sqrt{18} = 3\sqrt{2}$. However, there is no like terms, thus

$$(2\sqrt{27} - \sqrt{2})(\sqrt{18} + \sqrt{5}) = (6\sqrt{3} - \sqrt{2})(3\sqrt{2} + \sqrt{5}),$$

and we have to multiply the two factors, using the distributive law,

$$(6\sqrt{3} - \sqrt{2})(3\sqrt{2} + \sqrt{5}) = 6 \cdot 3\sqrt{3 \cdot 2} + 6\sqrt{3 \cdot 5} - 3\sqrt{2 \cdot 2} - \sqrt{2 \cdot 5}$$

$$= 18\sqrt{6} + 6\sqrt{15} - 3\sqrt{4} - \sqrt{10}.$$

Here only the second to the last radical can be simplified, $\sqrt{4} = 2$, $3\sqrt{4} = 3 \cdot 2 = 6$, and the final answer is

$$(2\sqrt{27} - \sqrt{2})(\sqrt{18} + \sqrt{5}) = 18\sqrt{6} + 6\sqrt{15} - 6 - \sqrt{10}.$$

$\square$

Exercise 3.1.7 *By making use of the distributive law, verify the following identity, where a and b are any numbers.*

$$(a - b) \cdot (a + b) = a^2 - b^2 \tag{3.1.3}$$

This identity is useful in many problems. Since any mathematical expression is a "two-way street", the identity can be also useful if we read it *from right to left*, as

The difference of two squares can be factored as the difference of the bases times the sum of these bases.

Exercise 3.1.8 *Factor the following expressions.*

$$x^2 - z^2 = \qquad a^2 - 9c^2 = \qquad d^4 - f^6 = \qquad a^8 - b^8 =$$

Warning. The sum of two squares cannot be factored, unless we use complex numbers.

Another transformation of algebraic fractions, which is useful in certain problems and considered sometimes as simplification, is called the *rationalization* of denominators. This means that given a fraction with radicals in the denominator, we have to find an equivalent fraction whose denominator does not contain any radical.

Example 3.1.9 *Rationalize the denominator of* $\frac{2}{\sqrt{2}}$.

Solution. By making use of the fundamental property of fractions, we multiply both the numerator and denominator of the fraction by $\sqrt{2}$, and get

$$\frac{2}{\sqrt{2}} = \frac{2 \cdot \sqrt{2}}{\sqrt{2} \cdot \sqrt{2}}.$$

Since $\sqrt{2} \cdot \sqrt{2} = (\sqrt{2})^2 = 2$, we have

$$\frac{2}{\sqrt{2}} = \frac{2 \cdot \sqrt{2}}{\sqrt{2} \cdot \sqrt{2}} = \frac{2 \cdot \sqrt{2}}{2} = \sqrt{2}.$$

We could also write $\frac{2}{\sqrt{2}} = \frac{\sqrt{2} \cdot \sqrt{2}}{\sqrt{2}} = \sqrt{2}$. In the same manner, $\frac{2}{\sqrt{3}} = \frac{2\sqrt{3}}{3}$.   □

Example 3.1.10 *Rationalize the denominator of* (1) $\frac{3\sqrt{2}}{\sqrt{5}}$; (2) $\frac{8\sqrt{3}}{3\sqrt{6}}$.

Solution. (1) $\frac{3\sqrt{2}}{\sqrt{5}} = \frac{3\sqrt{2}\sqrt{5}}{\sqrt{5}\sqrt{5}} = \frac{3\sqrt{10}}{5}$.

(2) $\frac{8\sqrt{3}}{3\sqrt{6}} = \frac{8\sqrt{3}\sqrt{6}}{3\sqrt{6}\sqrt{6}} = \frac{8\sqrt{3} \cdot \sqrt{63} \cdot \sqrt{2}}{3(\sqrt{6})^2} = \frac{8\sqrt{2}}{6} = \frac{4\sqrt{2}}{3}$.   □

Example 3.1.11 *Rationalize the denominator of*

$$\frac{3x^2 - 6}{x + \sqrt{2}}.$$

Solution. A simple method of solving this and similar problems is based on the identity (3.1.3), $(a+b)(a-b) = a^2 - b^2$. We factor out the 3 in the numerator and than multiply both the numerator and denominator of the given fraction by the difference $x - \sqrt{2}$ – the latter is called the *conjugate* expression to the denominator $x + \sqrt{2}$. If the denominator were $x - \sqrt{2}$, its conjugate would be $x + \sqrt{2}$. Thus the fraction in the example becomes

$$\frac{3(x^2 - 2)}{x + \sqrt{2}} = \frac{3(x^2 - 2)(x - \sqrt{2})}{(x + \sqrt{2})(x - \sqrt{2})} = \frac{3(x^2 - 2)(x - \sqrt{2})}{x^2 - 2}.$$

At the last step we have used (3.1.3) again:

$$(x + \sqrt{2})(x - \sqrt{2}) = x^2 - (\sqrt{2})^2 = x^2 - 2$$

– now we see how the radicals disappear. Finally we cancel out the common factor $x^2 - 2$ and get the answer $\frac{3x^2 - 6}{x + \sqrt{2}} = 3(x - \sqrt{2})$.   □

Exercise 3.1.9 *Rationalize numerators or denominators.*

$$\frac{3}{\sqrt{5}} = \qquad\qquad \frac{1}{2-\sqrt{2}} = \qquad\qquad \frac{5-\sqrt{2}}{\sqrt{5}} =$$

$$\frac{a+2}{a-\sqrt{3}} = \qquad\qquad \frac{x+\sqrt{2}}{3x-2} = \qquad\qquad \frac{3x-2}{\sqrt{2}} =$$

$$\frac{3x-2}{-3\sqrt{2}} = \qquad\qquad \frac{\sqrt{x}-2}{\sqrt{5}-3\sqrt{2}} = \qquad\qquad \frac{3\sqrt{x}-\sqrt{2a}}{x-3\sqrt{2}} =$$

Problem 3.1.6 *By using the distributive law, prove the following identities, which are also useful in algebraic transformations. Compare them with identity (3.1.3) and develop your own mnemonic rules which simplify memorizing these identities. Learn them by heart, since it makes problem solving faster and easier.*

$$(a - b)^2 = a^2 - 2a \cdot b + b^2 \qquad\qquad\qquad (3.1.4)$$

$$(a + b)^2 = a^2 + 2a \cdot b + b^2 \qquad\qquad\qquad (3.1.5)$$

Similarly to the square roots, we can define radicals of any natural degree. For example, since $2^3 = 8$, we write $\sqrt[3]{8} = 2$; since $2^4 = 16$, we write $\sqrt[4]{16} = 2$, etc.

However, we must remember that there is an essential distinction between *odd-degree* and *even-degree* radicals:

Indeed, unlike even degree, an *odd degree of a negative number is negative*, the odd-degree radicals of negative numbers also are negative, therefore, these are *real* numbers, $\sqrt[3]{-8} = -2$, $\sqrt[5]{-243} = -3$, etc. However, the even-degree roots of negative numbers, similarly to the square roots, are not real numbers.

Exercise 3.1.10 *Calculate.*

$$\sqrt[3]{8} = \qquad\qquad\qquad -\sqrt[3]{-8} = \qquad\qquad\qquad \sqrt[3]{-27} =$$

$$\sqrt[4]{|-81|} = \qquad\qquad |-\sqrt[7]{128}| = \qquad\qquad \sqrt[4]{81} =$$

$$\sqrt[3]{1000} = \qquad\qquad -\sqrt[3]{-125} = \qquad\qquad \sqrt[4]{625} =$$

Exercise 3.1.11 *Simplify. Represent the answer without negative exponents.*

$$\frac{45x^7(y^{-6})^4}{10x^{-2}y^{-13}z^2} = \qquad\qquad \frac{6v^{15}-8v^9-4v^4}{-2v^4} =$$

$$\frac{8k^{12}-20k^5-12k^3}{-4k^3} = \qquad\qquad \frac{12(x^5)^7y^{-6}}{4x^{-3}y^{-31}} =$$

Exercise 3.1.12 *Design and solve two more exercises similar to the previous one.*

Answers 3.1

Exercise 3.1.1. There are 11 perfect squares here: 0, 1, 4, 9, 16, 25, 36, 49, 64, 81, 100, and 91 non-squares.

Exercise 3.1.2.

$$\sqrt{0} = 0; \quad \sqrt{1} = 1; \quad \sqrt{4} = 2; \quad \sqrt{9} = 3; \quad \sqrt{16} = 4; \quad \sqrt{25} = 5;$$
$$\sqrt{36} = 6; \quad \sqrt{49} = 7; \quad \sqrt{64} = 8; \quad \sqrt{81} = 9; \quad \sqrt{100} = 10; \quad \sqrt{121} = 11;$$
$$\sqrt{144} = 12; \quad \sqrt{169} = 13; \quad \sqrt{196} = 14; \quad \sqrt{225} = 15.$$

Exercise 3.1.3. $\sqrt{14} \approx 3.741$, up to the thousandths, it is an approximation.

$\sqrt{\frac{1}{625}} = \frac{1}{25}$, this is an exact value. $\sqrt{\frac{9}{1234567891011121314}} \approx 0.000000003$, this is an approximation.

Exercise 3.1.4.

$-\sqrt{0} = 0;$ $\sqrt{-1} -$ Not real; $-\sqrt{4} = -2;$ $\sqrt{|9|} = 3;$

$\sqrt{|-16|} = 4;$ $-\sqrt{|-25|} = -5;$ $|\sqrt{|-36|}| = 6;$ $\sqrt{-49},$ Not real;

$|-\sqrt{64}| = 8;$ $\sqrt{81} = 9;$ $\sqrt{100-36} = 8;$ $\sqrt{121-122},$ Not real;

$\sqrt{144^2} = 144;$ $\sqrt{(-169)^2} = 169;$ $-\sqrt{(-196)^2} = -196;$ $\sqrt{225} = 15.$

Exercise 3.1.5.

$\sqrt{2^2} = 2;$ $\sqrt{(-17)^2} = 17;$ $\sqrt{234^2} = 234;$ $\sqrt{-2^2} -$ Not real;

$\left(\sqrt{3}\right)^2 = 3;$ $\sqrt{(-2)^2} = 2;$ $\left(\sqrt{453}\right)^2 = 453;$ $\left(\sqrt{234}\right)^2 = 234;$

$\sqrt{8} = 2\sqrt{2};$ $-\sqrt{8} = -2\sqrt{2};$ $\sqrt{98} = 7\sqrt{2};$ $\sqrt{|-32|} = 4\sqrt{2};$

$|-\sqrt{128}| = 8\sqrt{2};$ $\sqrt{18} = 3\sqrt{2};$ $\sqrt{1000} = 10\sqrt{10};$ $-\sqrt{75} = -5\sqrt{3};$

$\sqrt{675} = 15\sqrt{3};$ $\sqrt{\frac{1}{9}} = \frac{1}{3};$ $\sqrt{\frac{4}{4}} = 1;$ $\sqrt{\frac{9}{4}} = \frac{3}{2};$

$\sqrt{\frac{100}{144}} = \frac{5}{6};$ $\sqrt{\frac{36}{81}} = \frac{2}{3};$ $\sqrt{\frac{625}{1}} = 25;$ $\sqrt{\frac{1}{625}} = 1/25.$

Exercise 3.1.6.

$\sqrt{8} - \sqrt{8} = 0;$ $\sqrt{8} + \sqrt{8} = 4\sqrt{2};$

$\sqrt{8} - 2\sqrt{2} = 0;$ $\sqrt{8} - 3\sqrt{2} = -\sqrt{2};$

$\sqrt{8} - \sqrt{32} = -2\sqrt{2};$ $\sqrt{98} - \sqrt{|-32|} = 3\sqrt{2};$

$|-\sqrt{128}| + \sqrt{18} = 11\sqrt{2};$ $\sqrt{1000} - \sqrt{75} + \sqrt{675} = 10\sqrt{10} + 10\sqrt{3}.$

Exercise 3.1.8. $x^2 - z^2 = (x - z)(x + z);$ $a^2 - 9c^2 = (a - 3c)(a + 3c);$
$d^4 - f^6 = (d^2 - f^3)(d^2 + f^3);$
$a^8 - b^8 = (a^4 + b^4)(a^2 + b^2)(a + b)(a - b).$

Exercise 3.1.9.

$\frac{3}{\sqrt{5}} = \frac{3\sqrt{5}}{5};$ $\frac{1}{2-\sqrt{2}} = \frac{2+\sqrt{2}}{2};$ $\frac{5-\sqrt{2}}{\sqrt{5}} = \frac{5\sqrt{5}-\sqrt{10}}{5};$

$\frac{a+2}{a-\sqrt{3}} = \frac{(a+2)(a+\sqrt{3})}{a^2-3};$ $\frac{x+\sqrt{2}}{\sqrt{3}x-2} = \frac{(x+\sqrt{2})(\sqrt{3}x+2)}{3x^2-4};$ $\frac{3x-2}{\sqrt{2}} = \frac{\sqrt{2}(3x-2)}{2};$

$\frac{3x-2}{-3\sqrt{2}} = \frac{\sqrt{2}(2-3x)}{6};$ $\frac{\sqrt{x}-2}{\sqrt{5}-3\sqrt{2}} = \frac{(2-\sqrt{x})(\sqrt{5}+3\sqrt{2})}{13};$ $\frac{3\sqrt{x}-\sqrt{2a}}{x-3\sqrt{2}}.$

Exercise 3.1.10.

$\sqrt[3]{8} = 2;$ $-\sqrt[3]{-8} = 2;$ $\sqrt[3]{-27} = -3;$

$\sqrt[4]{|-81|} = 3;$ $|-\sqrt[7]{128}| = 2;$ $\sqrt[4]{81} = 3;$

$\sqrt[3]{1000} = 10;$ $-\sqrt[3]{-125} = 5;$ $\sqrt[4]{625} = 5.$

Exercise 3.1.11. $\frac{9x^9}{2y^{11}z^2} = 9 \cdot 2^{-1}x^9y^{-11}z^{-2};$ $-3y^{11} + 4y^5 + 2;$

$-2k^9 + 5k^2 + 3;$ $\frac{3x^{38}}{y^{37}} = 3x^{38}y^{-37}.$

3.2   Order of Operations. III

Now we have the full set of elementary operations, including *exponents* and *radicals*, and we review here the ordering of these operations, It follows three simple and logical rules.

- First perform operations inside *separators*

- Without any separator, more advanced operations should be done first

- If several operations of the same "tier" follow one another in a row without separators, proceed *from left to right*.

By separators we mean *parentheses* $(\ldots)$, *brackets* $[\ldots]$, (curly) *braces* $\{\ldots\}$, *fraction lines* $\frac{\cdot\cdot\cdot}{\cdot\cdot\cdot}$, *radicals* $\sqrt[n]{\cdots}$.

Addition and its inverse, subtraction, are the lowest level operations with regard to the ordering. Multiplication (at least of natural numbers) is a short-cut for addition, therefore, multiplication and its inverse, division, should be performed before the addition/subtraction. Powers with natural exponents are abbreviation of multiplication, thus, exponentiation and its inverse, radicals, must be done before multiplication/division.

Example 3.2.1 *Calculate*

$$\sqrt{\frac{1 + 5 \cdot \sqrt{25 - 16}}{3 \cdot 4 - [(|-5|-1)^2 - 14] + 6}}.$$

Solution. The expression looks cumbersome and complicated, but let us decompose it into simple components. First of all, we must compute the fraction in the radicand. The fraction line in the radicand is a *separator*, and this fraction can be written as

$$\frac{1 + 5 \cdot \sqrt{25 - 16}}{3 \cdot 4 - [(|-5|-1)^2 - 14] + 6} = [1 + 5 \cdot \sqrt{25 - 16}] \div [3 \cdot 4 - [(|-5|-1)^2 - 14] + 6],$$

thus we separately calculate the numerator and the denominator of the latter fraction. The numerator alone does not look too bad, it is

$$1 + 5 \cdot \sqrt{25 - 16}.$$

Here the internal radical is a separator itself, hence we compute its radicand, which is just the difference $25 - 16 = 9$, then the radical is $\sqrt{25 - 16} = \sqrt{9} = 3$, and the numerator inside the big radical collapses as

$$1 + 5 \cdot \sqrt{25 - 16} = 1 + 5 \cdot 3 = 1 + 15 = 16,$$

where we certainly first multiplied $5 \cdot 3 = 15$ and after that added $1 + 15 = 16$.

Now we take up the denominator, which consists of three "independent" terms. Namely, the product $3 \cdot 4$, the bracketed term $(|-5|-1)^2 - 14$, and the number 6. Thus, we compute separately the first term, $3 \cdot 4 = 12$, and then the second term, $(|-5|-1)^2 - 14$. In the latter, $|-5| = 5$, thus $(|-5|-1)^2 - 14 = (5-1)^2 - 14 = 4^2 - 14 = 16 - 14 = 2$. After that, the denominator becomes

$$3 \cdot 4 - [(|-5|-1)^2 - 14] + 6 = 12 - 2 + 6 = 10 + 6 = 16,$$

since we have to work here from left to right. Finally, the whole expression reads now

$$\sqrt{\frac{1 + 5 \cdot \sqrt{25 - 16}}{3 \cdot 4 - [(|-5|-1)^2 - 14] + 6}}$$

$$= \sqrt{\frac{1 + 5 \cdot \sqrt{9}}{3 \cdot 4 - [(5-1)^2 - 14] + 6}}$$

$$= \sqrt{\frac{1 + 5 \cdot 3}{12 - (16 - 14) + 6}} = \sqrt{\frac{1 + 15}{12 - 2 + 6}} = \sqrt{\frac{16}{16}} = 1.$$

We see that if we proceed slowly and carefully obey the rules, the example quickly simplifies. When gaining more experience, we see more and more short-cuts and opportunities to speed up solutions. For example, in this example we could from the very beginning to replace $|-5| = 5$, etc.   □

Exercise 3.2.1 *Compute.*

$1\,002\,345 - 70\,908 + \sqrt{81} =$ $709\,808 - \sqrt{2\,025} \cdot 33 =$

$3\,457 + (128\,345 - 9\,909) \div 2 =$ $2\,450\,067 - 801\,008 - 608^2 =$

$2\,450\,067 - (801\,008 - 50^3) =$ $\{870\,960 - (8\,456 + 123)\} - 31 =$

Exercise 3.2.2 *Design and solve two more exercises similar to the previous one.*

Answers 3.2

Exercise 3.2.1.

$1\,002\,345 - 70\,908 + \sqrt{81} = 931\,446;$ $709\,808 - \sqrt{2\,025} \cdot 33 = 708\,323;$
$3\,457 + (128\,345 - 9\,909) \div 2 = 62\,675;$ $2\,450\,067 - 801\,008 - 608^2 = 1\,279\,395;$
$2\,450\,067 - (801\,008 - 50^3) = 1\,774\,059;$ $\{870\,960 - (8\,456 + 123)\} - 31 = 862\,350.$

3.3   Radicals in Statistics
The Variance, Standard Deviation,
and Pearson's Correlation Coefficient

Square roots appear in many important formulas. In this section, as an example, we consider their occurrence in statistics. Let X be an arbitrary finite set of numbers, called in statistics *scores*. Depending upon the problem, the set can be called either a population or a sample. Here we call it a *population* and write it as $X = \{x_1, x_2, \ldots, x_n\}$, thus we suppose that the population consists of n items, or contains n *scores*. In Section 2.2.7 we defined the mean (the arithmetic average) of the population as

$$\bar{X} = \frac{1}{n} \sum_{i=1}^{n} x_i = \frac{1}{n} \{x_1 + x_2 + \cdots + x_n\}.$$

For example, consider the two small sets, $X_1 = \{9, 10, 11\}$ and $X_2 = \{0, 10, 20\}$, and compute their means. In both cases $n = 3$ and we easily have

$$\bar{X}_1 = \frac{9 + 10 + 11}{3} = 10 \text{ and } \bar{X}_2 = \frac{0 + 10 + 20}{3} = 10.$$

Thus $\bar{X}_1 = \bar{X}_2$, but the populations, clearly, are very different, one is strongly compressed to the mean, while another is very stretched, rarefied. A common measure of this tightness of a sample is the *standard deviation*. First it is convenient to define the *variance* V_X of the population.

Definition 3.3.1 *For the population* $X = \{x_1, x_2, \ldots, x_n\}$ *with the mean* $\bar{X}$ *its variance is*

$$V_X = \frac{1}{n} \sum_{i=1}^{n} \left(x_i - \bar{X}\right)^2 = \frac{1}{n} \left\{ \left(x_1 - \bar{X}\right)^2 + \left(x_2 - \bar{X}\right)^2 + \cdots + \left(x_n - \bar{X}\right)^2 \right\}$$

and its standard deviation is

$$\sigma_X = \sqrt{V_X} = \sqrt{\frac{1}{n} \left\{ \left(x_1 - \bar{X}\right)^2 + \left(x_2 - \bar{X}\right)^2 + \cdots + \left(x_n - \bar{X}\right)^2 \right\}}.$$

In the example above,

$$\sigma_{X_1} = \sqrt{\frac{(9 - 10)^2 + (10 - 10)^2 + (11 - 10)^2}{3}} = \sqrt{\frac{2}{3}},$$

while

$$\sigma_{X_2} = \sqrt{\frac{(0 - 10)^2 + (10 - 10)^2 + (20 - 10)^2}{3}} = \sqrt{\frac{200}{3}} = \frac{10\sqrt{2}}{3},$$

which is 10 times σ_{S_1}.

Exercise 3.3.1 *Find the variance and standard deviation of the following sets; round off to the nearest integer.*

$$\{870; 8\} = \qquad\qquad\qquad \{344; 0\} =$$

$$\{1\,002; 345; 71\} = \qquad\qquad \{709; 808; 2; 45\} =$$

$$\{128; 345; 9; 909\} = \qquad\qquad 3; 457; 128; 345; 9; 909\} =$$

To illustrate how the order of operations works in real problems, we consider another important statistical quantity, called the *Pearson coefficient of correlation*. Consider n pairs of *coupled data*,

$$(x_1, y_1), (x_2, y_2), \ldots, (x_n, y_n),$$

which means that the number y_1 corresponds to the number x_1, y_2 corresponds to x_2, etc., y_n corresponds to x_n. Suppose that $\{x_1, x_2, \ldots, x_n\}$ represent the independent variables (arguments), and $\{y_1, y_2, \ldots, y_n\}$ the dependent values, that is, y is the function of x, $y_1 = y(x_1)$, $y_2 = y(x_2)$, etc., $y_n = y(x_n)$. Compute their means as defined by (2.2.3), $\bar{x} = \sum_{i=1}^{n} x_i$ and $\bar{y} = \sum_{i=1}^{n} y_i$ and the standard deviations σ_x and σ_y as above. The correlation coefficient of these paired data is the number

$$r = \frac{1}{n\sigma_x \sigma_y} \sum_{i=1}^{n} \left((y_i - \bar{y}) \cdot (x_i - \bar{x})\right). \tag{3.3.1}$$

We are discussing this formula just to illustrate how the rules for order of operations work together:

We must first of all calculate the averages and standard deviations. Then we must evaluate the differences $y_i - \bar{y}$ and $x_i - \bar{x}$, and multiply each pair of the differences with the same subscript. After that we add all these pair-wise products and divide by $n\sigma_x\sigma_y$.

We do not practice formula (3.3.1), because after replacing the averages and standard deviations with their definitions and some simple but tedious algebra (we omit these computations) formula (3.3.1) can be transformed to the following one, which is more convenient for computations:

$$r = \frac{n\sum_{i=1}^{n} x_i \cdot y_i - \left(\sum_{i=1}^{n} x_i\right)\left(\sum_{i=1}^{n} y_i\right)}{\left(\sqrt{n\sum_{i=1}^{n} x_i^2 - \left(\sum_{i=1}^{n} x_i\right)^2}\right)\left(\sqrt{n\sum_{i=1}^{n} y_i^2 - \left(\sum_{i=1}^{n} y_i\right)^2}\right)}. \tag{3.3.2}$$

Example 3.3.1 *Use formula (3.3.2) to find the correlation coefficient for the sets* $x_1 = 1$, $x_2 = 3$, $y_1 = 7$, *and* $y_2 = -1$.

Solution. Here $n = 2$. The formula tells us that we need to compute both arithmetic means and both standard deviations. We have $\overline{X} = (1+3)/2 = 2$ and $\overline{Y} = (7-1)/2 = 3$. Next,

$$\sigma_X = \sqrt{\frac{(1-2)^2 + (3-2)^2}{2}} = \sqrt{\frac{2}{2}} = 1,$$

$$\sigma_Y = \sqrt{\frac{(7-3)^2 + (-1-3)^2}{2}} = \sqrt{\frac{32}{2}} = 4,$$

thus,

$$r = \frac{(1-2)(7-3) + (3-2)(-1-3)}{2 \cdot 1 \cdot 4} = \frac{-8}{8} = -1.$$

$\square$

Exercise 3.3.2 *Use formula (3.3.2) to find the correlation coefficients for the following three sets of coupled data, distinguished by the superscripts,* (x, y^1), (x, y^2), (x, y^3).

x	1	2	3	4	5	6	7	8	9	10
y^1	8	9	11	10	12	10	13	12	14	16
y^2	18	16	17	14	12	10	3	2	12	11
y^3	0	9	96	80	7	43	10	52	10	19

Problem 3.3.1 *Derive formula (3.3.2) from (3.3.1).*

Answers 3.3

Exercise 3.3.1.

$S = \{870; 8\}$, $V_S = 185\,761$, $\sigma_S = 431$ $S = \{344; 0\}$, $V_S = 29\,584$, $\sigma_S = 172$
$S = \{344; 71\}$, $V_S \approx 18\,632$, $\sigma_S \approx 137$ $S = \{709; 808; 2; 45\}$, $V_S = 391$, $\sigma_S \approx 137$

$$S = \{128; 345; 9; 909\}, V_S \approx 119\,513, \sigma_S \approx 346$$

$$S = \{3; 457; 128; 345; 9; 909\}, V_S \approx 99\,933, \sigma_S \approx 316$$

Exercise 3.3.2. In all three sets $n = 10$ and the $x-$values are the same, $\sum x_i = 55$, $\sum x_i^2 = 385$.

Set 1: $\sum y_i = 115$, $\sum y_i^2 = 1375$, $\sum x_i \cdot y_i = 6920$, $r^1 \approx 0.9$
Set 2: $\sum y_i = 115$, $\sum y_i^2 = 1587$, $\sum x_i \cdot y_i = 532$, $r^2 \approx -0.68$
Set 3: $\sum y_i = 326$, $\sum y_i^2 = 20860$, $\sum x_i \cdot y_i = 1685$, $r^3 \approx -0.18$.

3.4 Real Numbers

This short section introduces the reader into more advanced mathematical world. Most people have never heard about these topics, but if you got even a little bit interested in mathematics, then hopefully, reading this section may stimulate you to continue your mathematical education. So far, we studied several sets of numbers, natural numbers, integer numbers (both positive and negative), rational numbers. We know that every natural number is integer, but not every integer number is a natural one, since there are negative integers, which are not natural numbers. Then we studied even wider set of numbers, called rational numbers, and noticed that every natural number is rational, but there are rational numbers, say $\frac{1}{2}$, which are not integers.

It turns out that life in the number world is not limited to the rational numbers. In section 3.1 we introduced the irrational numbers. The rational and irrational numbers together make the set of numbers, called *Real Numbers* and traditionally denoted by $\mathbb{R}$. Thus, we have the hierarchy

$\{Natural Numbers\}$ are part of $\{Whole Numbers\}$ are part of $\{Integer Numbers\}$

are part of $\{Rational Numbers\}$ are part of $\{Real Numbers\}$ are part of ?

It is convenient to visualize these sets of numbers by making use of the *Number Line*. This is another *mental image*, because we cannot draw an infinite line. In practice, we draw a finite segment and pretend that it extends infinitely in both directions and represents the entire infinite line. On the number line, the integers correspond to only a few, even though infinitely many separated points. Some other points of the number line correspond to rational (non-integer) numbers, but even if we mark all the rational points, we still see many gaps between them. According to the accepted axioms, there is a one-to-one correspondence between the points of the number line and the set of real numbers – every real number has its corresponding point on the line, and vice versa, each point on the line is labeled by its own unique real number.

Here again we see that mathematics studies mental images – we can draw many-many different straight lines in our notebook or on the blackboard, however, we believe that all of them represent the same object, the unique abstract number line. Mathematicians, scientists have been working with this model of the system of real numbers for several centuries, applied it to endless applications, and still did not find any contradiction. Apparently this model correctly (to some extent) reflects properties of the world we live in, and real numbers, for example, can be made very realistic.

Problem 3.4.1 *Compute $\sqrt{2}$ up to the tenths.*

Solution. In this problem we show a typical *algorithm of consecutive approximation*, which allows the user to compute as many digits of the result as one needs. In practice people use more sophisticated and efficient algorithms, but the idea is the same. Since $1 < 2 < 4$, it must be $1 < \sqrt{2} < 2$, that is, $\sqrt{2} = 1 + a$, where a is a positive real number, which is less than 1. Then, and this is important, $a^2 < a < 1$. Let us square the equation $\sqrt{2} = 1 + a$, which gives $2 = 1 + 2a + a^2$, or $1 = 2a + a^2$. If we solve this quadratic equation, we will find another radical, thus, squaring does not work and we need another approach.

Let us notice, that since $0 < a < 1$, we have $a^2 < 2a$. Then we *neglect*, that is, just drop the smaller term a^2, and arrive at the *approximate equation* $1 = 2a$. We can easily solve this linear equation for a and get *approximately!* $1 \approx 2a$, thus $a \approx 1/2$, or $\sqrt{2} = 1 + a \approx 1 + 1/2 \approx 1.5$. Now we can repeat this step. We set $\sqrt{2} = 1.5 + b$, square this equation and again neglect b^2, resulting in $b \approx -0.08$ and $\sqrt{2} \approx 1.42$. If we make one more iteration, we see that it does not affect the 4, thus, $\sqrt{2} \approx 1.4$, which is correct value up to the tenths. $\square$

Problem 3.4.2 *Compute $\sqrt{1.21}$ up to the tenths.*

Solution. We want to explore in this example, how the algorithm works if the radicand is a perfect square; indeed, $1.21 = (1.1)^2$. We proceed exactly as in the previous example and set $\sqrt{1.21} = 1 + a$. Since $1 < 1.21 < 2$, then also $1 = \sqrt{1} < \sqrt{1.21} < \sqrt{2} < 2$, hence $0 < a < 1$. Squaring the equation for a, we get $1.21 = 1 + 2a + a^2$. However, $a < 1$, thus, $a^2 = a \cdot a < a < 2a$, and we neglect the a^2-term in the equation for a. The approximate equation for a is now $1.21 \approx 1 + 2a$, resulting in $a \approx 0.21 \div 2 = 0.105$.

To derive a better approximation, we repeat the procedure, that is, we set $a = 0.105 + b$, where definitely $b < 1$, so that, $\sqrt{1.21} = 1 + a = 1.105 + b$. Squaring the latter equation and dropping the smallest term b^2, we deduce the equation $1.21 = 1.221025 + 2.21b$. From here, $b = 0.00499$, and $\sqrt{1.21} \approx 1.10001$, with four correct decimal digits. $\square$

Exercise 3.4.1 *Compute $\sqrt{2}$ up to the thousandths and $\sqrt{3}$ up to the hundredths.*

Exercise 3.4.2 *Draw a "line" (we use the quotation marks here, because we can draw only a finite part of a line, which itself is infinite in both directions) and mark the numbers[2] $0, 6, -\pi, \sqrt{2}, -\sqrt{5}, 0.2, 0.75, 1\frac{3}{4}, -3/4$ on the line.*

Exercise 3.4.3 *Translate the sentences to equations.*
99 is 98 subtracted from 2 times a number.
57 subtracted from 11 times a number is 3 times 67.
78 is 37 less than 5 times a number.
94 subtracted from 8 times a number is 12.

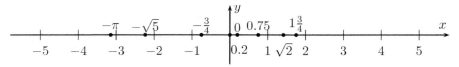

Figure 3.1: Exercise 3.4.2.

Answers 3.4

Exercise 3.4.1. $\sqrt{2} \approx 1.414$; $\sqrt{3} \approx 1.73$.

Exercise 3.4.2. The numbers $0, 6, -\pi, \sqrt{22}$, etc., are marked by bold dots.

Exercise 3.4.3. $99 = 2x - 98$; $11x - 57 = 3 \cdot 67$; $78 = 5x - 37$; $8x - 94 = 12$.

Part II

Minimal Plane Geometry

Chapter 4

Lines and Angles

4.1   Basic Definitions

Geometry, despite its fundamental importance in our life, is under-represented in high-school curriculum. That is why unlike Part I, we use in this part the more systematic approach. We have also included a few short proofs, for it might happen that the "Primer" is the first and only possibility for the reader to get a glimpse at a real beautiful mathematics.

Geometry began a few thousand years ago as the study of figures that can be drawn on a flat plane, for example, on the sand – we imagine the plane endless in any direction, and study, both to use them in our every-day activities and due to our human curiosity, various properties of these figures, like polygons, etc.

If we put a *dot* on paper or on a board, and look at the dot through a magnifier, we clearly observe an irregular spot having non-zero size. However, this does not bother us and does not prevent us from calling this image a *point*. This example emphasizes the difference between *mathematical* and *real-life* objects – mathematical notions are mental images, abstract ideas, reflecting some features that various real objects have in common, and neglecting certain particularities unimportant in the problem at hands. It is amazing and important, that many people, living in different times and places, with different backgrounds and education eventually develop the same mental images related to mathematics. In particular, we believe that mathematical points have no size.

Studying these geometrical figures, people have discovered certain features of different forms, and to describe them, introduced certain concepts. It is convenient to separate all geometrical concepts into two groups – a few *primary* (or *undefined*) items, and all the other concepts, called *secondary*, which must be defined through the primary concepts, even though sometimes certain definitions are not spelled out explicitly. Depending upon our problems, we can change the taxonomy, but the "Primer" follows more or less standard, high-school tradition. We study only *two-dimensional* (2D) geometry of the plane and need only two primary notions: the *point* and the *line*.

4.1.1   Lines and Angles

A line (*straight line*) is another ideal (mental) image abstracted from sun rays. Like the points, the lines have zero width, however, they have infinite length. The "infinite" here means that we *presume* that any line can be endlessly extended, without any obstacle in either of the two directions.

We study figures drawn using straight lines or pieces of those; these pieces are called (line)*segments* if they are finite in both directions, or *rays (half-lines)* if they are infinite in one direction. We imagine any line endless in either direction; on graphs, this boundlessness is sometimes indicated by arrows in one or both directions. We use logic to deduce (*to prove*) certain properties of these figures from the known ones. However, some properties are so obvious[1] that we accept them without any proof. Such properties are called *axioms* or *postulates*. One of such "self-evident" properties is the claim that given two points, there is *one and only one* line going through these two points – see the line $\mathcal{L}$ in Fig. 4.1, which goes through the points $\mathcal{A}$ and $\mathcal{B}$; sometimes we denote such a line as $\overline{\mathcal{AB}}$, or as $\overrightarrow{\mathcal{AB}}$. Some books use the symbol $\overline{\mathcal{AB}}$ for the *line segment* with the *end points* $\mathcal{A}$ and $\mathcal{B}$. to avoid any misunderstanding, familiarize yourself with the notations of the book you read!

If we have only one line, the picture (Fig. 4.1) is very simple – the line divides the plane into two disjoint half-planes, one above and another below the line. A line can also be vertical or slanted and split the plane in a *left* and a *right* half-plane – see, for instance, line $\mathcal{L}_2$ in Fig. 4.5.

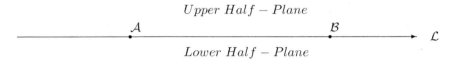

Figure 4.1: The line $\mathcal{L}$ is endless (boundless, infinite) in both directions and divides the plane in two half-planes.

Let us pick an arbitrary point on the line. This point, denoted in Fig. 4.2 by $\mathcal{O}$, splits the line into two *half-lines* or *rays*, each endless in one direction. The point $\mathcal{O}$ is called the *end-point* of these rays.

Figure 4.2: The line $\mathcal{L}$ through the points $\mathcal{A}$ and $\mathcal{B}$. The point $\mathcal{O}$ splits the line $\mathcal{L}$ in two half-lines (rays), $\mathcal{R}_r$ and $\mathcal{R}_l$ with the common end-point $\mathcal{O}$.

A part of a line between its two different points $\mathcal{A}$ and $\mathcal{B}$, including these points, is called a (closed) *segment* with the end-points $\mathcal{A}$ and $\mathcal{B}$ and is denoted as $\overline{\mathcal{AB}}$ - see Fig. 4.2. A segment is often written without an upper-bar, as $\mathcal{AB}$. The *length* of a segment $\overline{\mathcal{AB}}$ is denoted as $\left|\overline{\mathcal{AB}}\right| = \left|\mathcal{AB}\right|$.

A figure formed by two half-lines with the same end-point is called an *angle*. The common end-point of the rays is called the *vertex* of the angle, the rays are called its *sides*. Angles are denoted by the symbol $\angle\mathcal{O}$, where the character $\mathcal{O}$ always indicates the vertex of the angle.

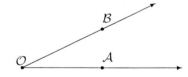

Figure 4.3: An angle $\angle\mathcal{AOB}$.

We can think of the angle as formed by rotating one or both of its sides about the end-point $\mathcal{O}$, as if there is a hinge at the vertex, and we can rotate the rays in either direction. If the side

---

[1]Eventually people have discovered cases that this self-evidence can be misleading, but we will not see such properties in this text.

$\overrightarrow{\mathcal{OA}}$ rests, it is called the *initial* side of the angle. The final location of the other (rotating) side, which is $\overrightarrow{\mathcal{OB}}$ in our example (Fig. 4.3), is called the *terminal* side. By an universal agreement (even if it may look counter-intuitive) a clockwise rotation is called *negative*, and a counter-clockwise rotation is called *positive*; therefore, the handles of a properly working watch rotate in the *negative* direction.

If two angles have the same vertex, to distinguish the angles, we must use three characters, like $\angle \mathcal{AOB}$, where $\mathcal{A}$ and $\mathcal{B}$ *must mark* different sides of the angle (Fig. 4.3); the middle character *always* refers to the vertex of the angle. See, for example, angles $\mathcal{AOB}$ and $\mathcal{BOD}$, Fig. 4.7.

When the two sides of an angle together make a *straight* line, they also form an angle. We know that the line divides the plane into two half-planes, and this line bounds both these half-planes – such a "half-plane angle" is called the *straight angle*; there are two straight angles $\angle \mathcal{O}$ in Fig. 4.2.

Any two half-lines with the common end-point form two angles. Thus, in Fig. 4.3 we can distinguish two angles, the angle $\angle \mathcal{BOA}$ with the initial side $\overrightarrow{\mathcal{OB}}$ and the terminal side $\overrightarrow{\mathcal{OA}}$, and the angle $\angle \mathcal{AOB}$, with the initial side $\overrightarrow{\mathcal{OA}}$, rotated in positive direction until it reaches the terminal side $\overrightarrow{\mathcal{OB}}$. The former angle is clearly wider than the latter one.

Given two lines in the plane, there are more options. The two lines can be parallel (Fig. 4.4) or can cross one another (Fig. 4.5). Two *different* lines in the same plane are said to be *parallel* if they do not intersect each other, no matter how far they are extended in both directions. In this case, no angle is formed. It is also possible to say that the parallel lines make *zero* angle. If the lines $\mathcal{L}_1$ and $\mathcal{L}_2$ are parallel, we denote this as $\mathcal{L}_1 \| \mathcal{L}_2$. Again, it is only a mental image, an idea abstracted from such examples as Sun rays.

Figure 4.4: Parallel lines $\mathcal{L}_1$ and $\mathcal{L}_2$.

We can also imagine a *degenerate* case, when both parallel lines merge, but it is not very interesting, since actually we have just one line. Therefore, while mentioning parallel lines, we always mean different lines.

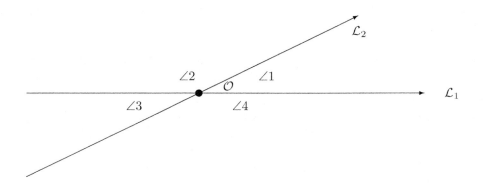

Figure 4.5: Two intersecting lines $\mathcal{L}_1$ and $\mathcal{L}_2$ form four angles $\angle 1$, $\angle 2$, $\angle 3$ and $\angle 4$.

When two lines intersect, they form two pairs of angles. In Fig. 4.5, the angles are numbered from $\angle 1$ to $\angle 4$ in positive direction (counter-clockwise).

We observe that the angles $\angle 1$ and $\angle 3$ have the same vertex, and the sides of either of them extend the sides of the other; such angles are called *vertical*. Thus, the two angles $\angle 1$ and $\angle 3$ are vertical, as well as the two angles $\angle 2$ and $\angle 4$. Looking at Fig. 4.5, one immediately gets an idea that vertical angles are equal. We prove this claim in the end of this section, but first we introduce a few more useful notions.

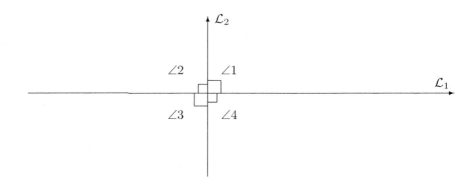

Figure 4.6: Perpendicular lines $\mathcal{L}_1$ and $\mathcal{L}_2$ form four right angles.

In section 4.2 we will learn how to assign a real number to any angle; this number is called the *measure* of the angle. Here we make only a few preliminary remarks.

Consider again four angles, made by two intersecting lines, like those in Fig. 4.5. It can happen, that all these angles are equal – see Fig. 4.6. In that case, the two lines are said to be *perpendicular*, and each of the four equal angles is called a *right* angle[2]. Due to some historical reasons (see the next section) the full rotation angle is assigned the measure of 360 *degrees*, denoted as 360°. Whence, the measure of a right angle is $360° \div 4 = 90°$.

In figures such as Fig. 4.6, right angles are indicated by a small square placed in the crook of the angle. Positive angles measuring less than 90°,
$0° < \angle \alpha < 90°$, are called *acute angles*, and angles measuring between 90° and 180°, $90° < \angle \alpha < 180°$, are called *obtuse angles*. For example, in Fig. 4.5, the $\angle 1$ and $\angle 3$ are acute and $\angle 2$ and $\angle 4$ are obtuse; we can write that $\angle 1 < 90°$ and $\angle 2 > 90°$.

When two angles have the same vertex, share a side, and are located on the opposite sides of the shared side, they are said to be *adjacent*. In Fig. 4.7, the adjacent angles $\angle \mathcal{COB}$ and $\angle \mathcal{BOD}$ share the side $\overrightarrow{\mathcal{OB}}$.

In Fig. 4.7, the right angle $\angle \mathcal{AOB}$ is split into two angles, $\angle \mathcal{AOC}$ and $\angle \mathcal{COB}$ by a ray $\overrightarrow{\mathcal{OC}}$, so that these two angles have the same vertex $\mathcal{O}$ and the common side $\overrightarrow{\mathcal{OC}}$. Angles such as $\angle \mathcal{AOC}$ and $\angle \mathcal{COB}$, are called *complementary angles*. Similarly, the ray $\overrightarrow{\mathcal{OC}}$ splits the straight angle $\angle \mathcal{AOD}$ (Fig. 4.7) into two angles, $\angle \mathcal{AOC}$ and $\angle \mathcal{COD}$, so that these two angles again have the same vertex $\mathcal{O}$ and the common side $\overrightarrow{\mathcal{OC}}$, and are located on the opposite sides of the side in common. Such angles, like $\angle \mathcal{AOC}$ and $\angle \mathcal{COD}$, are called *supplementary angles*. Two adjacent right angles form a straight angle. However in general, two adjacent angles do not have to be complementary nor supplementary.

Exercise 4.1.1 *Identify other pairs of adjacent angles in Fig. 4.5, 4.6, and 4.7.*

Exercise 4.1.2 *Prove that if two angles are supplementary, then either each of them is a right angle, or one of them is acute and another is obtuse.*

---

[2]This is just terminology, there is no left angle and no wrong angle.

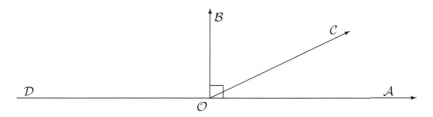

Figure 4.7: Complementary angles $\angle AOC$ and $\angle COB$ and supplementary angles $\angle AOC$ and $\angle COD$.

Now we can prove a simple but important property of vertical angles.

Theorem 4.1.1 *Vertical angles are equal.*

Proof. It is clear that whichever angle measure we use, $\angle 1$ and $\angle 2$ in Fig. 4.5 are adjacent and together make a straight angle, bounded by the line $\mathcal{L}_1$. The $\angle 2$ and $\angle 3$ are also adjacent and together make a straight angle, bounded by the line $\mathcal{L}_2$. Since $\angle 1$ and $\angle 3$ supplement the same angle $\angle 2$ to the straight angle, we conclude that $\angle 1 = \angle 3$.   □

Exercise 4.1.3 *In Fig. 4.5, denote $\angle 4 = \alpha$. Express $\angle 1$, $\angle 2$, and $\angle 3$ through α.*

4.1.2 Circles

Here we introduce only a few basic definitions regarding circles, needed in the sequel sections. Fix any point $\mathcal{O}$ in the plane and a positive number $R > 0$. A *circle* centered at $\mathcal{O}$ and of *radius* R is the *locus*[3] of all the points in the plane R−equidistant from the center $\mathcal{O}$, that is, the collection of all points in the plane, located at the distance R from $\mathcal{O}$, see Fig. 4.8.

Figure 4.8: Circle of radius R centered at point $\mathcal{O}$. The point $\mathcal{A}$ is the distance R from the center $\mathcal{O}$, $|\overline{\mathcal{O}\mathcal{A}}| = R$.

The collection of all points inside the circle of radius R is called the (open, that is, without the boundary) *disc* (spelled also *disk*) of radius R.

When we mention a radius of a circle, we sometimes mean the length of any radius, which is a unique number for the given circle, and sometimes we mean a specific geometric entity, that is, a straight segment, connecting the center of the circle with a particular point of the circle; usually this duality does not lead to any misunderstanding. A segment, connecting any two points of the circle, is called a *chord*. A longest chord, which must necessary go through the center of the circle, is called its *diameter*. It is clear that in any circle, the length of diameter is exactly twice the length of radius, $|\overline{\mathcal{BC}}| = 2R$.

Let us look again at Fig. 4.9. The three points $\mathcal{A}$, $\mathcal{B}$ and $\mathcal{C}$ divide the circle into three parts, called *arcs* and denoted as $\frown$: the arc $\frown (\mathcal{AB})$, the arc $\frown (\mathcal{BC})$ and the arc $\frown (\mathcal{CA})$.

[3]Locus means *collection* or the set of all the points satisfying the stated condition.

Figure 4.9: A chord $\overline{AB}$ and the diameter $\overline{BOC}$.

It is said that the arc $\frown (AC)$ *subtends* the angle $\angle ABC$ or vice versa, the angle $\angle ABC$ *is subtended* by the arc $\frown (AC)$.

Now let us look at Fig. 4.10, that shows a circle, centered at the point O, and two parallel lines, $\mathcal{L}_1$ and $\mathcal{L}_2$. The line $\mathcal{L}_1$ has two common points, A and B with the circle, while $\mathcal{L}_2$ does not intersect the circle at all. The *equal* radii $\overline{OA}$ and $\overline{OB}$ (since all radii of a cirle are equal to each other) and the chord $\overline{AB}$ make an isosceles triangle $\triangle AOB$. Its height OD is perpendicular to the base AB.

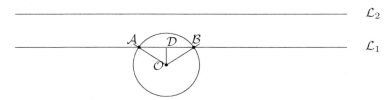

Figure 4.10: A circle and two parallel lines.

Let us move the line $\overleftrightarrow{AB}$ up, in a manner such that it remains parallel to itself, that is, horizontal. During the motion, the points A and B are sliding along the circle and approaching one another. At some instance, the points will merge at the point D, see Fig. 4.11, which is the only point in common for the line $\mathcal{L}$ and the circle. This line is called a *tangent line* to the circle at the *tangent point* D. When the line moves up, the height OD of the triangle $\triangle AOB$ does not rotate, it just gets longer, and when the line becomes a tangent line, the height remains perpendicular to the tangent and becomes the radius OD of the circle. We have discovered an important property of the tangent lines, see Fig. 4.11.

Theorem 4.1.2 *The radius of a circle at the tangent point is perpendicular to the tangent line at this point.*

Moreover, if a line is perpendicular to a radius OD of a circle, the line cannot have another common point B with the circle, since in this case, by the first statement, the triangle $\triangle OBD$ would have two right angles. □

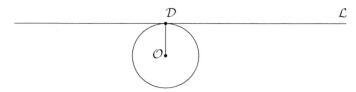

Figure 4.11: The radius $\overline{OD}$ is perpendicular to the tangent line $\mathcal{L}$.

Answers 4.1

Exercise 4.1.1. We list only some pairs of adjacent angles. Fig. 4.5: $\angle 2$ and $\angle 3$, $\angle 2$ and $\angle 1$. Fig. 4.6: $\angle 2$ and $\angle 3$, $\angle 2$ and $\angle 1$.

Exercise 4.1.2. Denote these angles $\angle \alpha$ and $\angle \beta$, thus $\angle \alpha + \angle \beta = 180°$. If $\angle \alpha = 90°$, then $\angle \beta = 180° - \angle \alpha = 180° - 90° = 90°$, hence each of them is a right angle. If $\angle \alpha$ is acute, that is, $\angle \alpha < 90°$, then $\angle \beta = 180° - \angle \alpha > 90°$, that is, $\angle \beta$ is obtuse, and vice versa.

Exercise 4.1.3. If $\angle 4 = \alpha$, then $\angle 2 = \angle 4 = \alpha$, and $\angle 1 = \angle 3 = 180° - \alpha$.

4.2 Measuring Angles and Arcs

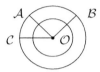

Figure 4.12: The degree measure of an arc does not depend upon the radius of a circle.

Angles are measured by the arcs they are subtended by. Let us look at Fig. 4.12 and compare the arcs $\frown (\mathcal{CA})$ and $\frown (\mathcal{CAB})$. They have a common end-point $\mathcal{C}$, therefore, the arc $\frown (\mathcal{CAB})$ is, clearly, *bigger* than the $\frown (\mathcal{CA})$, since the latter covers only a part of the former. Whence, the arc $\frown (\mathcal{CA})$ is *smaller* than the arc $\frown (\mathcal{CAB})$. Moreover, we observe that the relative size of arcs is the same on any *concentric* circle. Here, two or more circles are called *concentric* if they have the same center but different radii.

Thus, we measure both arcs and angles in the same units, called *degrees*.[4] According to some sources, more than twenty centuries ago people in ancient Babylon noticed that Sun disc fits 180 times[5] in its 12-hour path over sky; they assigned the measure of 180 *degrees* to the half of the circle, and correspondingly, the measure of $2 \cdot 180 = 360$ *degrees*, 360°, to the whole circle. Consider any angle and let its terminal side rotate counterclockwise until it collides first time with the initial side; such angle can be described as a *complete rotation*. This angle is subtended by the complete circle, whence it has the same measure as the entire circle itself.

To repeat, an angle contains as many angle degrees, as there are the angle degrees, in the subtended arc. Therefore, if we divide one complete rotation angle or, which is the same, the whole circle into 360 small equal arcs, then each of these small arcs or angles has the measure of one degree, 1°. As we have already mentioned, a half of the entire rotation angle, that is, an angle of $\frac{360°}{2} = 180°$, is called a *straight* angle.

If two lines are *perpendicular*, that is, all the four angles made by the lines, are equal, each of the four equal angles is a right angle. Therefore, the right angles are assigned a measure of $360 \div 4 = 90$ *degrees*, 90°.

If we divide 1°-angle into 60 equal parts, we get 1-*minute* angle, denoted as $1'$. If a 1-*minute* angle is divided into 60 equal parts, we get 1-*second* angle, denoted as $1''$. Since ancient times, we use the same units to measure time.

It should be also clear that if we divide an angle (an arc) into two parts, then the measure of the initial angle (arc) is equal to the sum of the measures of these parts – see, for instance,

---

[4]While studying trigonometry, in Section 9.1 we will learn another measure of angles, called *radian measure*, which is more convenient in calculus. In addition to degrees and radians, on your calculator you can find *grads*, which were invented to make the measurement of angles more "decimal", but are not commonly used.

[5]This was, of course, only an estimation.

angles $\angle BOA$, $\angle AOC$ and $\angle BOC$ in Fig. 4.13, where $\angle COA + \angle BOC = \angle BOA$. This property is called the *additive property* of the arc (angle) measure.

A half of a right angle is $\frac{1}{2} \cdot 90° = 45°$ angle, a one-third of a right angle is $\frac{1}{3} \cdot 90° = 30°$ angle; you see these angles in Fig. 4.15.

Remark 4.2.1 *Now the symbol $\angle\alpha$ is overloaded, it has two meanings. It stands for a geometrical figure - an angle, and also for the measure of this angle. In our problems this cannot lead to any misunderstanding.*

Let us sketch a number line, call it the x-axis, and the unit circle centered at the zero point 0, called also the *origin*, of the x-axis. Due to historical reasons, the right half-line, whose end-pointis 0, is called the *positive x-axis*. An angle is said to be in *standard position*, if its vertex is at the origin and its initial side coincides with the positive x-axis. For instance, in Fig. 4.13 the angles $\angle AOB$ and $\angle AOC$ are in standard position, but the angle $\angle BOC$ is not.

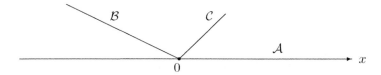

Figure 4.13: The angles $\angle AOB$ and $\angle AOC$ are in standard position, but $\angle BOC$ is not.

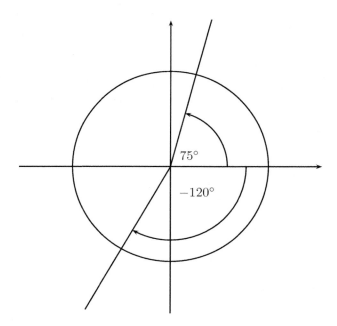

Figure 4.14: Angles of $75°$ and $-120°$ in standard position.

Exercise 4.2.1 *Sketch the angles of* $-45°$, $10°$, $30°$, $45°$, $60°$, $90°$, $135°$ *in standard position.*

Example 4.2.1 *If two angles are supplementary and one of them measures* $120°$, *what is the degree measure of the other?*

Solution. Because the two angles are supplementary, they make up a straight angle, that is, their measures add up to $180°$. Let x represent the degree measure of the unknown (acute) angle. Then

$$x + 120 = 180.$$

Thus we again arrive at a linear equation in unknown x. Transposing 120 from the left to the right-hand side, we get $x = 180 - 120 = 60$. Hence, the degree measure of the other angle is $60°$. ☐

Example 4.2.2 *If two angles are complementary and one of them is* $10°$ *less than three times the other, what are the degree measures of the angles?*

Solution. Because the two angles are complementary, they make up a right angle. That is, their measures add up to $90°$. Let x represent the degree measure of the first unknown angle. Then another angle is $3x - 10$, and since the angles are complementary, we have $x + 3x - 10 = 90$. Combining the like terms in this linear equation and transposing 10 from the left to the right-hand side, we obtain $4x = 90 + 10 = 100$, thus $x = 25$ and $3x - 10 = 65$. The degree measures of the angles are $25°$ and $65°$. ☐

Exercise 4.2.2 *If two angles are supplementary and one of them is* $20°$ *more than three times the other, what are the degree measures of the angles?*

Exercise 4.2.3 *If two angles are supplementary and one of them is a half of the other, what are the measures of the angles?*

Answers 4.2

Exercise 4.2.1. Fig. 4.14-4.15.
Exercise 4.2.2. $40°$, $140°$.
Exercise 4.2.3. $60°$, $120°$.

4.3   Two Parallel Lines and a Transversal

In this section we consider angles made by two parallel lines crossed by another line. The latter line is called a *transversal*, and the three lines create eight angles – see Fig. 4.16. We study this configuration in some detail, because for centuries it has been useful in many applications, for example, in navigation and currently in GPS devices; some of you know a *parallel ruler*, consisting of two pairs of parallel lines connected by four hinges – see Fig. 4.17.

By gradually "sliding" the line $\mathcal{L}_1$ in Fig. 4.16 onto the parallel line $\mathcal{L}_2 \| \mathcal{L}_1$, so that they always remain parallel to one another and then merge, you can see that the four angles on top of Fig. 4.16, $\angle 1$ through $\angle 4$, can be made to coincide with the four angles, $\angle 5$ through $\angle 8$, at the bottom.

Exercise 4.3.1 *Among the eight angles in Fig. 4.16, many are equal, for example,* $\angle 1 = \angle 5$. *What other pairs of angles in Fig. 4.16 are equal? In the equations below, replace the ? mark with the correct angle numbers.*

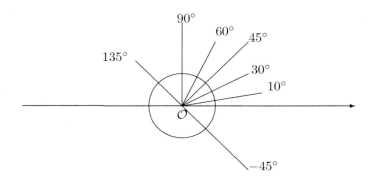

Figure 4.15: Angles of $-45°$, $10°$, $30°$, $45°$, $60°$, $90°$, $135°$ in standard position.

$\angle 1 = \angle?$	$\angle 1 = \angle?$	$\angle 1 = \angle?$
$\angle 3 = \angle?$	$\angle 3 = \angle?$	$\angle 3 = \angle?$
$\angle 3 = \angle?$		

Exercise 4.3.2 *Suppose the transversal in Fig. 4.16 is perpendicular to one of the parallel lines. Would it also be perpendicular to the other?*

Let us look one more time at Fig. 4.16. There are four pairs of vertical angles there, thus by Theorem 4.1.1 we conclude that

$$\angle 1 = \angle 3, \qquad\qquad \angle 2 = \angle 4$$
$$\angle 5 = \angle 7 \qquad\qquad \angle 6 = \angle 8.$$

Moreover, as we have noticed in Exercise 4.3.1, $\angle 1 = \angle 5$; the angles $\angle 1$ and $\angle 5$ are called *corresponding*, they are made by the transversal and two parallel lines, located at the same side of the transversal, and both open up in the same direction – up-right. Another pair of equal corresponding angles in Fig. 4.16 is $\angle 4 = \angle 8$. Thus, we have arrived at the following useful assertion.

Theorem 4.3.1 Corresponding angles are equal.

Example 4.3.1 *Find two other pairs of corresponding angles in Fig. 4.16.*

Solution. $\angle 2 = \angle 6$ and $\angle 3 = \angle 7$.   □

We have known already that $\angle 1 = \angle 5$. At the same time, $\angle 1 = \angle 3$ as vertical angles, therefore, $\angle 3 = \angle 5$. The pairs of angles like $\angle 3$ and $\angle 5$, which are located in the interior stripe between the parallel lines and on opposite sides of the transversal, are called *interior alternate angles*; we conclude that

Theorem 4.3.2 Interior alternate angles are equal.

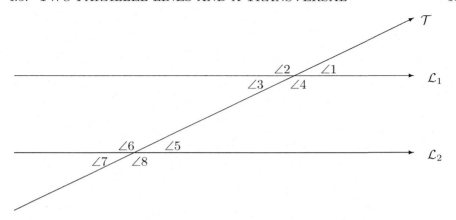

Figure 4.16: Parallel lines $\mathcal{L}_1 \| \mathcal{L}_2$ with a transversal $\mathcal{T}$. .

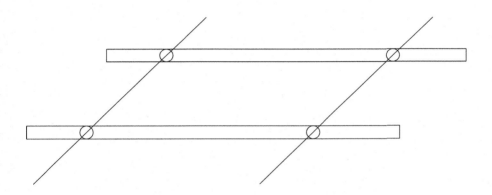

Figure 4.17: Parallel ruler.

Example 4.3.2 *Find another pair of interior alternate angles in Fig. 4.16.*

Solution. The angles $\angle 4 = \angle 6$. □

Example 4.3.3 *Give a definition of* exterior alternate angles. *Show all pairs of exterior alternate angles in Fig. 4.16, and state their major property.*

Solution. Indeed, $\angle 2 = \angle 8$ are exterior alternate angles; they are equal. □

Exercise 4.3.3 *Let in Fig. 4.16, $\angle 4 = 130^{o}$. Find the measures of the other seven angles in Fig. 4.16.*

Exercise 4.3.4 *Design and solve two more exercises similar to the previous one.*

Now we can prove the following remarkable property of plane triangles.

Theorem 4.3.3 *In any plane triangle, the sum of its three interior angles is $180°$.*

Proof. Given a triangle $\triangle ABC$, we draw (see Fig. 4.18) a line $\overline{DE}$ through the vertex B parallel to the *base* $\overline{AC}$. The side $\overline{AB}$ is a transversal relative to these two parallel lines, thus $\angle CAB$ and $\angle DBA$ are alternate interior angles, therefore, they are equal, $\angle CAB = \angle DBA$. By the same reason, $\angle CBE = \angle BCA$. Clearly, the three angles $\angle DBA$, $\angle ABC$, and $\angle CBE$ together make a straight angle, therefore,

$$\angle DBA + \angle ABC + \angle CBE = 180°.$$

Replacing in the latter equation angles $\angle DBA$ and $\angle CBE$ with equal angles $\angle CAB$ and $\angle BCA$, respectively, we derive the equation we sought for, that is,

$$\angle CAB + \angle ABC + \angle BCA = 180°. \qquad \square$$

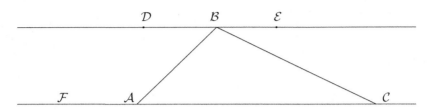

Figure 4.18: The sum of the three interior angles in a triangle is 180°.

Example 4.3.4 *Find the angles of a triangle $\triangle ABC$ if $\angle A$ is three times $\angle B$ and the latter angle is $20°$ less than $\angle C$.*

Solution. Denote the degree measure of $\angle B$ by x; we will write $\angle B = x$, where $\angle B$ stands for the measure of the angle. Then, since $\angle A$ is three times $\angle B$, we have $\angle A = 3x$. In addition, since $\angle B$ is $20°$ less than $\angle C$, that is, $\angle B = \angle C - 20$, we can rewrite the latter equation as $x = \angle C - 20$, or $\angle C = x + 20$. By Theorem 4.3.3, $\angle A + \angle B + \angle C = 180°$. In this problem, this equation becomes $3x + x + x + 20 = 180$, or combining the like terms on the left, $5x + 20 = 180$. Solving this linear equation, we have $5x = 180 - 20$, then $5x = 160$, and finally $x = 32$. Thus, $\angle B = 32°$, $\angle A = 96°$, and $\angle C = 52°$. We can check that $96° + 32° + 52° = 180°$. $\qquad \square$

Let us consider the angle $\angle FAB$ – see Fig. 4.18. It is called an *exterior angle* of the triangle $\triangle ABC$.

Exercise 4.3.5 *Draw another exterior angle of $\triangle ABC$, Fig. 4.18, at the same vertex A.*

The exterior angle $\angle FAB$ and the interior angle $\angle A$ are supplementary angles, thus their sum is $180°$. At the same time, the sum of the three interior angles, including $\angle A$, is also $180°$. As a corollary, we arrive at the following useful result.

Theorem 4.3.4 *An exterior angle of a triangle is equal to the sum of the two interior angles of the triangle, not adjacent with the given exterior angle.* $\qquad \square$

Problem 4.3.1 *Prove this theorem.*

Remark 4.3.1 *It is useful to know the following terms. If a statement claims that a condition $\aleph$ implies a condition $\beth$, then this statement is called the implication and is denoted as $\aleph \Rightarrow \beth$. The symbol $\neg\aleph$ or $\overline{\aleph}$ stands for the negation of the statement $\aleph$; for example, if $\aleph$ means "x is a negative number", then $\neg\aleph$ means "x is not a negative number" (but not the statement "x is a positive number"!). The implication $\beth \Rightarrow \aleph$ is called the converse of the implication $\aleph \Rightarrow \beth$, the implication $\neg\aleph \Rightarrow \neg\beth$ is called the inverse of the implication $\aleph \Rightarrow \beth$, and the implication $\neg\beth \Rightarrow \neg\aleph$ is called the contrapositive of the implication $\aleph \Rightarrow \beth$.*

For some of the theorems above, their *converses* are also true. For instance, we prove the following result.

Theorem 4.3.5 *Given two lines and a transversal that crosses both of them. If two corresponding angles (any pair of these angles) are equal, the lines are parallel.*

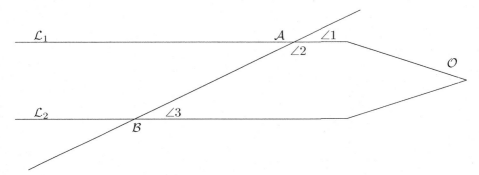

Figure 4.19: Proof of Theorem 4.3.5.

Proof. Suppose $\angle 1 = \angle 3$ - see Fig. 4.19, but the lines $\mathcal{L}_1$ and $\mathcal{L}_2$ are not parallel. This means that the lines must intersect either to the left or to the right of the transversal; let they intersect at a point $\mathcal{O}$ to the right, otherwise the proof goes exactly the same. Since the angles $\angle 1$ and $\angle 2$ are supplementary, we have $\angle 1 + \angle 2 = 180°$. Replacing here $\angle 1$ with the equal angle $\angle 3$, we deduce that $\angle 2 + \angle 3 = 180°$, therefore, the sum of the angles in the triangle $\triangle \mathcal{ABO}$ is $180° + \angle O$, which is clearly larger than $180°$. But this *contradicts* to the Theorem 4.3.3. The contradiction derived proves that our assumption, namely that the lines $\mathcal{L}_1$ and $\mathcal{L}_2$ are not parallel, cannot be valid, and we must conclude that these lines indeed are parallel. □

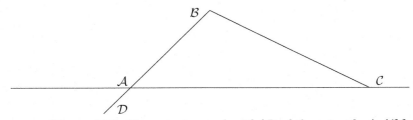

Figure 4.20: The exterior angle $\angle \mathcal{CAD}$ of the triangle $\triangle \mathcal{ABC}$.

Remark 4.3.2 *Exactly in the same way we can prove that if there is a pair of non-equal alternate interior angles or non-equal alternate exterior angles, the lines cannot be parallel.*

Remark 4.3.3 *The method of proof, used in this theorem, is called proof by contradiction. If we want to prove a statement $\aleph$ by contradiction, we assume that the statement $\aleph$ is false, thus its opposite statement $\neg \aleph$ is to be true. Then we try to deduce from the negation $\neg \aleph$ some conclusions contradicting either to our assumptions or certain known results. If we manage to arrive at this contradiction, we conclude that our assumption $\neg \aleph$ cannot be true, therefore, $\aleph$ itself is true.*

Of course, we assume in this method that no statement can be true simultaneously with its negation.

Answers 4.3

Exercise 4.3.1. $\angle 1 = \angle 3 = \angle 5 = \angle 7$; $\angle 2 = \angle 4 = \angle 6 = \angle 8$.
Exercise 4.3.2. Yes, all of these angles are right angles.
Exercise 4.3.3. $\angle 2 = \angle 6 = \angle 8 = \angle 4 = 130°$; $\angle 1 = \angle 3 = \angle 5 = \angle 7 = 180° - 130° = 50°$.
Exercise 4.3.5. For example, the angle $\angle CAD$ in Fig. 4.20.

Chapter 5

Polygons

5.1 Basic Definitions

We remind that any connected finite part of a line is called a (straight) *segment*. We assume that the segment contains its end-points, say A and B, and denote this segment by $\overline{AB}$. The *length* of a segment is denoted by two vertical bars, similar to the symbol of the absolute value. Thus, $\overline{AB}$ is the segment with the *end-points* A and B, that is, a geometrical image, a collection of points in the plane, and $\left|\overline{AB}\right|$ is a non-negative number, the length of this segment. Segments

$$\overline{AB}, \overline{BC}, \overline{CD}, \ldots, \overline{KL},$$

where every two consecutive segments, except for the first and the last one, have a common end-point, compose a *broken line*. A broken line $\overline{ABCDE}$ in Fig. 5.1 consists of four segments $\overline{AB}, \overline{BC}, \overline{CD}, \overline{DE}$. We assume that the segments, composing a broken line, can have only their end-points in common, that is, they *cannot intersect* one another.

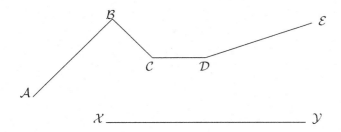

Figure 5.1: A segment $\overline{XY}$ and a broken line $\overline{ABCDE}$.

Exercise 5.1.1 *Can two segments with a common end-point be parallel?*

In the broken line $\overline{ABCDE}$ (Fig. 5.1) the points B, C, and D each belong to two neighboring segments, while the end-points A and E belong to one segment each. If we connect these end-points, A and E, with a new segment $\overline{AE}$, we get a *closed broken line*. A closed broken line without self-intersections, consisting of n segments, is called a *polygon* with n vertices and n sides, or an $n-$gon. The polygon $\overline{ABCDE}$ in Fig. 5.2 has $n = 5$ sides and $n = 5$ vertices, it is called a *pentagon*.

Definition 5.1.1 *A straight segment connecting any two vertices of a polygon, which is not a side of the polygon, is called a* diagonal *of the polygon.*

Hereafter, we consider only *convex polygons,* that is, the polygons such that any its diagonal lies entirely inside the polygon. The polygon $\overline{ABCDE}$ in Fig. 5.2 is not convex since its diagonal $\overline{BD}$ lies in its exterior.

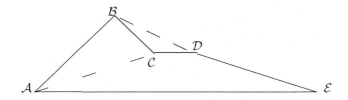

Figure 5.2: A pentagon $\overline{ABCDE}$ and its diagonals $\overline{AC}$ and $\overline{BD}$.

A few more polygons are shown in Fig. 5.3.

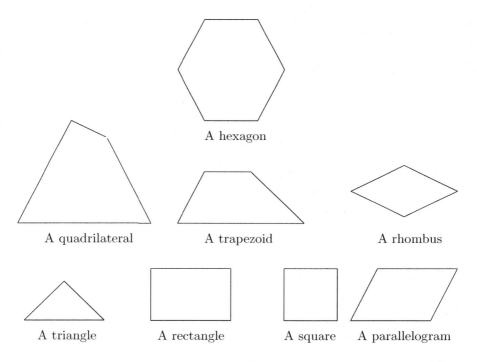

Figure 5.3: A triangle, six quadrilaterals and a hexagon.

Example 5.1.1 *In all the examples of polygons above compare the number of sides with the number of vertices, and draw the conclusion regarding these quantities in any polygon.*

Solution. In any polygon, the number of sides is the same as the number of vertices.   □

Exercise 5.1.2 *Does there exist a 2-gon, that is, a polygon with 2 sides and 2 vertices?*

Exercise 5.1.3 *How many diagonals emanate from every vertex of each polygon in Fig. 5.2 - 5.3?How many diagonals does each polygon in Fig. 5.2 - 5.3 have in total? Analyze these examples and try to derive a general formula for the number of diagonals of a polygon.*

Example 5.1.2 *For example, if we fix a vertex, say A, in a convex quadrilateral $\overline{ABCD}$, then there are three other vertices, B, C, and D, but B and D are connected with A by sides, which are not diagonals, therefore there is only one diagonal, starting at A, namely, $\overline{AC}$. We can observe one more diagonal, $\overline{BD}$. Thus, a quadrilateral has two diagonals.*

Draw more examples of polygons and count diagonals in your examples and in a pentagon, a hexagon, and in a $7-gon$. □

Exercise 5.1.4 *Can a polygon have exactly one diagonal?*

The most common type of polygons are those with $n = 3$, called *triangles*. We will study triangles in the next section. Polygons with $n = 4$ (4-gons) are called *quadrilaterals*. Several special quadrilaterals occur often in architectural designs and many other occasions, and have special names. If the opposite sides of a quadrilateral are pair-wise parallel and pair-wise equal, the quadrilateral is called a *parallelogram*, see Fig. 5.3. We study the parallelograms in Section 5.3.

A quadrilateral with two (opposite) parallel, but not necessarily equal sides is called a *trapezoid*, see Fig. 5.3. The two parallel sides are called the *bases* of the trapezoid. Two other sides are called *lateral* sides. If the lateral sides are equal, the trapezoid is called *isosceles*. If one lateral side is perpendicular to the bases, the trapezoid is called *right trapezoid*.

A parallelogram, whose adjacent sides are perpendicular to one another, so that it has four right angles, is called a *rectangle*, Fig. 5.3. If all the four sides of a rectangle are equal, the rectangle is called *square*, Fig. 5.3.

A parallelogram with four equal sides is called a *rhombus*, Fig. 5.3. Thus, a square is both a parallelogram and a rhombus.

Answers 5.1

Exercise 5.1.1. If they have another common point, then one of these segments is a part of the other one. Another degenerate case is when they belong to a line and extend from the common end-point to the opposite directions.
Exercise 5.1.2. No, it does not exist.
Exercise 5.1.3. The pentagon (Fig. 5.2) has 4 proper (internal) diagonals, AC, AD, BC, CE, and 2 diagonals, BD and BE, that lie outside the polygon. A triangle has no diagonal. Any convex quadrilateral, like those in Fig. 5.3, has 2 diagonals. A hexagon has 9 diagonals.
Exercise 5.1.4. No, such polygon does not exist.

5.2   Triangles

The simplest polygons are triangles, and we shall study them in more detail. Any triangle has six major elements, three sides and three *interior* angles, and the vertices of the angles are called the vertices of the triangle. Triangles are denoted by symbols $\triangle ABC$, where the characters refer to the vertices of the triangle – see Fig. 5.4.

Exercise 5.2.1 *Taking the ordering into account, into how many ordered triples can the three characters $\{A, B, C\}$ be arranged? For example, (A, B, C) and (B, A, C) are two different arrangements.*

Exercise 5.2.2 *In Fig. 5.4, what angles are opposite to the sides $\overline{AC}$ and $\overline{BC}$? What sides are opposite to the angles $\angle A$ and $\angle B$?*

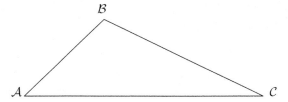

Figure 5.4: A triangle $\triangle ABC$. Here side $\overline{AB}$ is *opposite* to angle $\angle C$ and vice versa, angle $\angle C$ is *opposite* to the side $\overline{AB}$.

If all the three angles of a triangle are acute, the triangle itself is called *acute*. If a triangle has an obtuse angle, the triangle is called *obtuse*. A triangle with a right angle is called a *right* triangle – see Fig. 5.5.

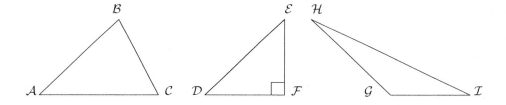

Figure 5.5: An acute triangle $\triangle ABC$, a right triangle $\triangle DEF$ with a right angle $\angle F$, and an obtuse triangle $\triangle GHI$ with an obtuse angle $\angle G$.

Exercise 5.2.3 *Can a triangle have two obtuse angles? An obtuse and a right angle? Two right angles? The angle of 180°? The angle of 179°?*

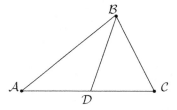

Figure 5.6: $\overline{BD}$ is the median of the side $\overline{AC}$, $|\overline{AD}| = |\overline{DC}|$.

There are several important line segments, associated with each vertex in any triangle, especially, bisectrices, medians, and heights. Consider a triangle $\triangle ABC$, see Fig. 5.6, where the vertex B is opposite to the side $\overline{AC}$, divide the latter side in halves by the point D, that is, $|\overline{AD}| = |\overline{DC}|$, and connect the vertex B and the middle-point D by a segment $\overline{BD}$ (Fig. 5.6); this segment is called the *median* corresponding to the vertex B and the side $\overline{AC}$.

In Fig. 5.7, you see the three medians of the triangle $\triangle ABC$, the points $\mathcal{D}$, $\mathcal{E}$, and $\mathcal{F}$ are the middle points of the sides $\overline{AC}$, $\overline{AB}$, $\overline{BC}$, respectively, that is, $|\overline{A\mathcal{D}}| = |\overline{\mathcal{D}C}|$, $|\overline{A\mathcal{E}}| = |\overline{B\mathcal{E}}|$, $|\overline{B\mathcal{F}}| = |\overline{C\mathcal{F}}|$.

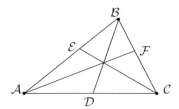

Figure 5.7: $\overline{B\mathcal{D}}$, $\overline{C\mathcal{E}}$, $\overline{A\mathcal{F}}$ are the medians of the triangle $\triangle ABC$.

The three medians in Fig. 5.7 seem to intersect at the same point. Later on we prove that this is not just an optical illusion, but a true mathematical result.

A triangle is called *isosceles* if it has two equal sides. The third side is usually called the *base* of the triangle and drawn horizontally. We establish a few important properties of isosceles triangles.

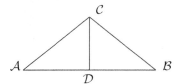

Figure 5.8: An isosceles triangle $\triangle ABC$, $|\overline{AC}| = |\overline{BC}|$.

Consider an isosceles triangle $\triangle ABC$, Fig. 5.8, with equal sides $|\overline{AC}| = |\overline{BC}|$, and let $\overline{CD}$ be the *bisectrix* of the angle $\angle C$, that is, the line, which divides the angle into two equal halves; the point $\mathcal{D}$ belongs to the base $\overline{AB}$. Thus by construction, $\angle ACD = \angle DCB$.

Draw an isosceles triangle on a sheet of paper and fold the paper along the bisectrix $\overline{CD}$ – you will immediately see for yourself that, up to our unprecise drawing, the side $\overline{AC}$ goes along the side $\overline{BC}$, the angle $\angle BAC$ covers the angle $\angle ABC$, and the half-side $\overline{AD}$ goes along $\overline{BD}$. Hence, $\angle ABC = \angle BAC$ and we have discovered (and almost proved) an important though simple result.

Theorem 5.2.1 *In an isosceles triangle, the angles by the base are equal.* □

Moreover, we observe that the angle $\angle ADC$ precisely covers the angle $\angle BDC$, so that these two angles become indistinguishable. Hence, these two angles are equal, and since they are supplementary angles, each of them is a half of the straight angle of 180°, that is, each is the right angle, $\angle ADC = \angle BDC = 90^\circ$. Due to this observation, in an isosceles triangle, the bisectrix of the angle opposite to the base, is perpendicular to the base of the triangle, that is, $\overline{CD} \perp \overline{AB}$ – such a perpendicular to a side of a triangle is called the *height* (or the *altitude*) corresponding to that side. We have proved that

Theorem 5.2.2 *The bisectrix of the angle opposite to the base of an isosceles triangle is also the height and the median of the base.* □

If the base of an isosceles triangle is equal to its equal sides as well, therefore, all the three sides of a triangle are equal, then the triangle is called *equilateral*. In an equilateral triangle every side can be designated as the base with two its adjacent angles equal. Therefore,

Theorem 5.2.3 *In an equilateral triangle all its three angles are equal, and by Theorem 4.3.3, each is equal to* $180° \div 3 = 60°$. □

Before moving on we state without a proof an important property of any, not necessarily right triangle. Consider an arbitrary triangle $\triangle ABC$ and let its angle $\angle C$ be bigger than its $\angle A$, $\angle C > \angle A$ – see Fig.5.9. We claim then that the side opposite to a larger angle $\angle C$, that is, the side $\overline{AB}$ is also bigger (longer) than the side $\overline{BC}$, which is opposite to $\angle A$. And vice versa, if, say, side $\overline{AC}$ is smaller than side $\overline{AB}$, $|\overline{AC}| < |\overline{AB}|$, then the opposite angles preserve the same inequality, $\angle B < \angle C$. We leave a proof of this theorem to the reader, see Theorem 5.2.4 and Exercise 5.2.4.

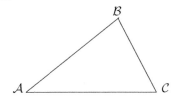

Figure 5.9: $\angle A < \angle C$.

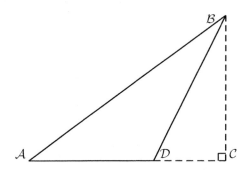

Figure 5.10: In an obtuse triangle $\triangle ABD$, $\angle A < \angle ADB$ and $|\overline{AB}| > |\overline{BD}|$. In a right triangle $\triangle BCD$, $\angle BDC < \angle C$ and $|\overline{BD}| > |\overline{BC}|$.

Theorem 5.2.4 *If in a triangle* $\triangle ABD$, $\angle A > \angle B$, *then* $\overline{BD}$, *the opposite side of the angle* $\angle A$ *is larger than* $\overline{AD}$, *the opposite side of the angle* $\angle B$. □

Exercise 5.2.4 *Considering Fig. 5.10 and a few more examples, convince yourself that the following Theorem 5.2.4 is correct and try to prove it or at least give a plausible explanation why its statement must be true.*

Exercise 5.2.5 *Draw two other heights of the triangle* $\triangle ABD$, *Fig. 5.10.*

Exercise 5.2.6 *In the triangle* $\triangle ABD$, *Fig. 5.10, let angle* $\angle A = 40°$ *and the external angle* $\angle BDC = 80°$. *Find the angles* $\angle B$, $\angle D = \angle ADB$, *and* $\angle DBC$.

5.2.1 Congruent and Similar Triangles

If the "Primer" were a regular full-sized textbook, we would give here a detailed exposition of congruent triangles, and systematically used them hereafter. It is not a regular text though. Moreover, the only valid reason for introducing this very term, *congruent*, is to distinguish two "congruent" triangles as the sets of points in the plane, since all their actual geometrical properties are identical. This is more appropriate in the Bourbaki-like treatise than in this "Primer". There is no harm, if we would call these triangles and other congruent figures just *equal*, and we sometimes do that. To avoid any confusion though, we follow the tradition and use the term *congruent*, but state these very intuitive results as problems for the reader.

Definition 5.2.1 *Two triangle are called congruent if we can completely merge them (make indistinguishable) by a movement in the three-dimensional space, in particular, by a translation in the plane.*

Since congruent triangles can be superposed on one another, so that we see only one triangle, all their corresponding elements are equal (congruent), their corresponding angles are equal, their corresponding sides are equal, they have equal corresponding heights, medians, bisectrices, etc. But it is convenient to have tests for congruence, where we do not have to check, that all the *six* elements, the three angles and three sides, are equal. It is enough to have only three elements equal, but at least one of them must be a *side*. These tests are given in the sequel problem.

Problem 5.2.1 *Prove that two triangles are congruent if*
(1) *Two sides and the enclosed angle of one triangle are equal respectively to two sides and the enclosed angle of another triangle – This property is often referred to as the SAS-test of congruence.*
(2) *A side and the two adjacent angles of one triangle are equal (*congruent – sic!*) respectively to a side and two adjacent angles of another triangle – ASA-test.*
(3) *Three sides of one triangle are equal respectively to three sides of another triangle – SSS-test.*
(4) *It is useful to specialize the ASA-test in the case of right triangles. Namely, if a leg and an adjacent acute angle of one right triangle are equal to a leg and an adjacent acute angle of another right triangle, then the triangles are congruent.*

Problem 5.2.2 (1) *Show by an example, that the SAS-test fails if the angle is not the angle enclosed between the two given sides.*
(2) *Analyze from this point of view the would-be AAS-test.*
(3) *Show by an example, that the specialized ASA-test for right triangles fails if the given angle is opposite rather than adjacent to the given leg.*

Exercise 5.2.7 *A quadrilateral* $\overline{ABCD}$ *in Fig. 5.11 is a parallelogram,* $\overline{AC}$ *is its diagonal. Identify congruent triangles in this figure.*

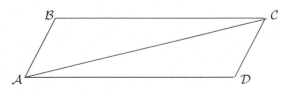

Figure 5.11: Exercise 5.2.7.

Exercise 5.2.8 *Prove that the two angles at a base of a isosceles trapezoid are equal.*

One can say that the *congruent* triangles have the *same shape* and the *same size*. The triangles $\triangle ABC$ and $\triangle DEF$ in Fig. 5.12 are not congruent, they have the same shape but different sizes - such triangles are called *similar*.

Definition 5.2.2 *Two triangles are called similar, denoted $\triangle ABC \sim \triangle DEF$, if their angles are pairwise equal. The sides opposite to equal angles in two similar triangles are called corresponding sides.*

We see that, unlike their opposite angles, the corresponding sides in similar triangles are not, in general, equal.

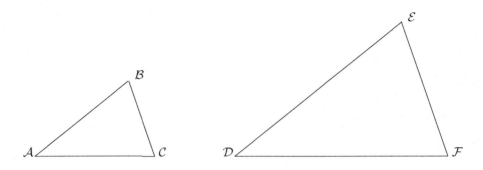

Figure 5.12: Similar triangles $\triangle ABC \sim \triangle DEF$.

Example 5.2.1 *In Fig. 5.12, $\angle A = \angle D$, $\angle B = \angle E$, and $\angle C = \angle F$; the pairs of corresponding sides are $\overline{AB}$ and $\overline{DE}$, $\overline{AC}$ and $\overline{DF}$, $\overline{BC}$ and $\overline{EF}$.* □

Corollary 5.2.1 *Any two equilateral triangles are similar since all their angles are $60° -$ angles.*

The definition of similar triangles involves three equations, since such triangles have three pairs of equal angles. But if we know any two angles of a triangle, then by Theorem 4.3.3 we can calculate the third angle by subtracting these two angles from $180°$. We conclude that if two triangles have only *two* pairs of equal angles, their third angles are also equal. Therefore, if two triangles have two pairs of equal angles they actually have *three* pairs of equal angles, hence, they are similar.

Corollary 5.2.2 *To conclude that two triangles are similar, it is enough to check that they have two pairs of equal angles. Then the third angles in the triangles will be equal automatically, and we do not have to verify this.*

Example 5.2.2 *A triangle $\triangle ABC$ has angles $\angle A = 35°$ and $\angle B = 85°$. A triangle $\triangle DEF$ has angles $\angle D = 35°$ and $\angle E = 60°$. Are these triangles similar?*

Solution. By Theorem 4.3.3, in triangle $\triangle ABC$, the third angle is $\angle C = 180 - 35 - 85 = 60°$, while in triangle $\triangle DEF$ the third angle is $\angle F = 180 - 35 - 60 = 85°$. Therefore, $\angle A = \angle D$, $\angle B = \angle F$, $\angle C = \angle E$, thus, the triangles are similar, $\triangle ABC \sim \triangle DEF$. □

Example 5.2.3 *A triangle $\triangle ABC$ has angles $\angle A = 35°$ and $\angle B = 85°$. A triangle $\triangle DEF \sim \triangle ABC$. Find the angles of $\triangle DEF$.*

Solution. By Theorem 4.3.3, in $\triangle ABC$, $\angle C = 180 - 35 - 85 = 60°$. Thus, $\triangle DEF$ also has angles of $35°$, $85°$, and $60°$, but without some additional information we cannot conclude which of them is, say, $35°$-angle. □

Example 5.2.4 *Are triangles* $\triangle ABC$ *and* $\triangle DEF$ *similar if* $\angle A = 35°$ *and* $\angle B = 85°$, *while* $\angle D = 35°$ *and* $\angle E = 65°$ *?*

Solution. No, because $\angle C = 180 - 35 - 85 = 60°$ and $\angle F = 180 - 35 - 65 = 80°$, thus, these triangles have only one pair of equal angles. □

The most important property of similar triangles is the *proportionality* of their corresponding sides. We state it and the sequel corollary, which is a traditional similarity test, without a proof.

Theorem 5.2.5 *Let* $\triangle ABC$ *and* $\triangle DEF$ *be similar triangles*, $\triangle ABC \sim \triangle DEF$, *such that* $\angle A = \angle D$, $\angle B = \angle E$, *and* $\angle C = \angle F$. *Then their corresponding sides are in proportion, that is,*

$$\frac{|\overline{AB}|}{|\overline{DE}|} = \frac{|\overline{AC}|}{|\overline{DF}|} = \frac{|\overline{BC}|}{|\overline{EF}|}.$$

Corollary 5.2.3 *If an angle of a triangle is equal to an angle of another triangle, and the adjacent sides of these angles are proportional, the triangles are similar.*

Problem 5.2.3 *Prove the Theorem 5.2.5 and Corollary 5.2.3.*

Exercise 5.2.9 *A line segment, connecting the middle points of any two sides of a triangle, is called the midline of the triangle. Prove that the midline is parallel to the third side and is equal to a half of it.*

Problem 5.2.4 *Define the midline of a trapezoid and state its properties similarly to the previous exercise.*

Example 5.2.5 *A triangle* $\triangle ABC$ *has the angles* $\angle A = 35°$ *and* $\angle B = 85°$. *A triangle* $\triangle DEF$ *has the angles* $\angle D = 35°$ *and* $\angle E = 60°$. *Find* $|\overline{DF}|$ *and* $|\overline{EF}|$, *given the sides* $|\overline{AB}| = 4$, $|\overline{BC}| = 7$, $|\overline{AC}| = 9$, *and* $|\overline{DE}| = 99$.

Solution. We proved in Example 5.2.2 that $\triangle ABC \sim \triangle DEF$. Therefore, by Theorem 5.2.5, $\frac{9}{4} = \frac{99}{|\overline{DF}|}$, hence $|\overline{DF}| = \frac{4 \cdot 99}{9} = 44$ and $\frac{|\overline{FE}|}{7} = \frac{44}{4}$, thus $|\overline{FE}| = 77$. □

In Section 4.3 we considered two parallel lines intersected by a transversal. An extensive source of problems about the similar triangles, both in real life, like GPS systems, and at tests of all level is a configuration consisting of two parallel lines $\mathcal{L}_1$ and $\mathcal{L}_2$ and two transversals, $\mathcal{T}_1$ and $\mathcal{T}_2$, see Fig. 5.13 – 5.14. The difference between these figures is that the transversals in Fig. 5.14 intersect at the point $\mathcal{O}_2$ *between* the parallel lines, while the transversals in Fig. 5.13 intersect at the point $\mathcal{O}_1$ *outside* the parallel lines.

Two transversals can be parallel and never intersect, like $\mathcal{T}_4 \| \mathcal{T}_5$ in Fig. 5.15. In this case we can regard the lines $\mathcal{L}_1$ and $\mathcal{L}_2$ as transversals of the parallel lines $\mathcal{T}_4$ and $\mathcal{T}_5$.

Let us look at triangles $\triangle AC\mathcal{O}_1$ and $\triangle BD\mathcal{O}_1$ in Fig. 5.13. They share the angle $\angle B\mathcal{O}_1D$. Moreover, $\angle \mathcal{O}_1BD = \angle \mathcal{O}_1AC$ as corresponding angles – see Section 4.3, and, even though this is not necessary by virtue Corollary 5.2.1, since there are already two pairs of equal angles, $\angle \mathcal{O}_1DB = \angle \mathcal{O}_1CA$ as another pair of corresponding angles. Thus, in Fig. 5.13 we have two similar triangles, $\triangle AC\mathcal{O}_1 \sim \triangle BD\mathcal{O}_1$.

Next, we determine what sides of these triangles correspond to one another. Recalling that the corresponding sides *oppose* equal angles, we pick any side, say, side $\overline{BD}$. In the smaller triangle $\triangle BD\mathcal{O}_1$, the side $\overline{BD}$ is opposite to the angle $\angle \mathcal{O}_1$. However, in the larger triangle $\triangle AC\mathcal{O}_1$ this very angle is opposite to the side $\overline{AC}$, thus, the sides $\overline{BD}$ and $\overline{AC}$ are *corresponding sides* in the similar triangles $\triangle AC\mathcal{O}_1 \sim \triangle BD\mathcal{O}_1$.

We have demonstrated in this example how to identify pairs of the corresponding sides in two similar triangles. We can describe the algorithm as follows:

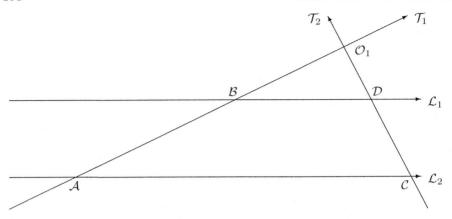

Figure 5.13: Parallel lines $\mathcal{L}_1\|\mathcal{L}_2$ with transversals $\mathcal{T}_1$ and $\mathcal{T}_2$.

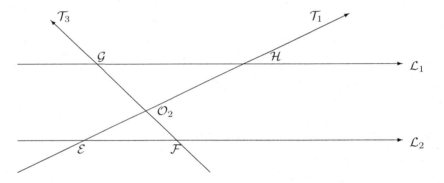

Figure 5.14: Parallel lines $\mathcal{L}_1\|\mathcal{L}_2$ with transversals $\mathcal{T}_1$ and $\mathcal{T}_3$.

Given a side of any triangle,
- GO TO the opposite angle in this triangle
- GO TO the equal angle in the other similar triangle
- GO TO the opposite side of the latter angle
– This is the corresponding side to the given one.

Let us practice the algorithm above and identify two other pairs of corresponding sides in the similar triangles

$$\triangle \mathcal{ACO}_1 \sim \triangle \mathcal{BDO}_1.$$

To do this, we start with the bigger triangle $\triangle \mathcal{ACO}_1$ and pick its side $\overline{\mathcal{AO}_1}$. It is opposite to the angle $\angle \mathcal{ACO}_1$, which is equal to the angle $\angle \mathcal{D}$ in $\triangle \mathcal{BDO}_1$. The opposite side to the angle $\angle \mathcal{D}$ in $\triangle \mathcal{BDO}_1$ is $\overline{\mathcal{BO}_1}$, thus $\overline{\mathcal{AO}_1}$ and $\overline{\mathcal{BO}_1}$ are corresponding sides. If we repeat this reasoning one more time, we find the third pair of corresponding sides in these triangles, $\overline{\mathcal{CO}_1}$ and $\overline{\mathcal{DO}_1}$. Applying the major property of similar triangles, we claim that the sides of the similar triangles $\triangle \mathcal{ACO}_1 \sim \triangle \mathcal{BDO}_1$ make a double proportion

$$\frac{|\overline{\mathcal{BD}}|}{|\overline{\mathcal{AC}}|} = \frac{|\overline{\mathcal{BO}_1}|}{|\overline{\mathcal{AO}_1}|} = \frac{|\overline{\mathcal{DO}_1}|}{|\overline{\mathcal{CO}_1}|}.$$

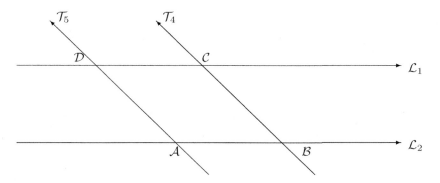

Figure 5.15: Two pairs of parallel lines $\mathcal{L}_1\|\mathcal{L}_2$ and $\mathcal{T}_4\|\mathcal{T}_5$.

While composing these proportions, we must be consistent: if in the first ratio we placed a side of the triangle $\triangle BD\mathcal{O}_1$ on top (in the numerator) and a side of the triangle $\triangle A\mathcal{C}\mathcal{O}_1$ at the bottom (in the denominator), we must follow this order in all of the sequel ratios. We can change the order of the triangles and write the first ratio as $\frac{AC}{BD}$, but then we must follow *this order* throughout the entire proportion. Actually, we just flipped all the ratios simultaneously. For example, in this problem we can compose the next proportion with the same results:

$$\frac{|AC|}{|BD|} = \frac{|A\mathcal{O}_1|}{|B\mathcal{O}_1|} = \frac{|C\mathcal{O}_1|}{|D\mathcal{O}_1|}. \tag{5.2.1}$$

Example 5.2.6 *In this example, we refer to Fig. 5.13. Given $|B\mathcal{O}_1| = 5$, $|BD| = 6$, and $|A\mathcal{O}_1| = 30$, find $|AC|$ and $|AB|$.*

Solution. The ratio $\frac{|C\mathcal{O}_1|}{|D\mathcal{O}_1|}$ is useless in this problem, since both these sides are not given and are not among the sides to compute. Thus, we drop this ratio and extract from the proportion (5.2.1) an equation, containing the other two ratios, the ratios which contain the three given sides and the unknown,

$$\frac{|AC|}{|BD|} = \frac{|A\mathcal{O}_1|}{|B\mathcal{O}_1|}.$$

Inserting the given numbers, we derive the proportion

$$\frac{|AC|}{6} = \frac{30}{5}.$$

By the fundamental property of proportions, we get from here $5 \cdot |AC| = 6 \cdot 30$, which is a linear equation for the unknown $|AC|$. Dividing both sides by the coefficient 5 and computing the fraction $\frac{6 \cdot 30}{5} = 36$ in the right-hand side, we find $|AC| = 36$.

To find $|AB|$, we notice that the side $|A\mathcal{O}_1|$ consists of two parts, and

$$|A\mathcal{O}_1| = |AB| + |B\mathcal{O}_1|,$$

hence $|AB| = |A\mathcal{O}_1| - |B\mathcal{O}_1| = 30 - 5 = 25$.   □

Example 5.2.7 *We again refer to Fig. 5.13. To find either $|C\mathcal{O}_1|$, or $|CD|$, or $|D\mathcal{O}_1|$, we need some information, pertinent to the side $|C\mathcal{O}_1|$. For example, let us find the segment $|CD|$, given the side $|D\mathcal{O}_1| = 3$.*

Solution. Now we have to use another ratio, containing the given side $|D\mathcal{O}_1|$. For example, we can use the proportion

$$\frac{|AC|}{|BD|} = \frac{|C\mathcal{O}_1|}{|D\mathcal{O}_1|},$$

since we have already found $|\mathcal{AC}|$. Inserting the known numbers, we get the proportion

$$\frac{36}{6} = \frac{|\mathcal{CO}_1|}{3}.$$

Solving the latter, we find $|\mathcal{CO}_1| = 18$, and finally,

$$|\mathcal{CD}| = |\mathcal{CO}_1| - |\mathcal{DO}_1| = 18 - 3 = 15.$$

$\square$

The major property of similar triangles used in the solutions above, also can be reversed; we leave the proof of the following claim to the reader.

Theorem 5.2.6 *Given triangles* $\triangle \mathcal{ABC}$ *and* $\triangle \mathcal{DEF}$. *If their sides are proportional, that is,*

$$\frac{|\overline{\mathcal{AB}}|}{|\overline{\mathcal{DE}}|} = \frac{|\overline{\mathcal{AC}}|}{|\overline{\mathcal{DF}}|} = \frac{|\overline{\mathcal{BC}}|}{|\overline{\mathcal{EF}}|},$$

then the angles of the triangles are pairwise equal, that is,

$$\angle A = \angle D, \ \angle B = \angle E, \ \angle C = \angle F,$$

hence, the triangles $\triangle \mathcal{ABC}$ *and* $\triangle \mathcal{DEF}$ *are similar,* $\triangle \mathcal{ABC} \sim \triangle \mathcal{DEF}$. $\square$

In Fig. 5.14, we also have a pair of similar triangles, $\triangle \mathcal{GHO}_2$ and $\triangle \mathcal{EFO}_2$, however they are "flipped over" with respect to one another. Indeed, the angles $\angle \mathcal{GO}_2 \mathcal{H}$ and $\angle \mathcal{EO}_2 \mathcal{F}$ are equal, for they are vertical angles, the angles $\angle \mathcal{HGO}_2 = \angle \mathcal{EFO}_2$ by Corollary 5.2.1, since they are alternate interior angles, and the angles $\angle \mathcal{GHO}_2 = \angle \mathcal{FEO}_2$ by the same reason. Therefore, the pairs of corresponding sides are now $\mathcal{GH}$ and $\mathcal{EF}$, $\mathcal{GO}_2$ and $\mathcal{FO}_2$, $\mathcal{HO}_2$ and $\mathcal{EO}_2$, and the principal proportion for these triangles is

$$\frac{\mathcal{GH}}{\mathcal{EF}} = \frac{\mathcal{GO}_2}{\mathcal{FO}_2} = \frac{\mathcal{HO}_2}{\mathcal{EO}_2}.$$

Example 5.2.8 *Here we refer to Fig. 5.14. Given* $|\mathcal{GO}_2| = 5$, $|\mathcal{GH}| = 6$, $|\mathcal{HO}_2| = 4$,, *and* $|\mathcal{EO}_2| = 30$, *find* $|\mathcal{EF}|$ *and* $|\mathcal{FO}_2|$.

Solution. From the proportion above we immediately compute $|\mathcal{EF}| = 45$ and $|\mathcal{FO}_2| = 37\frac{1}{2}$. $\square$

Example 5.2.9 *[6, No. 15] - see Fig. 5.16. A surveillance photo was taken from a plane with a camera having a focal length of F=10 inches. The representative fraction, that is, the ratio of a distance A on the photograph to the corresponding distance B on the ground, is 1 : 12,000. How high over the ground level was the plane?*

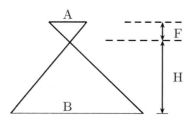

Figure 5.16: Example 5.2.9. The altitude of the plane is H.

Solution. Focal length $= 10" = \frac{5}{6}$ ft. Thus, $\frac{A}{B} = \frac{F}{H}$, or $\frac{1}{12,000} = \frac{5/6}{H}$. From this proportion, $H = 10,000$ ft. $\square$

As an application of the properties of similar triangles, we prove the following beautiful and useful result.

Theorem 5.2.7 *In a triangle, two medians intersect one another at a point, which divides each of them in the ratio 1 : 2, that is, the smaller part of each median is exactly $\frac{1}{3}$ of the entire median – see Fig. 5.16.*

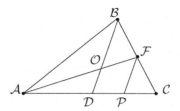

Figure 5.17: $\mathcal{BD}$ and $\mathcal{AF}$ are two medians of the triangle $\triangle\mathcal{ABC}$; $\mathcal{OD} = \frac{1}{3}\mathcal{BD}$, $\mathcal{OF} = \frac{1}{3}\mathcal{AF}$.

Proof. Draw a segment $\mathcal{FP}$ parallel to the median $\mathcal{BD}$; the triangles $\triangle\mathcal{BDC}$ and $\triangle\mathcal{FPC}$ with the parallel bases share the angle $\angle\mathcal{C}$, therefore they are similar. Since $\mathcal{AF}$ is a median, the point $\mathcal{F}$ divides the side $\mathcal{BC}$ in halves. Thus $\mathcal{FC}$ is a half of $\mathcal{BC}$, and due to the similarity, $\mathcal{PC} = \frac{1}{2}\mathcal{DC}$. However, $\mathcal{BD}$ is a median as well, $\mathcal{AD} = \mathcal{DC}$, hence, $\mathcal{AD} = \frac{2}{3}\mathcal{AP}$. Finally, since $\triangle\mathcal{AOD} \sim \triangle\mathcal{AFP}$ (Prove it!)$\mathcal{OD} = \frac{2}{3}\mathcal{FP}$, and the latter, in turn, is $\frac{1}{2}\mathcal{BD}$. That together with the previous equation, gives

$$\mathcal{OD} = \frac{2}{3}\mathcal{FP} = \frac{2}{3} \cdot \frac{1}{2}\mathcal{BD} = \frac{1}{3}\mathcal{BD}.$$

$\square$

Since this reasoning applies to any pair of the medians in a triangle, and the point, cutting one-third of the median, is unique and does not depend upon another median, we immediately deduce an important corollary.

Theorem 5.2.8 *The three medians of any triangle intersect at the same point, called the barycenter of the triangle.* $\square$

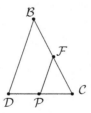

Figure 5.18: $\mathcal{BD}\|\mathcal{PF}$, $\mathcal{PF} = 12$, $\mathcal{BF} = \mathcal{CF} = 11$.

Exercise 5.2.10 *Given two parallel lines, see Fig. 5.17, $\mathcal{BD}\|\mathcal{PF}$, find $\mathcal{BD}$ if $\mathcal{PF} = 12$ and $\mathcal{BF} = \mathcal{CF} = 11$.*

Exercise 5.2.11 *Given two parallel lines $\mathcal{GH}\|\mathcal{EF}$, see Fig. 5.18, find $\mathcal{GO}$ and $\mathcal{GH}$ if $\mathcal{OE} = 10$, $\mathcal{OF} = 8$, $\mathcal{OF} = 12$, and $\mathcal{OH} = 20$.*

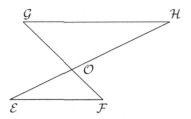

Figure 5.19: Parallel lines $\mathcal{EF}\|\mathcal{GH}$ with transversals $\mathcal{EH}$ and $\mathcal{FG}$.

5.2.2   Right Triangles. The Pythagorean Theorem

There are two major types of problems about right triangles – those involving angles and involving sides. The first type is straightforward. Consider a right triangle $\triangle ABC$, Fig. 5.20. Since the sum of the three angles is $180°$ and $\angle C = 90°$, two other acute angles add up to $90°$ as well, $\angle A + \angle B = 90°$.

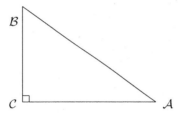

Figure 5.20: A right triangle $\triangle ABC$.

Example 5.2.10 *In a right triangle $\triangle ABC$ with right angle $\angle C = 90°$, angle $\angle A$ is four times $\angle B$. Find the angles $\angle A$ and $\angle B$.*

Solution. Set $\angle B = x$. Then $\angle A = 4x$, thus $x + 4x = 5x = 90°$, $\angle B = x = 90/5 = 18°$ and $\angle A = 4x = 72°$.   □

Exercise 5.2.12 *The difference of the acute angles of a right triangle is $20°$. Find the angles of the triangle.*

Exercise 5.2.13 *The difference of the acute angles of a right triangle is a half of their sum. Find the angles of the triangle.*

Exercise 5.2.14 *Design and solve two more exercises similar to the previous ones.*

Now we tackle problems involving the sides of a right triangle $\triangle ABC$; to be specific let angle C be the right angle, $\angle C = 90°$. The longest side, opposite to the right angle $\angle C$, is called the *hypotenuse*, two other sides are called *legs* or catheti[1]. Since an acute angle, by Theorem 5.2.4, is smaller than the right angle, both legs, which are opposite to acute angles, are shorter than the hypotenuse. The major fact regarding the sides of a right triangle, is the following.

---

[1]The plural for *cathetus*.

Theorem 5.2.9 Pythagorean Theorem. *Denote the lengths of the sides of a right triangle* $\triangle \mathcal{ABC}$ *with right angle* $\angle \mathcal{C} = 90°$ *as* $|\overline{AB}| = c$, $|\overline{BC}| = a$ *and* $|\overline{AC}| = b$, *respectively. Then*

$$a^2 + b^2 = c^2,$$

that is, in a right triangle, the sum of the squares of the two legs is equal to the square of the hypotenuse.

The converse statement is also valid: In any plain triangle, if the sum of the squares of two sides is equal to the square of the third side, then this is a right triangle, and the longest side is the hypotenuse of the triangle.

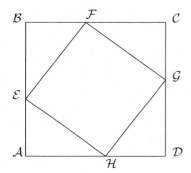 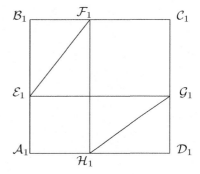

Figure 5.21: A Proof of the Pythagorean Theorem.

Proof. We prove only the first statement of the theorem. Consider a right triangle with legs a and b and the hypotenuse c, and draw a square $\mathcal{ABCD}$ with the side $a + b$, and also an equal (congruent!) square $\mathcal{A}_1\mathcal{B}_1\mathcal{C}_1\mathcal{D}_1$, see Fig. 5.21. The proof is clear from this figure, where

$$\mathcal{AE} = \mathcal{BF} = \mathcal{CG} = \mathcal{DH} = a$$

and

$$\mathcal{BE} = \mathcal{CF} = \mathcal{DG} = \mathcal{AH} = b.$$

On the one hand, the four inscribed right triangles inside $\mathcal{ABCD}$ are equal, thus the area of the square $\mathcal{EFGH}$ is c^2 – that claim must be proved, see Exercise 5.2.15.

On the other hand, draw the segment $\mathcal{E}_1\mathcal{G}_1$ parallel to the side $\mathcal{A}_1\mathcal{D}_1$ in the square $\mathcal{A}_1\mathcal{B}_1\mathcal{C}_1\mathcal{D}_1$, such that $|\mathcal{B}_1\mathcal{E}_1| = |\mathcal{BE}|$ and the segment $\mathcal{F}_1\mathcal{H}_1$ parallel to the side $\mathcal{A}_1\mathcal{B}_1$, such that $|\mathcal{B}_1\mathcal{F}_1| = |\mathcal{BF}|$. Hence the square $\mathcal{A}_1\mathcal{B}_1\mathcal{C}_1\mathcal{D}_1$ consists of the same four right triangles and the two smaller squares, whose areas are a^2 and b^2. Removing the four triangles from the area of $\mathcal{ABCD}$, we literally see the statement of the Pythagorean Theorem: $a^2 + b^2 = c^2$. □

Exercise 5.2.15 *Prove that the quadrilateral* $\mathcal{EFGH}$ *(Fig. 5.21) is a square.*

Exercise 5.2.16 *Find the hypotenuse of a right triangle with the legs of 3 ft. and 4 ft. - This is called the Egyptian triangle.*

Exercise 5.2.17 *Find a leg of a right triangle with another leg of 3 ft. and the hypotenuse of 6 ft.*

Exercise 5.2.18 *Design and solve two more exercises similar to the previous ones.*

Exercise 5.2.19 *A triangle has two sides of 2 in and 4 in, respectively, and the third side is the half-sum of these two. Is it a right triangle?*

Exercise 5.2.20 *Does there exist a right triangle with a leg of 2 ft. and the hypotenuse of 1ft.? Give a general statement generalizing this exercise.*

Exercise 5.2.21 *A triangle has two sides of 1 ft. and the third side of 3 ft. What is wrong with these data?*

Consider a right triangle $\triangle ABC$ (Fig. 5.22), where CD is the height to the side AB, that is, $CD \perp AB$.

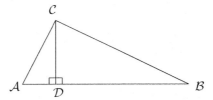

Figure 5.22: A right triangle $\triangle ABC$, $\angle ACB = 90°$, the height $CD \perp AB$.

Both triangles $\triangle ADC$ and $\triangle BDC$ are right triangles, for the height $CD \perp AB$. Since the two acute angles in a right triangle add up to $90°$, and there are three right triangles in Fig. 5.21, we have $\angle A + \angle B = 90°$, $\angle ACD + \angle CAD = 90°$, and $\angle BCD + \angle DBC = 90°$. From these equations we deduce

$$\angle A = \angle BCD \text{ and } \angle B = \angle ACD.$$

Therefore, the angles in these triangles are pair-wise equal and the triangles are similar:

$$\triangle ABC \sim \triangle ACD \sim \triangle BCD.$$

Recasting the similarity into the proportionality of the corresponding sides, we prove the following claim.

Theorem 5.2.10 *Consider a right triangle $\triangle ABC$ with the right angle $\angle C$ and the height $CD \perp AB$ – see again Fig. 5.22. Then the height is the mid-proportional between the parts it splits the side AB, that is,*

$$\frac{|AD|}{|CD|} = \frac{|CD|}{|BD|}.$$

In some problems it is convenient to rewrite the latter as

$$|CD|^2 = |AD| \cdot |DB|.$$

Problem 5.2.5 *What other proportions are valid for these similar triangles?*

Let us look again at Fig. 5.22, and compare the angles $\angle A$ and $\angle BCD$ – we have known already that they have pair-wise perpendicular sides. Indeed, $AC \perp BC$ and $CD \perp AB$. What is more, they are equal. This is a special instance of the following theorem, whose proof we leave as a problem to the reader.

Problem 5.2.6 *Prove that any two angles with the mutually pair-wise perpendicular sides are equal.*

We finish the section by presenting one more useful property of right triangles. Now we consider a special triangle with acute angle of $30°$, therefore, the other acute angle is $90 - 30 = 60°$; see the triangle $\triangle ABC$ in Fig. 5.23, where the angle $\angle ACD = 30°$ and the angle $\angle A = 60°$. The dashed triangle $\triangle BDC$ is the mirror reflection of the given triangle $\triangle ADC$ with respect to the vertical line DC. The two triangles are congruent, therefore, angle

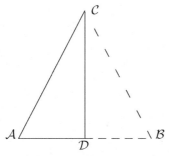

Figure 5.23: A $30° - 60°$-right triangle $\triangle\mathcal{ADC}$.

$\angle\mathcal{ABC} = 60°$, $\angle\mathcal{BCD} = 30°$, and so that the angle $\angle\mathcal{ACB} = 60°$. We have proved that triangle $\triangle\mathcal{ABC}$ is equilateral triangle.

Next, since $\mathcal{AD} = \mathcal{BD}$ by construction, and $\mathcal{AB} = \mathcal{AC}$, $\mathcal{AD}$ is exactly half of the side $\mathcal{AC}$. We proved the following statement.

Proposition 5.2.1 *In a $30° - 60°$-right triangle, the leg opposite to the $30°$ angle is equal to the half of the hypotenuse.*   □

Exercise 5.2.22 *Smart Mouse has to walk from her house $\mathcal{A}$ to her country house $\mathcal{F}$ – see Fig. 5.24. There are two routes, either directly from $\mathcal{A}$ to $\mathcal{E}$ and then to $\mathcal{F}$, or go from $\mathcal{A}$ to an intermediate point $\mathcal{C}$, then to $\mathcal{D}$, and from here directly to $\mathcal{F}$. The GPS gives the following distances, in miles, $|\mathcal{AB}| = 2$, $|\mathcal{AE}| = 4$, $|\mathcal{BD}| = 1$, $|\mathcal{BC}| = 1$, and $|\mathcal{EF}| = 3$. Which way is shorter, $\mathcal{AEF}$ or $\mathcal{ACDF}$?*

Problem 5.2.7 *This problem also refers to Fig. 5.24. Smart Mouse loves mathematics and she decided to find what the vertical distance $|\mathcal{BC}|$ should be to make the two routes of equal length. Can you help her to solve the problem?*

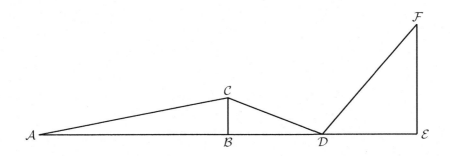

Figure 5.24: Exercise 5.2.22 and Problem 5.2.7.

5.2.3 More Triangles

The bisectrix (or *bisector*) of an angle was defined in Section 5.1, before Theorem 5.2.1; it has many uses. In Fig. 5.24, $\overrightarrow{\mathcal{OD}}$ is the bisectrix of the angle $\angle\mathcal{AOB}$, $\mathcal{D}$ is its arbitrary point.

Drop perpendiculars from that point onto the sides of the angle, $\mathcal{DK} \perp \mathcal{OA}$ and $\mathcal{DL} \perp \mathcal{OB}$. The right triangles $\mathcal{ODK}$ and $\mathcal{ODL}$ are equal, because they share the hypotenuse $\mathcal{OD}$ and,

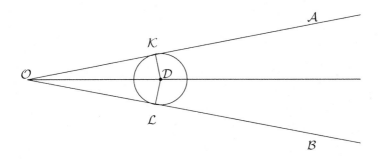

Figure 5.25: The bisectrix $\overline{\mathcal{OD}}$ of angle $\angle\mathcal{AOB}$ and perpendiculars $\overline{\mathcal{DK}} \perp \overline{\mathcal{OA}}$ and $\overline{\mathcal{DL}} \perp \overline{\mathcal{OB}}$.

by the definition of bisectrix, have equal acute angles $\angle\mathcal{AOD} = \angle\mathcal{DOB}$. Therefore, the other acute angles of these triangles are also equal, $\angle\mathcal{KDO} = \angle\mathcal{LDO}$.

Thus, if we draw a circle centered at the point $\mathcal{D}$ of radius $\mathcal{DK} = \mathcal{DL}$, it touches both sides $\mathcal{OA}$ and $\mathcal{OB}$ of the angle; if both sides of an angle are tangent lines to the circle, the circle is said to be *inscribed* in the angle. We repeat that the center of the inscribed circle lies on the bisectrix of the angle.

Another useful observation is that if we have to measure the distance from an external point to a line, we mean, of course, the shortest distance, and this shortest distance is given by the perpendicular dropped from the point onto the line. Indeed, the slanted segments $\mathcal{AB}$ and $\mathcal{CB}$ (Fig 5.25) are obviously longer than the perpendicular $\mathcal{BD}$ to the line.

Remark 5.2.1 *Any claim that something is "obvious" can be dangerous and misleading. The "obviously longer" claim above must be proved – it follows from Theorem 5.2.4.*

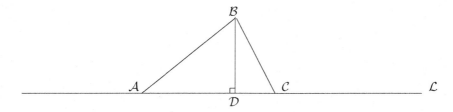

Figure 5.26: The distance from the point $\mathcal{B}$ to the line $\mathcal{L}$ is given by the perpendicular $\mathcal{BD} \perp \mathcal{L}$.

Problem 5.2.8 *Let $\mathcal{B}$ be a point outside a line. Drop a perpendicular $\mathcal{BD}$ from the point onto the line, and connect $\mathcal{B}$ with two other points $\mathcal{A}$ and $\mathcal{C}$ on the line by segments $\mathcal{AB}$ and $\mathcal{CB}$. The segment $\mathcal{AD}$ is called the projection of the slanted (or oblique) line $\mathcal{AB}$ on the line; $\mathcal{CD}$ is the projection of the oblique line $\mathcal{AC}$ on the same line. Prove that a longer slanted line has the longer projection, and vice versa, the longer projection corresponds to the longer slanted line.*

Consider now a triangle $\triangle\mathcal{ABC}$ (Fig. 5.26) and draw the bisectrices of its angles $\angle\mathcal{A}$ and $\angle\mathcal{C}$. They are inside the triangle and therefore cannot be parallel and must intersect at some interior point $\mathcal{O}$. Next, we draw a segment through this point $\mathcal{O}$ and the vertex $\mathcal{B}$, and extend it till the intersection with the opposite side $\mathcal{AC}$ at some point $\mathcal{K}$. We claim that the segment $\overline{\mathcal{BK}}$ is the bisectrix of $\angle\mathcal{B}$.

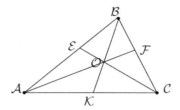

Figure 5.27: $\overline{\mathcal{BK}}$, $\overline{\mathcal{CE}}$, $\overline{\mathcal{AF}}$ are the bisectrices of the triangle $\triangle\mathcal{ABC}$.

Theorem 5.2.11 *In any triangle, the three bisectrices of its interior angles intersect at the same point.*

Proof – see Fig. 5.26. Indeed, since the point $\mathcal{O}$ is on the bisectrix $\mathcal{AO}$, it is equidistant from the sides $\mathcal{AB}$ and $\mathcal{AC}$. Similarly, $\mathcal{O}$ is equidistant from the sides $\mathcal{CB}$ and $\mathcal{AC}$. Thus, $\mathcal{O}$ is equidistant from the sides $\mathcal{AB}$ and $\mathcal{BC}$, that is, the point $\mathcal{O}$ is on the bisectrix $\mathcal{BK}$.   □

Answers 5.2

Exercise 5.2.1. There are 6 such arrangements: $(\mathcal{A},\mathcal{B},\mathcal{C})$, $(\mathcal{A},\mathcal{C},\mathcal{B})$, $(\mathcal{B},\mathcal{A},\mathcal{C})$, $(\mathcal{B},\mathcal{C},\mathcal{A})$, $(\mathcal{C},\mathcal{A},\mathcal{B})$, $(\mathcal{C},\mathcal{B},\mathcal{A})$.
Exercise 5.2.2. The angle $\angle\mathcal{A}$ is opposite to the side $\overline{\mathcal{BC}}$ and vice versa, the angle $\angle\mathcal{B}$ is opposite to the side $\overline{\mathcal{AC}}$, the angle $\angle\mathcal{C}$ is opposite to the side $\overline{\mathcal{AB}}$.
Exercise 5.2.3. No. No. No. No. Yes, for example, a triangle can have the angle of $179°$ and two angles of $0.5°$.
Exercise 5.2.4. Let us look at Fig. 5.9 and imagine that there is a hinge at the vertex $(\mathcal{B})$ and we can rotate the side $\overline{\mathcal{BD}}$ counter-clock-wise, until it covers the vertical side $\overline{\mathcal{BC}}$. It looks obvious that the point $\mathcal{D}$ will go below the point $\mathcal{C}$, therefore, $\overline{\mathcal{BD}}$ is longer (bigger) than $\overline{\mathcal{BC}}$. However, $\overline{\mathcal{BD}}$ is opposite to the right angle $\angle\mathcal{C}$, while $\overline{\mathcal{BC}}$ is opposite to the acute, that is, smaller angle $\angle\mathcal{BDC}$. All the other possible relationships between sides and opposite angles can be studied exactly in the same way.
Exercise 5.2.5. See Fig. 5.27.
 Exercise 5.2.6. $\angle\mathcal{B} = 40°$, $\angle\mathcal{ADB} = 100°$, $\angle\mathcal{DBC} = 10°$.
Exercise 5.2.7. $\triangle\mathcal{ABC} \sim \triangle\mathcal{ACD}$.
Exercise 5.2.10. $\mathcal{BD} = 24$.
Exercise 5.2.11. $\mathcal{GO} = 16$, $\mathcal{GH} = 24$.
Exercise 5.2.12. The acute angles satisfy the linear system $\alpha - \beta = 20°$ and $\alpha + \beta = 90°$. Hence, $\alpha = 55°$ and $\beta = 35°$.
Exercise 5.2.13. The angles are $22.5°$ and $67.5°$.
Exercise 5.2.15. The right triangles $\triangle\mathcal{AEH}$ and triangle $\triangle\mathcal{DGH}$ are similar, since $\mathcal{AH} = \mathcal{DG}$ and $\mathcal{AE} = \mathcal{DH}$. Therefore, $\angle\mathcal{AEH} + \angle\mathcal{AHE} = 90°$, or $\angle\mathcal{DHG} + \angle\mathcal{AHE} = 90°$, and finally, $\angle\mathcal{EHG} = 180° - (\angle\mathcal{DHG} + \angle\mathcal{AHE}) = 90°$.
Exercise 5.2.16. $\mathcal{H} = \sqrt{3^2 + 4^2} = 5$ ft.
Exercise 5.2.17. $l = \sqrt{6^2 - 3^2} = 3\sqrt{3}$ ft.
Exercise 5.2.19. The third side is $(2 + 4)/2 = 3$, which is less than 4, thus 4 could be the hypotenuse only. But $2^2 + 3^2 = 13 \neq 4^2 = 16$, therefore, this is not a right triangle.
Exercise 5.2.20. No, a leg cannot be longer than the hypotenuse.
Exercise 5.2.21. The sum of any two sides of a triangle must be larger than the third

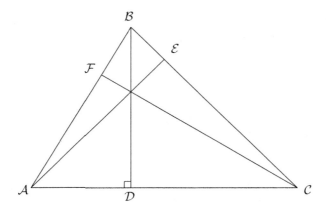

Figure 5.28: Exercise 5.2.5. In the triangle $\triangle ABC$, height $BD \perp AC$, height $AE \perp BC$, height $CF \perp AB$.

side.

Exercise 5.2.22. $|AE| + |EF| = 7$, while $|AC| + |CD| + |DE| = \sqrt{5} + \sqrt{2} + \sqrt{10} \approx 6.8$.
Problem 5.2.7. Let $|BC| = x$. Then the condition of equal lengths becomes a quadratic equation for x^2. Solving this equation, we get

$$x = \frac{1}{13}\sqrt{2085 - 588\sqrt{10}} \approx 1.155.$$

5.3 Parallelograms

Quadrilaterals or 4-gons were introduced above. Here we consider in more details *parallelograms*, Fig. 5.28. We remind the definition, which was given implicitly on p. 184.

Definition 5.3.1 *A quadrilateral is called a parallelogram if its opposite sides are pair-wise equal[2] and parallel.*

For example, in Fig. 5.28, $|AB| = |CD|$, $|AD| = |BC|$, $AB \| CD$, and $AD \| BC$.

Exercise 5.3.1 *What is the sum of the two angles adjacent to a lateral side of a trapezoid?*

Consider again a parallelogram $ABCD$ and erect a perpendicular DE from the vertex D onto its side BC – see Fig. 5.28. This perpendicular is called a *height* of the parallelogram $ABCD$, and often its length $|DE|$ is also called the *height* of the parallelogram. Moreover, we can drop a perpendicular CF from the vertex C onto the (extension of) the side AB or drop a perpendicular BG from the vertex B onto the side CD – then CF and BG are also heights of the parallelogram $ABCD$ and have the same length.

Theorem 5.3.1 *The opposite angles of a parallelogram are pairwise equal; thus in Fig. 5.28, $\angle A = \angle C$ and $\angle B = \angle D$. The opposite sides of a parallelogram are also pairwise equal – in Fig. 5.28, $AB = CD$ and $AD = BC$. Moreover, in a parallelogram the two angles adjacent to any side, are supplementary; thus, in Fig. 5.28, $\angle A + \angle B = \angle A + \angle D = 180°$, etc.*

---

[2]Here again, instead of a technical term *congruent* we say *equal*.

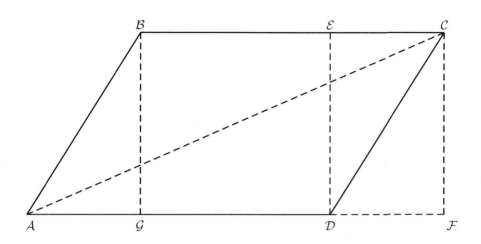

Figure 5.29: Parallelogram $\mathcal{ABCD}$, $\mathcal{AC}$ is its diagonal, $\mathcal{BG}$, $\mathcal{ED}$, and $\mathcal{CF}$ are its heights; $\mathcal{DE} \perp \mathcal{BC}$, it is also perpendicular to the other side, $\mathcal{DE} \perp \mathcal{AD}$; also $\mathcal{FC} \perp \mathcal{BC}$ and $\mathcal{BG} \perp \mathcal{BC}$.

Proof. These properties follow immediately from the properties of similar triangles. Indeed, consider a diagonal $\mathcal{AC}$ – it makes two triangles $\triangle \mathcal{ABC}$ and $\triangle \mathcal{ADC}$. The triangles are similar since the sides $\mathcal{AB}$ and $\mathcal{DC}$ are parallel by the definition of a parallelogram, and the diagonal $\mathcal{AC}$ is transversal. Therefore, $\angle \mathcal{DCA} = \angle \mathcal{CAB}$ as interior alternate angles. By the same reason, $\angle \mathcal{ACB} = \angle \mathcal{DAC}$. Therefore the triangles are similar, $\triangle \mathcal{ABC} \sim \triangle \mathcal{ADC}$, implying the equation $\angle \mathcal{B} = \angle \mathcal{D}$. The equation $\angle \mathcal{A} = \angle \mathcal{C}$ follows the same way if we consider another diagonal $\mathcal{BD}$.

To prove that the opposite sides of a parallelogram are equal, we consider the similar triangles[3] $\triangle \mathcal{ABC} \sim \triangle \mathcal{ADC}$, which share a side $\mathcal{AC}$. Composing a proportion

$$\frac{|\mathcal{CD}|}{|\mathcal{AC}|} = \frac{|\mathcal{AB}|}{|\mathcal{AC}|},$$

we observe that both ratios have the same denominator $\mathcal{AC}$, therefore the numerators must also be the same, $|\mathcal{AB}| = |\mathcal{CD}|$. The equation $|\mathcal{AD}| = |\mathcal{BC}|$ can be proved the same way. $\square$

Corollary 5.3.1 *Since a rectangle is a special case of a parallelogram, all statements of Theorem 5.3.1 hold true for any rectangle.*

Exercise 5.3.2 *Prove that in the parallelogram $\mathcal{ABCD}$, Fig. 5.25, $\angle \mathcal{A} = \angle \mathcal{C}$.*

Exercise 5.3.3 *Prove that in the parallelogram $\mathcal{ABCD}$, Fig. 5.25, $\angle \mathcal{ACB} = \angle \mathcal{DAC}$.*

Exercise 5.3.4 *See Fig. 5.28: Prove that $|\mathcal{AD}| = |\mathcal{BC}|$.*

Exercise 5.3.5 *Prove that in a parallelogram, each diagonal divides it into two equal triangles.*

---

[3]These triangles are actually congruent.

Exercise 5.3.6 *Prove that in a parallelogram, the diagonals at the intersection point are divided in halves.*

Exercise 5.3.7 *Does there exist a parallelogram with exactly one right angle?*

Exercise 5.3.8 *Can a parallelogram have all four acute angles?*

Exercise 5.3.9 *Can a parallelogram have all four obtuse angles?*

Definition 5.3.2 *A parallelogram with all four sides equal is called a rhombus.*

Exercise 5.3.10 *Prove that the diagonals of a rhombus are mutually perpendicular.*

Exercise 5.3.11 *Prove that the diagonals of a rhombus divide it into four equal triangles.*

Example 5.3.1 *Prove that in any quadrilateral the sum of four interior angles is 360°.*

Solution. We assume in the proof that there is a point inside the rectangle, which can be connected with all the four vertices of the rectangle by segments, such that none of the segments intersects any side of the rectangle. Then these four segments together with four sides make four triangles lying entirely in the interior of the rectangle. To find the sum of the interior angles at question, we have to add the sums of the angles of the four triangles and subtract the $360°$−degree angle about the point fixed. □

Problem 5.3.1 *Prove that in any pentagon the sum of five interior angles is 540°.*

Problem 5.3.2 *Guess and prove the formula for the sum of n interior angles in any $n-gon$.*

Example 5.3.2 *This example refers to Fig. 5.28. Prove that $|\mathcal{DE}| = |\mathcal{CF}| = |\mathcal{BG}|$.*

Solution. Since $\mathcal{DE}, \mathcal{CF}$, and $\mathcal{BG}$ are perpendicular to $\mathcal{AB}$, they are parallel and both $\mathcal{DEFC}$ and $\mathcal{DEGB}$ are parallelograms; actually, they are rectangles. Thus by Theorem 5.3.1 they are equal as the opposite sides of a parallelogram. □

Answers 5.3

Exercise 5.3.1. $180°$.
Exercise 5.3.7. No.
Exercise 5.3.8. No.
Exercise 5.3.9. No.
Problem 5.3.2. $(n-2)180°$.

5.4 Perimeter and Area

5.4.1 Perimeter

The *perimeter* of a geometrical figure is the total length of the boundary of a figure, that is, the total distance when one travels along the boundary of the figure. Specifically, the *perimeter of a polygon* is the sum of the lengths of all the sides of the polygon. For example, the perimeter of a triangle $\triangle ABC$ in Fig. 5.29 is $|\mathcal{AB}| + |\mathcal{BC}| + |\mathcal{AC}| = 6 + 4.5 + 5.5 = 16$. Since a quadrilateral has four sides, its perimeter is the total length of the four sides. Hence, for any rectangle with the length l and width w, the perimeter is $P = 2l + 2w$. Thus, the perimeter of the rectangle $\mathcal{DEFG}$ in Fig. 5.29 is $2(2+3) = 10$.

In particular, if a rectangle is a square with the side s, then $l = w = s$, hence, the perimeter of a square is $P = 4s$.

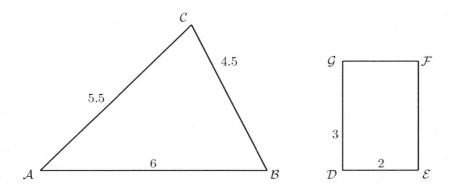

Figure 5.30: The triangle $\triangle ABC$ and the rectangle $\mathcal{DEFG}$.

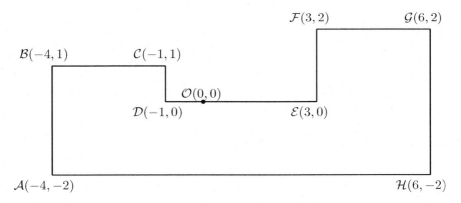

Figure 5.31: Example 5.4.1.

Example 5.4.1 *Find the perimeter of the polygon $ABCDEFGH$ in Fig. 5.31, where the coordinates of the vertices are given, assuming that all its sides are either horizontal or vertical, thus, all its interior angles are either right angles or $270°-$angles, as $\angle CDE$ and $\angle DEF$.*

Solution. The boundary of the polygon $ABCDEFGH$ consists of 4 horizontal and 4 vertical segments AB, BC, CD, DE, EF, FG, GH, and AH. The lengths of the segments can be found by comparing the coordinates of their end-points shown in Fig. 5.31. For instance, the bottom horizontal side AH begins at the point $A(-4,-2)$ and goes to the point $H(6,-2)$, thus its length is $6 - (-4) = 10$ unspecified units. The left-most vertical side AB connects the points $A(-4,-2)$ and $B(-4,1)$, therefore, its length is $1 - (-2) = 3$ units. Hence, the perimeter is

$$|AB| + |BC| + |CD| + |DE| + |EF| + |FG| + |GH| + |AH|$$

$$= 3 + 3 + 1 + 4 + 2 + 3 + 4 + 10 = 30.$$
$\square$

Example 5.4.2 *Find the perimeter of the polygon in Fig. 5.32.*

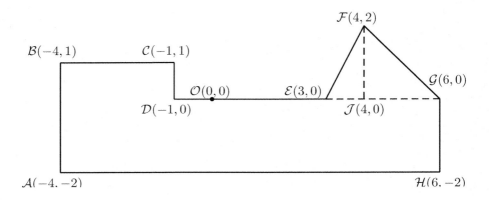

Figure 5.32: Example 5.4.2.

Solution. Instead of the horizontal segment $\mathcal{FG}$, we now have two slanted sides $\mathcal{EF}$ and $\mathcal{FG}$. The altitude $\mathcal{FJ}$ of the triangle $\triangle\mathcal{EFG}$ is perpendicular to the horizontal segment $\mathcal{EG}$; the latter shown as a dashed line since *it is not a part of the perimeter*. The points $\mathcal{F}$ and $\mathcal{J}$ lie on the same vertical line, therefore they have the same horizontal coordinate 4. Moreover, the point $\mathcal{J}$ has the same vertical coordinate as $\mathcal{E}$ or $\mathcal{G}$, which is 0. Whence, we found the coordinates of the point $\mathcal{J}(4,0)$, and we can compute the length of the segment $\mathcal{EF}$, which is the hypotenuse of the right triangle $\triangle\mathcal{EFJ}$. (We can also apply formula (6.1.2) from Section 6.1.1 for the distance between two points in the plane, which is, of course, the same Pythagorean theorem.) Since $|\mathcal{EJ}| = 4 - 3 = 1$ and $|\mathcal{FJ}| = 2 - 0 = 2$; either way, we get $|\mathcal{EF}| = \sqrt{1^2 + 2^2} = \sqrt{5}$. Quite similarly, $|\mathcal{GF}| = \sqrt{2^2 + 2^2} = 2\sqrt{2}$. Finally, the perimeter of the polygon $\mathcal{ABCDEFGH}$ (Fig. 5.32) is

$$|\mathcal{AB}| + |\mathcal{BC}| + |\mathcal{CD}| + |\mathcal{DE}| + |\mathcal{EF}| + |\mathcal{FG}| + |\mathcal{GH}| + |\mathcal{AH}|$$
$$= 3 + 3 + 1 + 4 + \sqrt{5} + 2\sqrt{2} + 2 + 10 = 23 + \sqrt{5} + 2\sqrt{2}.$$

□

Exercise 5.4.1 *Find the perimeter of the polygon $\mathcal{ABCDEFGHIJKA}$ in Fig. 5.33.*

Exercise 5.4.2 *Design and solve two more exercises similar to the previous one.*

5.4.2   Area

The area of a figure is the measure of space inside the boundary of this figure. We must remember that when we want to *fence* our backyard, we have to measure the *perimeter* of the backyard, but when we want to *carpet* our bedroom, we have to measure the *area* of the bedroom.

The area is always measured in square units.

To compute areas, we must know a few formulas. We start with the simplest figure, a square with the unit side, called the *unit square* - Fig. 5.34.

It is reasonable to assign to this square the area of one square unit – if the side is 1 foot, then the area is 1 square foot, if the side is 1 meter, then the area is 1 square meter, etc.

Thus, area can be measured in *square feet, square inches, square miles, square meters*, etc., often written as sq. ft. or ft^2, etc., while the perimeter is always measured in linear

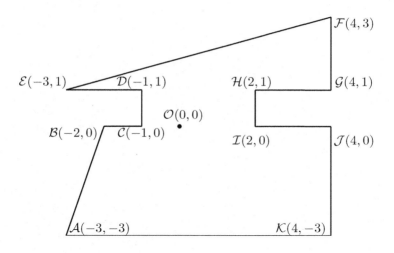

Figure 5.33: Exercise 5.4.1.

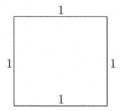

Figure 5.34: A unit square.

units, like feet, meters, etc.

The major principle used in dealing with areas says that

*If a figure consists of several **non-overlapping** parts, the total area is the sum of the areas of the parts.*

For example, the rectangle in Fig. 5.35 can be decomposed into 6 unit squares, it *comprises* 6 unit squares, thus its area is $1 + 1 + 1 + 1 + 1 + 1 = 6 \cdot 1 = 6$ square units.

Generalizing this example, we may use the same reasoning to convince ourselves that the area of any rectangle is given by the following well-known formula.

Theorem 5.4.1 *The area A of a rectangle with width w and length l is equal to the product*

$$A = w \cdot l. \tag{5.4.1}$$

Example 5.4.3 *If the width of a rectangle is $w = 3$ inches and the length $l = 5$ inches, then the area of this rectangle is $A = 3 \cdot 5 = 15$ square inches.* □

From here, we can immediately derive the formula for the area of a triangle.

Indeed, given a triangle $\triangle ACE$, let $CF \perp AE$ be its height, see Fig. 5.36. We embed the triangle in the rectangle $ABDE$ and see that the rectangle $ABCF$ consists of two congruent

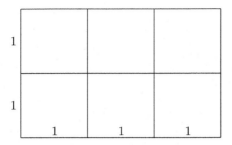

Figure 5.35: A $2 \cdot 3$ rectangle consists of $2 \cdot 3 = 6$ unit squares. Its area is 6 square units.

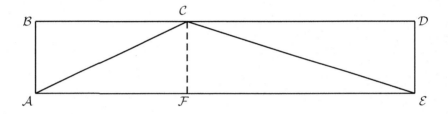

Figure 5.36: The area of a triangle $\triangle \mathcal{ACE}$.

triangles $\triangle \mathcal{ACF}$ and $\triangle \mathcal{ACB}$, so that the area of the triangle $\triangle \mathcal{ACF}$ is exactly a half of the area of the rectangle $\mathcal{ABCF}$. Whence by formula (5.4.1), the area of this triangle is

$$A_{\triangle \mathcal{ACF}} = \frac{1}{2}|\mathcal{AF}| \cdot |\mathcal{CF}|.$$

Quite similarly, the area of the triangle $\triangle \mathcal{CFE}$ is

$$A_{\triangle \mathcal{CFE}} = \frac{1}{2}|\mathcal{EF}| \cdot |\mathcal{CF}|.$$

Adding these two equations, we conclude that the area of the given triangle $\triangle \mathcal{ACE}$ is

$$A_{\triangle \mathcal{ACE}} = \frac{1}{2}|\mathcal{AF}| \cdot |\mathcal{CF}| + \frac{1}{2}|\mathcal{EF}| \cdot |\mathcal{CF}| = \frac{1}{2}(|\mathcal{AF}| + |\mathcal{EF}|) \cdot |\mathcal{CF}| = \frac{1}{2}|\mathcal{AE}| \cdot |\mathcal{CF}|.$$

Since $\mathcal{AE}$ is the base and $\mathcal{CF}$ is the height of the triangle $\triangle \mathcal{ACE}$, we can read this formula as follows:

Theorem 5.4.2 *The area A of a triangle with base b and height h is equal to the half of the product base times height,*

$$A = \frac{1}{2}b \cdot h = \frac{b \cdot h}{2}.$$

We see that the area *does not* depend on the location of the triangle or any other figure.

Example 5.4.4 *For instance, the area of a triangle with the base of 4 units and the height of 3 units is $\frac{1}{2} \cdot 4 \cdot 3 = 6$ square units.*   □

Figure 5.37: The area of a parallelogram $\mathcal{ABCD}$.

We can also easily find the area of a parallelogram. Let $\mathcal{BE} \perp \mathcal{AD}$ be its height and $\mathcal{CF} \perp \mathcal{AD}$ another height of a parallelogram $\mathcal{ABCD}$, Fig. 5.37. Then the right triangles $\triangle \mathcal{ABE}$ and $\triangle \mathcal{DCF}$ are congruent, thus, if we cut off the triangle $\triangle \mathcal{ABE}$ and move it to the right to cover the triangle $\triangle \mathcal{DCF}$, the parallelogram $\mathcal{ABCD}$ becomes the rectangle $\mathcal{EBCF}$ with the same area. Since these quadrilaterals have equal horizontal bases and equal heights, we conclude that the area of any parallelogram is given by the formula, similar to (5.4.1), it is *the product of the base times the height.*

Exercise 5.4.3 *Prove that the triangles $\triangle \mathcal{ABE}$ and $\triangle \mathcal{DCF}$ in Fig. 5.37 – see the proof above, are indeed congruent.*

Example 5.4.5 *For instance, the area of a parallelogram with the base of 4 units and the height of 3 units is $4 \cdot 3 = 12$ square units.*   □

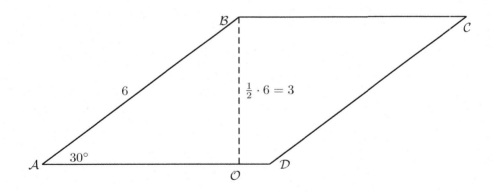

Figure 5.38: Example 5.4.6.

Example 5.4.6 *Find the area of the rhombus with the side of 6 and the acute angle of $30°$, Fig. 5.38.*

Solution. The height of the rhombus is not given in the problem, thus we have to compute it. Analyzing Fig. 5.38, we see that the height $\mathcal{BO}$ is a leg of the right triangle $\triangle \mathcal{AOB}$ with the hypotenuse 6 (because all the sides of a rhombus are equal) and with an acute angle of $30°$. We remember (Proposition 5.3.1) that the leg, opposite to a $30°$−angle, is a half of the hypotenuse of this right triangle; thus in example 5.4.6 the leg is $(1/2)6 = 3$. Since any rhombus is a parallelogram, by formula (5.4.1) we compute the area, $3 \cdot 6 = 18$ sq. units.   □

Exercise 5.4.4 *Use Fig. 5.39 and properties of similar triangles to prove that the area of a trapezoid $\mathcal{ABCD}$ with bases b_1 and b_2 and the height h is*

$$A = \frac{b_1 + b_2}{h}.$$

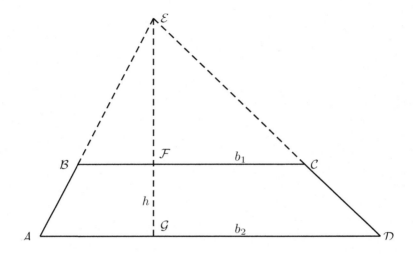

Figure 5.39: The area of a trapezoid $\mathcal{ABCD}$.

Example 5.4.7 *Find the area of the polygon in Fig. 5.40.*

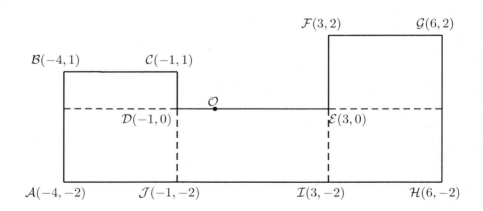

Figure 5.40: Example 5.4.7.

Solution. We emphasize that the *dashed lines* here do not belong to the perimeter of the figure, they only help us to distinguish segments, which are inside the polygon, from its boundary.

Since the polygon is not of any familiar shape, we must split it into simpler parts. For example, we can divide it into three rectangles, $\mathcal{ABCJ}$, $\mathcal{DEIJ}$, and $\mathcal{FGHI}$, compute these three area independently, and then add them up; surely, there are other partitions, all leading to the same total area.

To find the area of the rectangle $\mathcal{ABCJ}$, we observe that its height is the vertical distance between the points $\mathcal{A}$ and $\mathcal{B}$, that is, $1 - (-2) = 1 + 2 = 3$ units. The base is the horizontal distance between the points $\mathcal{B}$ and $\mathcal{C}$, or between $\mathcal{A}$ and $\mathcal{J}$, that is, $-1 - (-4) = -1 + 4 = 3$ units. Hence, the area of the rectangle $\mathcal{ABCJ}$ is $3 \cdot 3 = 9$ square units. In the same way, the height of the rectangle $\mathcal{DEIJ}$ is $0 - (-2) = 2$, and the base is $3 - (-1) = 3 + 1 = 4$, therefore, the area of the rectangle $\mathcal{DEIJ}$ is $2 \cdot 4 = 8$ square units, and the height of the rectangle $\mathcal{FGHI}$ is $2 - (-2) = 4$, and its base is $6 - 3 = 3$, whence the area of this rectangle is $3 \cdot 4 = 12$ square units. Finally, the total area of the polygon $\mathcal{ABCDEFGH}$ is $9 + 8 + 12 = 29$ square units. $\square$

Remark 5.4.1 *Pay attention to order of operations. To compute horizontal distances, we always subtract the left measurement from the right one, and to find vertical distances, we always take away the lower measurement from the upper one, otherwise, the result could be negative.*

Exercise 5.4.5 *Find the area of a rectangle, whose length is 4 ft. 4 in. and the width is 11 in.*

Exercise 5.4.6 *Find the area of a rectangle, whose width is 5 meters and the diagonal is 13 meters.*

Answers 5.4

Exercise 5.4.1. $21 + \sqrt{10} + \sqrt{53}$.
Exercise 5.4.5. 575 sq. in. $= 3\frac{35}{36}$ sq. ft.
Exercise 5.4.6. 60 sq. meters.

Chapter 6

Disc, Circle, Circumference

6.1 The Circumference of a Circle

Not all the animals have needles as porcupines, and not all geometrical figures have sharp parts like vertices–corners. This short chapter is devoted to some roundish things, like circles. If we look at several circles of different radii, especially if they are *concentric*, that is, have the same center, we observe that if we increase the radius, the *length of the circle*, (that is, the *perimeter* of the disc, called also the *circumference*), also increases. We can say that all circles are *similar*.

The following result, where $C = C(r)$ stands for the circumference of the circle of radius r, gives the precise meaning of this statement, which can be traced back at least to Ancient Greece.

Fact. *For any circle, the ratio*

$$\frac{C}{2r} = \pi$$

of its length to its radius is a constant. This ratio is the real number, which does not depend on the radius r of the circle, on the location of the circle, on the units of measurement, etc.

This real number is traditionally denoted by the Greek letter[1] π; it is irrational number, *approximately* $\pi \approx 3.14159...$. The equation above can be written as

$$C = \pi d = 2\pi r,$$

where d stands for the (length of) diameter of the circle.

Example 6.1.1 *Find the circumference of a circle of radius 3 inches.*

Solution. By the formula above, $C = 2\pi \cdot 3 = 6\pi$ inches. This is the precise answer, called also *the answer in terms of* π.

If we need a decimal approximation, the problem should specify the required accuracy, and then the symbol π must be replaced by its decimal approximation. Unless a problem requires another precision, we round π off to the hundredths, that is, *approximately* $\pi \approx 3.14$. Thus, in this example the answer would be $C \approx 6 \cdot 3.14 = 18.84$ inches. If a problem requires another precision, it must be clearly stated. □

Example 6.1.2 *Find the radius of a circle, if its circumference is 3 inches.*

---

[1] Pronounced [pi].

Solution. By the same formula, we have now $3 = 2\pi \cdot r$. From this equation, $r = \frac{3}{2\pi}$ inches, or approximately, $r \approx \frac{3}{2\cdot 3.14} \approx 0.48$ inches. □

The length of the entire circle of radius r is $C = 2\pi \cdot r$ units. In this formula, 2π is the *radian* measure of the central angle subtending the whole circle. If we consider the semi-circle, its length is evidently a half of the whole circle, that is, $\frac{2\pi\cdot r}{2} = \pi \cdot r$. Here π is the radian measure of the corresponding central angle, which is $180° = \pi$. In general, a central angle of Θ radians in a circle of radius r cuts from the circle the arc of length (Fig. 6.1)

$$S = \theta \cdot r. \tag{6.1.1}$$

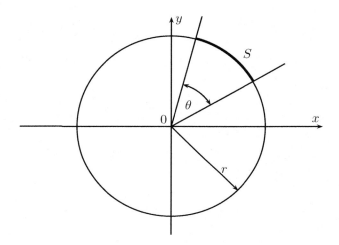

Figure 6.1: The circle of radius r, the central angle θ and the subtended arc of length $S = \theta \cdot r$.

Example 6.1.3 (1) *What arc is subtended from the circle of radius 4 feet by a central angle of 2 radians?*

(2) *What arc is subtended from the circle of radius 4 feet by a central angle of 2° ?*

(3) *Find the central angle, which subtends 1-foot arc from the circle of radius 4 feet.*

Solution. (1) We must find the length of the arc, because its angular measure[2] is the same 2 radians. By formula (6.1.1), $c = \theta \cdot r$, thus, in this problem $S = 2 \cdot 4 = 8$ feet.

(2) Since the angle in this formula is measured in the radians, we must convert 2° into radians, therefore $S = \left(\frac{2\pi}{180}\right) \cdot 4 \approx 0.035 \cdot 4 = 0.14$ feet.

(3) This is the inverse problem, and we have to solve the equation $4 = \theta \cdot 4$ for θ. Hence, $\theta = 4 \div 4 = 1$ radian. □

Exercise 6.1.1 (1) *Which arc is longer, a 30°-arc in a circle of radius 6 or a 60°-arc in a circle of radius 3?*

(2) *An arc of the circle of radius 4 centimeters subtends the central angle of 45°. Into how many times should we increase the radius of the circle, so that the corresponding arc becomes 4 meters long?*

---

[2]The angular measure is dimensionless.

Exercise 6.1.2 *The radius of a circle is 2 inches bigger than the radius r of another circle. How much longer is the circumference of the big circle than the circumference of the smaller one?*

Exercise 6.1.3 *Suppose that our Earth is a perfect ball. A cord surrounds the Earth by equator. The cord was cut, made longer by one meter, and again stretched over the Earth, so that the distance between the Earth and cord is everywhere the same. Can an elephant crawl under the cord? What about the Smart Mouse?*

Answers 6.1

Exercise 6.1.1. **(1)**. They are equal. **(2)**. The arc is proportional to the radius, but we compare them in "twisted" way. The first arc is π cm. long. If the new radius is r, then the length of the corresponding arc is $\pi \cdot r/4 = 4$, hence from this linear equation, the radius must be $16/\pi$ meters or $1600/\pi$ centimeters. The ratio of the radii is $1600/\pi$.
Exercise 6.1.2. The difference is $2\pi(r+2) - 2\pi r = 4\pi$.
Exercise 6.1.3. Let R be the radius of Earth. Then its circumference, increased by 1 meter, is $2\pi R + 1$, and the new radius is $\frac{2\pi R + 1}{2\pi} = R + \frac{1}{2\pi}$. We see that the radius becomes $1/(2\pi)$ meters or $100/(2\pi) \approx 15.9$ centimeters longer. Probably, this is not enough for an elephant, but more then enough for a mouse.

6.2 The Area of a Disc

A *disc* (sometimes *disk*) of radius r is the interior of the circle of radius r.. Finally we compute the *area of a disc*. We have already learnt that areas are measured in square units, therefore, the dependence of the area of a disc of its radius must be quadratic. That is, unlike formula (6.1.1) for the circumference, where the radius is to be to the first degree (linear dependence), the formula for the area of a disc must contain the square of the radius. Indeed, the area of a disc of radius r is given by the following formula, which is derived in calculus,

$$A = \pi r^2,$$

where π is the same constant as before; up to the five places after the decimal point, $\pi \approx 3.14159....$

Example 6.2.1 *Find the area of the disc of radius 3 inches.*

Solution. By the latter formula, the area is $A = \pi \cdot 3^2 = 9\pi$, or if we need a decimal approximation, $A \approx 9 \cdot 3.14 = 28.26$ square inches. □

Example 6.2.2 *Find the area and the perimeter of the sector of the disc of radius 3 inches, subtended by the central angle of 40°.*

Solution. The area of a sector is proportional by its central angle, that is, the area is

$$\frac{40}{360}\pi \cdot r^2 = \pi \frac{3^2}{9} = \pi \text{ sq. in.}$$

The perimeter consists of three parts, two radii and an arc, that is,

$$2 \cdot 3 + \frac{40}{360} 2 \cdot \pi \cdot 3 = 6 + (2/3)\pi.$$

□

Exercise 6.2.1 *The radius R of a disc is twice the radius r of another disc. How many times is the area of the small disc to the area of the large disc?*

Exercise 6.2.2 *Find the circumference and the area of the disc of radius 3 feet and 4 inches.*

Answers 6.2

Exercise 6.2.1. Since $R = 2r$, the area is $\pi R^2 = \pi(2r)^2 = 4(\pi r^2)$. Therefore, the larger area is 4 times the smaller one.

Exercise 6.2.2. To avoid fractions, we do computations in inches, keeping in mind that 1 foot is 12 inches. Thus, the radius is $3 \cdot 12 + 4 = 40$ inches, the circumference is $C = 2\pi \cdot 40 = 80\pi \approx 251.2$ inches, and the area is $A = \pi 40^2 \approx 5,024$ square inches.

Contents of Volume 2

Part III. Elementary Functions

7 Cartesian Coordinates and Complex Numbers
7.1 Cartesian Coordinates
7.1.1 The Distance Between Two Points
Answers 7.1
7.2 Complex Numbers
7.2.1 Introduction
7.2.2 Complex Numbers in Algebraic Form
Answers 7.2
8 Functional Dependence
8.1 Functions and Their Graphs
Answers 8.1
8.2 Superposition and Inverse Functions
Answers 8.2
9 Power Functions
9.1 Linear Functions and Their Graphs
9.1.1 Graphing Linear Equations
9.1.2 Collinear Points
9.1.3 Linear Functions as Mathematical Models
A. Uniform Motion
B. Simple Interest
C. Linear Correlation and the Least-Squares Line
Answers 9.1
9.2 Systems of Linear equations and Inequalities
9.2.1 Systems of Two Linear Equations in Two Unknowns. Analytic Solution
9.2.2 Graphical Solution of Linear Inequalities in Two Variables
9.2.3 Systems of Three Linear Equations With Three Unknowns
Answers 9.2
9.3 Determinants and Cramer's Rule
Answers 9.3
9.4 Quadratic Functions and Their Graphs
9.4.1 Graphing Parabolas
9.4.2 Quadratic Equations and Inequalities
Answers 9.4
9.5 Circles
Answers 9.5
9.6 Power Functions Beyond Quadratics
Answers 9.6
10 Polynomials and Rational Functions
10.1 Polynomials
10.1.1 Algebra of Polynomials
10.1.2 Division of Polynomials
A. Synthetic Division or Horner Scheme
10.1.3 Roots of Polynomials
10.1.4 Graphs of Polynomials
Answers 10.1

10.2 Rational Functions
10.2.1 Domain and Range, Asymptotic Behavior and Graphs of Rational Functions
10.2.2 Equations and Inequalities With Polynomials and Rational Functions
Answers 10.2
11 Exponential and Logarithmic Functions
11.1 Exponential Functions
11.1.1 Properties of Exponential Functions, Their Graphs
11.1.2 The Number e
Answers 11.1
11.2 Logarithmic Functions
11.2.1 Logarithms and Their Properties
11.2.2 Change of Base Formula
11.2.3 Logarithmic Functions and their Graphs
11.2.4 Exponential and Logarithmic Equations
Answers 11.2
12 Sequences. Progressions. Applications
12.1 Sequences
12.2 Arithmetic and Geometric Progressions
12.2.1 Arithmetic Progression
12.2.2 Geometric Progression
Answers 12.2
12.3 Compound Interest and Annuities
Answers 12.3

Part IV. Trigonometry and Two-Dimensional Vectors

13 Trigonometric Functions
13.1 Radian Measure of Angles
13.1.1 Radians to Degrees and Back. The Length of an Arc
Answers 13.1
13.2 Trigonometric Functions of Acute Angles
13.2.1 Trigonometric Ratios
13.2.2 Trigonometric Functions of Acute Angles
Answers 13.2
13.3 Trigonometric Functions of Any Argument
13.3.1 Definitions of Trigonometric Functions of Any Real Argument
13.3.2 Trigonometric Identities
Reduction Formulas
13.3.3 Calculators in Trigonometry
13.3.4 Inverse Trigonometric Functions
13.3.5 Trigonometric Equations
Answers 13.3
13.4 Applications
13.4.1 The Laws of Sines and Cosines
13.4.2 Solving Triangles
13.4.3 Angles of Depression and Elevation
Answers 13.4
13.5 Geometry of Complex Numbers
13.5.1 Geometric Interpretation of Complex Numbers
13.5.2 Trigonometric and Exponential Forms of Complex Numbers
Answers 13.5
13.6 Two-DimensionalVectors
13.6.1 Introduction
13.6.2 Plane Vectors as Ordered Pairs of Components. Addition/Subtraction of Vectors
13.6.3 Polar Form of Plane Vectors
Answers 13.6

Bibliography

[1] A. Borovik, *Mathematics under the Microscope*. The Amer. Math. Soc., Providence, RI, 2010.

[2] S. Feferman, *The Number Systems. Foundations of Algebra and Analysis*. Addison-Wesley Publ. Co., Inc. Reading, Mass.-Palo Alto-London, 1963.

[3] A. Kheyfits *A Primer in Combinatorics*. De Gruyter, Berlin, 2010.

[4] M. Kimball, N. Smith, The Myth of 'I'm Bad in Math', *The Atlantic*, Posted on Oct. 28, 2013, at 10:30 AM ET, accessed on Oct. 30, at 9:57 AM ET.

[5] L. Koopman, N. Brouwer, A. Heck, W. J. Buma, Remedial Mathematics for Quantum Chemistry, *J. Chemical Education*, Vol. 85 (20080, 1233-1236.

[6] *Some Military Applications of Elementary Mathematics*. The Institute of Military Studies. The University of Chicago. Chicago, 1942.

[7] G. Polya, *How to Solve It*. Princeton Univ. Press, Princeton, 1945.

[8] D. T. Willingham, Is It True That Some People Just Can't Do Math?, *American Educator*, Vol. 33 (2009-2010), No. 4, 14-19,39.

[9] H. Wu, The Mis-Education of Mathematics Teachers, *Notices of the Amer. Math. Soc.*, Vol. 58 (2011), 372-384.

Index

π, 1-219
e, 2-168

absolute value, 1-57
addition, 1-22
    addends, 1-22
    associative property, 1-53
    commutative property, 1-24
    neutral element, 1-23
    sum, 1-22
addition of whole numbers, 1-26
additive inverse, 1-51
algebraic expression, 1-135
algorithm, 2-72
angle, 1-176
    1-degree angle, 1-181
    acute, 1-178
    adjacent, 1-178
    complementary, 1-178
    corresponding, 1-184
    coterminal angle, 2-207
    degree measure, 1-181
    depression/elevation, 2-235
    exterior alternate, 1-184
    interior alternate, 1-188
    obtuse, 1-178
    radian measure, 2-195
    right, 1-178
    sides, 1-176
      initial, 1-176
      terminal, 1-176
    standard position, 1-182
    straight, 1-177
    subtend, 1-180, 220
    supplementary, 1-178
    vertex, 1-176
    vertical, 1-178
annuity ordinary, 2-190
area, 1-212
arithmetic average, 1-113
arithmetic progression (sequence), 2-183
    characteristic property, 2-185
    difference, 2-183
    general term, 2-183
    sum, 2-184
asymptote, 2-121

    horizontal, 2-121
    slanted, 2-121
    vertical, 2-121
parallel lines axiom 1-39

binomial coefficient, 2-182
borrowing in subtraction, 1-29
broken line, 1-189
    closed, 1-190

carry-on, 1-26
circle, 1-179, 2-114
    arc, 1-181
      subtends, 1-181
    chord, 1-179
    circumference, 1-219
    diameter, 1-179
    disc (disk), 1-179
    equation, 2-114
    radius of circle or disc, 1-179
    tangent line, 1-180
circles concentric, 1-181
collinear points, 2-51
common factor, 1-88
complex numbers, 2-26
    algebraic form, 2-27
    argument, 2-239
    arithmetic operations, 2-28
    conjugate, 2-29
    geometric interpretation (Argand-Bessel diagram), 2-238
    imaginary part, 2-27
    modulus, 2-29
    real part, 2-27
composite function, 2-35
composite number, 1-88
compound interest, 2-187
consecutive integers, 1-52
coordinate axes, 2-22
cosines law, 2-230
counting numbers, 1-21
Cramer's rule, 2-82

decimals, 1-122
    arithmetic operations, 1-124
    comparison, 1-124

determinant, 2-82
diagonal, 1-190
digits, 1-21
digits addition, 1-22
    digit-addition table, 1-23
disc area, 1-221
distance between points, 2-24
division, 1-79
    dividend, 1-79
    divisor, 1-79
    long division algorithm, 1-80
    quotient, 1-79
    remainder, 1-79

ellipsis, 1-40
equality, 1-22
    transitivity, 1-22
equation with unknowns, 1-138
    roots, 1-138
Euler's formula, 2-239
exponential and logarithmic equations, 2-174
exponential function, 2-163
    base, 2-163
    graph, 2-165
    properties, 2-164

factorial, 2-52, 182
factorization, 1-88
    proper factor, 1-88
following (preceding) integer, 1-22
fractions, 1-97
    aliquot, 1-111
    arithmetic operations, 1-103
    canceling, 1-101
    comparison, 1-111
    denominator, 1-96
    equivalent, 1-100
    fundamental property, 1-100
    improper, 1-108
    in lowest terms, 1-101
    irreducible, 1-101
    like, 1-102
    meaning of, 1-97
    numerator, 1-96
    proper, 1-108
    unlike, 1-102
frequency (in statistics), 1-115
functional notation, 2-33
function, 2-32
    convex/concave, 2-119
    dependent variable (function), 2-32
    domain, 2-32
    even, 2-117
    graph, 2-32
    image, 2-32
    increasing/decreasing/monotone, 2-120
    independent variable (argument), 2-32
    inverse, 2-36
    odd, 2-117
    one-to-one, 2-36
    pre-image, 2-32
    range, 2-32
    target space, 2-32
Fundamental Assumption of School Mathematics, 1-10
Fundamental Theorem of Algebra, 2-136

GCF, 1-90
    Euclidean algorithm, 1-91
geometric progression (sequence), 2-185
    characteristic property, 2-186
    common ratio, 2-185
    general term, 2-185
    sum, 2-186
graph transformations, 2-91
    horizontal translation(shift), 2-93
    reflection, 2-95
    vertical stretch (compression), 2-96
    vertical translation (shift), 2-92
grouping symbols (separators), 1-64

hexagon, 1-190
Horner scheme, 2-133

"if and only is" statement, 1-66
implication, 1-186
    contrapositive, 1-186
    converse, 1-186
    inverse, 1-186
    negation, 1-186
inequalities, 1-41
    addition and subtraction, 1-44
    additive property, 1-44
    multiplicative property, 1-45
    of the opposite sense, 1-46
    of the same sense, 1-42
    transitive property, 1-43
integer numbers, 1-39
    consecutive odd or consecutive even, 1-67
    even, 1-66
    odd, 1-66
interval notation, 1-145
inverse operations, 1-54, 79
    division, 1-79
    subtraction, 1-54
inverse proportionality, 2-119
irrational numbers, 1-156

LCD, 1-104
LCM, 1-92
least-squares line, 2-57
like terms, 1-135
    combining like terms, 1-138

line, 1-175
    broken line, 1-189
    half-line (ray), 1-176
    segment, 1-176
linear correlation, 2-57
linear equations, 1-140
    equivalent, 1-141
    root (solution), 1-141
linear function, 2-39
    horizontal, 2-47
    intercepts, 2-44, 45
    rise-over-run ratio, 2-47
    slope, 2-45
    slope-intercept form, 2-46
    standard form, 2-40
    through two points, 2-48
linear inequalities, 1-146
    equivalent, 1-147
linear inequality with two unknowns, 2-70
    graphical solution, 2-70
lines, 1-175
    parallel, 1-177
    perpendicular, 1-178
    transversal, 1-183
logarithmic function, 2-173
    graphs, 2-174
    properties, 2-173
logarithms, 2-169
    change of base formula, 2-172
    common (decimal), 2-170
    natural, 2-170
    properties, 2-169
"long addition", 1-26
"long division", 1-79

mean, 1-113
median, 1-115
mixed numbers, 1-108
    arithmetic operations, 1-109
mode, 1-115
monomial, 2-129
    degree, 2-129
multiplication, 1-33
    associativity, 1-68
    by zero, 1-34
    commutativity, 1-34
    digits multiplication table, 1-34
    distributive property, 1-68
    neutral element, 1-34
    symbols for, 1-33
multiplication of many-digit numbers, 1-75

Napierian number e, 2-168
natural numbers, 1-40
necessary and sufficient conditions, 1-66
negative numbers, 1-50
nested separators, 1-64

neutral element of addition, 1-23
number line, 1-41
    segment, 1-97

opposite numbers, 1-50
order
    ascending, 1-112
    decreasing, 1-112
    descending, 1-112
    increasing, 1-112
order of operations, 1-64, 86, 164
    separators, 1-165
ordered pair, 2-21

parabola, 2-85
    symmetry axis, 2-85
    vertex, 2-86
Parallel Lines Axiom, 1-39
parallelogram, 1-190, 208
parallel ruler, 1-185
Pearson correlation coefficient, 1-167
percents, 1-131
perfect squares, 1-156
perimeter, 1-210
polygon, 1-189
    convex, 1-190
    diagonal, 1-190
    hexagon, 1-190
    pentagon, 1-190
    quadrilateral, 1-190
        rectangle, 1-190
        rhombus, 1-190
        square, 1-190
        trapezoid, 1-190
polynomial, 2-129
    degree, 2-129
population (in statistics), 1-115
    frequency, 1-115
    mean, 1-115
    median, 1-115
    mode, 1-115
    outlier, 1-114
power function, 2-41
    base, 2-39
    cubic function, 2-116, 117
    exponent, 2-39
power, 1-72
    base, 1-72
    exponent, 1-72
    negative exponents, 1-150
    of ten, 1-74
    operations with powers, 1-149
    zero exponent, 1-73
prime factorization, 1-88
prime number, 1-88
    mutually prime, 1-91
promille, 1-131

proof by contradiction, 1-187
proportion, 1-118
    fundamental property, 1-118
Pythagorean Theorem, 1-203

quadratic equation, 2-96
    incomplete, 2-101
    quadratic formula, 2-103
        reduced, 2-106
    roots, 2-96
        roots as the x-intercepts, 2-89
    solution set, 2-100
    general form, 2-97
quadratic function (trinomial), 2-84
    domain, 2-85
    range, 2-91
    discriminant, 2-104

radicals, 1-155
    simplest radical form, 1-159
ratio, 1-118
rational numbers, 1-95
rationalization of numerators or denominators, 1-162
    conjugate expression, 1-162
real numbers, 1-169
reduction formulas, 2-217
reference angle, 2-217
root (solution) of the equation, 1-138
rounding-off, 1-47

scalar, 2-238
scatter diagram (scatter plot), 2-33
scientific notation, 1-151
segment, 1-176
set, 1-40
    element, 1-40
    empty set, 1-40
    finite, 1-40
    infinite, 1-40
signed numbers, 1-52
simple interest, 2-56
sines law, 2-229
sinusoid, 2-204
speed, 2-53
square root, 1-155
    principal value, 1-156
    radicand, 1-156
standard deviation, 1-167
subtraction, 1-29
    borrowing, 1-29
    difference, 1-29
    minuend, 1-29
    subtrahend, 1-29
superposition, 2-35
synthetic division (Horner scheme), 2-133
systems of linear equations, 2-60

algebraic addition, 2-68
consistent, 2-66
dependent, 2-67
graphical solution, 2-70
inconsistent, 2-66

tangents law, 2-231
transposition, 1-136
triangle, 1-191
    acute, 1-192
    bisectrix, 1-192
    congruent, 1-195
        tests for congruence, 1-195
    equal, 1-195
    equilateral, 1-193
    exterior angle, 1-186
    height, 1-184, 193
    isosceles, 1-193
    median, 1-192
    obtuse, 1-192
    right, 1-192, 202
        cathetus (leg), 1-202
        hypotenuse, 1-202
    similar, 1-196
    solving tringles, 2-231
trigonometric equations, 2-225
trigonometric functions, 2-198
    of any angle, 2-207
    graphs, 2-204, 210, 214
    inverse, 2-220
    of acute angles, 2-198
trigonometric identities, 2-214
    addition formulas, 2-216
trigonometric ratios, 2-198
    cosecant (csc), 2-200
    cosine (cos), 2-199
    cotangent (ctg or cot), 2-200
    secant (sec), 2-200
    sine (sin), 2-199
    tangent (tan or tg), 2-200

uniform motion, 2-52

variance, 1-167
vector, 2-240
    components, 2-240
    resultant, 2-241
velocity, 2-53
    rate of change, 2-53
vertical line test, 2-34

whole numbers, 1-22

zero, 1-23
zero denominator, 1-97